POLAND BETWEEN THE WARS, 1918–1939

Also by Peter D. Stachura

NAZI YOUTH IN THE WEIMAR REPUBLIC

THE WEIMAR ERA AND HITLER
A Select Bibliography

THE SHAPING OF THE NAZI STATE (*editor*)

THE GERMAN YOUTH MOVEMENT, 1900–1945
An Interpretative and Documentary History

THE NAZI MACHTERGREIFUNG (*editor*)

GREGOR STRASSER AND THE RISE OF NAZISM

UNEMPLOYMENT AND THE GREAT DEPRESSION IN WEIMAR
GERMANY (*editor*)

THE WEIMAR REPUBLIC AND THE YOUNGER PROLETARIAT
An Economic and Social Analysis

POLITICAL LEADERS IN WEIMAR GERMANY

THEMES OF MODERN POLISH HISTORY (*editor*)

Poland between the Wars, 1918–1939

Edited by

Peter D. Stachura
Reader in History
University of Stirling
Scotland

First published in Great Britain 1998 by
MACMILLAN PRESS LTD
Houndmills, Basingstoke, Hampshire RG21 6XS and London
Companies and representatives throughout the world

A catalogue record for this book is available from the British Library.

ISBN 0–333–73680–X

First published in the United States of America 1998 by
ST. MARTIN'S PRESS, INC.,
Scholarly and Reference Division,
175 Fifth Avenue, New York, N.Y. 10010

ISBN 0–312–21680–7

Library of Congress Cataloging-in-Publication Data
Poland between the wars, 1918–1939 / edited by Peter D. Stachura.
p.   cm.
"Most of the contributions in this volume were originally
presented in abbreviated form at a conference "Poland Between the
Wars, 1918–1939," organized by the Polish Society at the University
of Stirling on 11 October 1997"—Pref.
Includes bibliographical references and index.
ISBN 0–312–21680–7
1. Poland—History—1918–1945—Congresses.   I. Stachura, Peter D.
II. Conference "Poland Between the Wars, 1918–1939" (1997 :
University of Stirling)
DK4400.P627   1998
943.8'04—dc21   98–7134
                                                                CIP

This book is printed on paper suitable for recycling and made from fully managed and
sustained forest sources.

10   9   8   7   6   5   4   3   2   1
07   06   05   04   03   02   01   00   99   98

Printed and bound in Great Britain by
Antony Rowe Ltd, Chippenham, Wiltshire

For Gregory and Madeleine
as another gentle reminder of their Polish heritage

Contents

Preface

Most of the contributions in this volume were originally presented in abbreviated form at a conference, 'Poland between the Wars, 1918–1939', organized by The Polish Society at the University of Stirling on 11 October 1997. The society has no affiliation with the University.

The Polish Society was formed in September 1996 as an academic discussion forum for those interested in the best traditions of Polish history, culture and contemporary affairs, and it has already forged meaningful links with a number of university and research bodies, cultural and historical organizations and archives in the United Kingdom. Meetings, usually with an invited speaker, are held at least quarterly, and invariably take place at the University of Glasgow. Members of all ages are drawn from both a Polish and non-Polish background across Scotland.

I should like to thank my fellow Committee members, Mr Joseph T. Devine (Treasurer) and Mrs Stella K. Neil (Secretary), for their invaluable assistance in the administration of the Society's affairs since its inception, and in the preparation for the Conference.

The Royal Historical Society, of which I am a Fellow, is thanked most sincerely for awarding a grant towards the conference expenses, and the University of Stirling kindly provided excellent accommodation for the Conference free of charge, as well as the splendid surroundings of its campus.

I am very pleased to record my gratitude to the Polonia Aid Foundation Trust, London, for providing a generous subsidy towards the publication costs of this volume.

Dr Peter D. Stachura
Chairman

Bridge of Allan
Polish Independence Day, 11 November 1997

Notes on Contributors

John M. Bates studied Russian at Cambridge before taking an M.Phil. and Ph.D. at the University of Glasgow, where he is at present Lecturer in Polish. His research interests lie in Polish censorship, particularly under the Communist regime in Poland, and the transformation of Polish media since 1989. He has several articles in press.

Peter Leśniewski served in the Royal Air Force and worked as an engineer in the aerospace industry before commencing his studies in 1989 at the University of Dundee. Since graduating in 1993 he has been preparing a doctoral thesis on Britain's role in Upper Silesia, 1919–22.

Peter D. Stachura is Reader in History at the University of Stirling. His numerous publications on the history of Weimar Germany, including, most recently, *The Weimar Republic and the Younger Proletariat* (1989) and *Political Leaders in Weimar Germany* (1992), led to the award in 1994 of the Degree of Doctor of Letters (D. Litt.). His research interests have been extended to the Second Polish Republic, on which he is presently completing a book. He is Chairman of The Polish Society.

Andrzej Suchcitz, a graduate of the University of London (SSEES), is Keeper of Archives at the Polish Institute and Sikorski Museum, London. His primary research interest is in Polish military history, 1918–46, on which he has written, edited and co-edited several books, mainly in Polish. He is a member of a number of editorial committees, including that of *Teki Historyczne*, published by The Polish Historical Society in Great Britain.

Abbreviations and Glossary

Agudat Israel	A conservative, pro-assimilationist Jewish political party (Poland)
Ausgleich	Compromise between the Hapsburgs and Magyars, resulting in the establishment of the Dual Monarchy in 1867
BBWR	*Bezpartyjny Blok dla Współpracy z Rządem* (Non-Party Bloc for Cooperation with the Government)
Blitzkrieg	'Lightning war', the ultra-rapid strategic operation of the German Army
BRT	Ship tonnage measurement
Bund	Abbreviation of the 'General Jewish Workers' Union', a Jewish Marxist and anti-Zionist political party
Chadecja	*Chrześcijańska Demokracja* (Christian Democratic Party)
C-in-C	Commander-in-Chief
COP	*Centralny Okręg Przemysłowy* (Central Industrial Area)
DBFP	Documents on British Foreign Policy
Duma	Russian parliament
Endecja	Polish name for the National Democratic Party and its successors
Endek	Polish abbreviation for member/follower of the National Democratic Party
FO	Foreign Office (British)
Folkists	Small Jewish political party in the Second Republic
Freikorps	Right-wing German paramilitary groups after 1918
General Zionists	Jewish political movement straddling Socialism and Orthodoxy
GHQ	General Headquarters
Grenzschutz	Border Guard units
H-K-T Society	German right-wing, imperialist pressure group in Prussian Poland before 1914
HMSO	Her Majesty's Stationery Office
KNP	*Komitet Narodowy Polski* (Polish National Committee)
KPD	*Kommunistische Partei Deutschlands* (German Communist Party)

KPP	*Komunistyczna Partia Polski* (Communist Party of Poland)
KPRP	*Komunistyczna Partia Robotnicza Polski* (Communist Workers' Party of Poland)
Kreis	Small German administrative district
Kresy	Polish term for the eastern borderlands
Kulturkampf	The somewhat grandiose term used to describe Reich Chancellor Otto von Bismarck's struggle against the Catholic Church in Germany after 1871
Landschutz	German provincial militia
Landtag	German provincial parliament
Litvak	Polish (derogatory) term for Jews from Lithuania and environs
Luftwaffe	German Air Force
NBKR	Noel Baker Papers (Churchill College, Cambridge)
OUN	*Organizacja Ukraińskich Nacjonalistów* (Organization of Ukrainian Nationalists)
OWP	*Obóz Wielkiej Polski* (Camp of Great Poland)
OZON	*Obóz Zjednoczenia Narodowego* (Camp of National Unity)
PAT	Polish Telecommunications Agency
People's Poland	The Soviet-imposed Communist regime in Poland (1944/5–89)
Pogrom	A massacre of Jews
POW	*Polska Organizacja Wojskowa* (Polish Military Organization, 1914–19)
PPS	*Polska Partia Socjalistyczna* (Polish Socialist Party)
PRO	Public Record Office, London
PSL	*Polskie Stronnictwo Ludowe* (Polish Peasant Movement)
PSL-*Piast*	The largest peasant party until 1931
PSL-*Wyzwolenie*	'Liberation', a radical peasant party until 1931
PWW	Papers of President Woodrow Wilson of the USA
RAF	Royal Air Force
Reichstag	Federal German Parliament
Reichswehr	The name of the German Army, 1918–34, when it became the *Wehrmacht*
Ruch	Association of Railway Bookshops (Polish)
Saisonstaat	Prusso-German term used to denigrate Poland
Sanacja	Name given to the post-1926 regime in Poland (denoting a 'moral purification')

Schutzbund	German paramilitary organization
Selbstschutz	German self-defence militia
Sejm	Polish parliament
Shtetl	Small Jewish town in Eastern Europe
Sicherheitspolizei	German Security Police
Siegfried Line	German military defensive line in the West
SL	*Stronnictwo Ludowe* (united Peasant Party set up in 1931)
Solidarność	Solidarity movement
Spartacists	Radical leftists, precursors of Bolsheviks and Communists in Germany
SRO	Scottish Record Office, Edinburgh
Starosta	District Administrator (Polish)
Szlachta	Polish landed nobility and gentry
Ugoda	Polish Government–Jewish agreement in 1925
USSR	United Soviet Socialist Republics (Soviet Union)
UVO	Ukrainian Military Organization
Voievode	Regional Governor (Polish)
Voievodship	Regional administrative unit
Wehrmacht	Name of the German Armed Forces during the Third Reich
YIVO	Jewish Scientific Institute for Research on Judaism, Wilno
Złoty	Polish currency from 1924 (gold crown)

Map of Poland 1939

1 The Second Republic in Historiographical Outline

Peter D. Stachura

For the vast majority of Poles, the re-establishment in November 1918 of an independent and sovereign Polish state – the Second Republic – represented the culmination of their struggle throughout the nineteenth century and during the First World War to regain what had been cynically stripped from them by the Partitions of 1772, 1793 and 1795. Their endeavours had taken different forms at different times: the Romantic-insurrectionist tradition led, most notably, to the unsuccessful Risings of 1830–1 and 1863–4 against the Russians, while the Positivist years of 'Organic Work' in the second half of the nineteenth century had ensured that the economic, cultural, religious and educational foundations were in place when the moment for further political and military struggle arrived towards the end of the century. In particular, the revolutionary Socialist movement, whose leading personality was Józef Piłsudski, and the Nationalist movement, in the form of the National Democratic Party under Roman Dmowski, spearheaded in their separate ways the quest for independence in a Europe plunged into war in 1914 by the competing ambitions and interests of the Great Powers.

The 'Polish Question', which had effectively disappeared from the agenda of international diplomacy after the 1863–4 Rising, did not contribute to the outbreak of war, but it received growing recognition as an issue as the conflict dragged on, partly due to the varied military and diplomatic efforts of the Poles themselves, but also as a consequence of the changing fortunes of war, especially as they affected the position of the partitionist powers, Russia, Germany and Austria-Hungary. The Bolshevik Revolution and, more importantly, the crusading intervention of the United States both, in 1917, created the broader political and diplomatic framework within which the 'Polish Question' was at last definitively addressed. The final outcome was brought about by a powerful combination of, on the one hand, the Polish people's resilience amidst every conceivable type of adversity, their physical and moral courage and unquenchable belief in their right to determine their own destiny and, on the other, of the triumph of Western democracy and liberalism over authoritarianism and reaction.

The euphoria of independence, with its manifestations of intense patriotism and joyful expectation that the interminable, repressive years of partition were now be succeeded by a fresh new era of hope and progress, was rapidly displaced by the sober realization that Poland was immediately confronted by a plethora of difficult problems and a veritable fight for survival. The profound economic, social and political instability of the interwar era ensured a rough passage for all the newly independent countries in East-Central Europe which were created by the Treaty of Versailles, but few Poles could have anticipated that their independence would prove to be such an ephemeral experience. After a mere 20 years or so, Poland was once again made to vanish from the map of Europe, this time through the most nefarious totalitarian aggression.

The Second Republic has been, and continues to be, the subject of intense, often controversial and polemical historical assessment, which has passed through various phases, most of them critical, some even denunciatory. Contemporary interpretations of it, however, tended to be favourable, even if they were often coloured in Poland by the bitter rivalry between the Piłsudski and Dmowski camps, with their contrasting interpretations of the course and meaning of modern Polish history, the first influenced by the insurrectionist tradition, the other by the Positivist outlook. The small number of Western-based scholars interested in Polish affairs had very limited access to sources, as revealed, for example, in the studies by Buell, Machray and Sarolea,[1] and much the same criticism may be made of the numerous biographies of Piłsudski, who was widely perceived, especially abroad, as personifying the Polish state. Works by, for example, Bartel, Humphrey, Lipiński, Reddaway and Starszewski were characterized by an eulogistic, descriptive tone. They also invariably expressed admiration for Poland's development in general, stressing her few resources.[2]

During the Second World War, when the Poles were initially feted in Britain as gallant allies against Nazi tyranny, William Rose, who held the Chair of Polish History at the School of Slavonic and East European Studies at the University of London, was a prominent producer of sympathetic outlines.[3] Other wartime accounts, often by Polish émigrés, continued in this friendly vein,[4] though one or two, disapproving of the authoritarian character of the post-1926 Piłsudski (*Sanacja*) regime, were anxious to stress Poland's democratic credentials.[5] In this, they reflected the views of General Władysław Sikorski, a pre-war opponent of Piłsudski and leader of the exiled Polish government in London until his death in 1943.[6]

While after 1945 the study of Poland by Western historians proceeded according to established criteria of scholarship, a distinctive if largely regrettable historiographical trend regarding Poland's most recent development emerged as a direct consequence of the Soviet imposition of a Communist system of government from 1944/5, which very much determined the nature of historical scholarship in Poland for the next 40 years or so. In particular, during the period of Stalinist terror from the late 1940s until the mid-1950s, verdicts on the Second Republic were comprehensively negative. It was dismissed as a 'bourgeois-capitalist-landowner' state, in which the only worthwhile political element had been the Communist Party (KPP).[7] A spate of works ignored the circumstances of the KPP's dissolution by Stalin in 1938, and instead extolled the party as a progressive force which now had the historic task of bringing 'People's Poland' into the modern age in loyal partnership with the Soviet Union. In aid of this purpose documents were freely falsified, records distorted or fabricated, and there was an unashamed recourse to outright propaganda.[8]

The Gomułka era after 1956 did not change this situation fundamentally, despite a degree of early hope for a more relaxed air about the regime. While the Marxist-Leninist ideology has had the benefit of opening up valuable social and economic perspectives on historical developments of the inter-war period,[9] too many works continued to forsake objectivity in favour of a politically acceptable exposition. The Republic's alleged failures were often denounced in scathing, sometimes rather crude terms. These included the volatile parliamentary system before 1926, the growing authoritarianism of the *Sanacja* regime, the poverty of many peasants and industrial workers, the treatment of the national minorities (except the Germans and Jews) and the conduct of foreign policy, where a pro-German bias was alleged.[10] Only the indisputable cultural and educational achievements attracted any degree of appreciation: the works of Polish writers such as Witold Gombrowicz and Stanisław Witkiewicz, and the brilliance of mathematicians, philosophers and linguists in the universities were particularly acknowledged.[11] However, these were comparatively minor deviations from the norm and the overall partisan and tendentious trend extended into the 1960s and 1970s, though perhaps with diminishing frequency and intensity. None the less, it meant that too many studies were dubious because they were so obviously serving, to one extent or another, the political imperatives of the regime, above all to somehow legitimize either the Communist system as a whole or certain developments within it that occurred from time to time. These works have to be read very carefully, therefore, not only in terms of their interpretative analysis, but also in relation to their factual reliability.

One of the most notorious examples of this genre is Micewski's study published in 1964, which argues that 'People's Poland' represented the realization of the nationalist ideology of the inter-war *Endecja*, in that it embodied antagonism towards Germany and the reality of an ethnically homogeneous, Catholic Poland that was allied to Russia.[12] The absurdity of this proposition is plain enough, and if its underlying purpose was to somehow undermine popular admiration for the Second Republic and to act as an apologist for the Communist regime, it was a complete miscalculation. None the less, others in Poland were undeterred, and authored a series of works which sought unconvincingly to demonstrate, on the basis of inter-war developments, that liberal Catholicism and Communism were intrinsically compatible.[13]

Another major feature of this era of sullied scholarship was that certain topics were taboo – the infamous 'Blank Pages' – because of their political sensitivity, notably the Polish–Soviet War of 1920, the Nazi–Soviet Pact of 1939 and relations generally between Poland and the Soviet Union.[14] It was thus left to historians in the West such as Wandycz, Korbel, Davies and Zamoyski to fill these important gaps.[15] Foreign policy in general during the Second Republic is more extensively and satisfactorily covered by accounts published in the West, with Wandycz, Cienciała and Karski among the most prominent and distinguished contributors.[16]

The growing unrest in Poland in the 1970s, and particularly the reverberations of the election in 1978 of the Archbishop of Kraków, Karol Wojtyła, to head the Vatican as Pope John Paul II, and the subsequent rise of *Solidarność*, exerted an ameliorative influence on historical scholarship in Poland. Interest in the Second Republic was further stimulated, particularly with a view to understanding the leading political figures of that era, as well as to drawing comparisons between the social and political crises of the late 1970s and early 1980s and those of the 1920s and 1930s. This led to a spate of biographies of noteworthy political personalities, including Wincenty Witos, Wojciech Korfanty, Roman Dmowski, Herman Lieberman and Ignacy Paderewski.[17] At long last, Polish historical scholarship became less observant of Marxist-Leninist prescriptions and began slowly and circumspectly to breathe a new air of traditional scholarship. In the post-Communist era of the 1990s, the latter trend has been accentuated, so that for the first time in half a century Polish historians and their works are able to be read in the confident expectation that they are no longer purveying a discredited political message at the ultimate behest of a foreign power, the Soviet Union.

Reference may be made to works in specific areas of scholarship in Poland and the West which are illustrative of the trends noted above. In the first instance, the manifold weaknesses of the inter-war economy, already crippled at the outset to a considerable extent by exploitative partitionist policies, and the devastation of the First World War, have received detailed attention in monographs by, for example, Taylor, Landau and Tomaszewski, Roszkowski and Kofman.[18] There is a consensus that in Poland in 1918 the infrastructure was rudimentary at best, there was little capital or industry, no settled currency, an overpopulated and inefficient agrarian sector, and few foreign markets, especially following the collapse of trade with Russia. As government expenditure vastly outstripped income the early 1920s saw an inflationary trend which reached a climax in autumn 1923, when the currency was rendered virtually worthless on a scale comparable with that of Weimar Germany. A brief period of respite followed the establishment in early 1924 of the Bank of Poland and the introduction of a new currency, the *złoty*. Fiscal, budgetary and investment problems soon resurfaced, however, contributing to the crisis that prompted a *coup d'état* by Piłsudski in May 1926.

The late 1920s saw clear signs of economic recovery in Poland, reflecting a general upturn in the European economy, only for the Depression to obliterate any gains from 1930 until about 1935. Poland then suffered severely from rising unemployment, plummeting living standards and social and ethnic unrest, a situation exacerbated by the government's rigid pursuit of a deflationary strategy to protect the currency in international markets. The problems of agriculture had not been significantly alleviated by reformist legislation in 1920 and 1925, so that peasant unrest perceptibly increased.[19] From 1935/6, however, with the worst of the Depression over, the economy began another, largely state-directed revival, epitomized by the creation within a four-year programme of the Central Industrial Region, serving both industrial and military needs. In the last years before the Second World War it is noted that Poland was beginning to exploit more successfully her resources in raw materials, increase production levels, reduce unemployment and begin to raise the living standards of many social groups. Taylor's assessment is the most optimistic of all; while affirming that the Polish economy in 1939 still lagged far behind that of the major industrialized countries of the West, he salutes the advances that were made.[20]

The political development of the Second Republic was particularly turbulent between 1918 and 1926, by which time more than 90 parties had been set up, about one-third of which were represented at one time or another in parliament, thanks to the system of proportional representation. As a result of the political immaturity of both the emergent political class and the electorate, a weakness compounded by widespread graft, corruption and scandal, ethnic tension and external threat from Germany and the Soviet Union, government changed no fewer than 14 times. Only following Piłsudski's coup was this volatility brought under control, though at the expense of an incremental emasculation of parliamentary democracy within an authoritarian (but not dictatorial) system, and a series of tough measures against certain political opponents. Marshal Piłsudski at once dominated and personified the *Sanacja* regime.

In the post-Piłsudski era of the mid- and late 1930s, the regime drifted more and more decisively to the Right in response to rising nationalist and international tensions, and, paradoxically, took on many of the views of its erstwhile enemy, the *Endecja*. Among the comparatively few Polish works offering informed insights into specific developments are those by Ajnenkiel, Garlicki and Majchrowski,[21] though the most trustworthy and valuable accounts are undoubtedly by scholars from Britain and the United States, especially Davies, Polonsky, Leslie, Rothschild and Wynot.[22] The central figures and influences of the period, Piłsudski and Dmowski, have yet to find a wholly satisfactory biographer. Jędrzejewicz, a former camp follower of the Marshal, is too obviously adulatory, while the more recent work by Garlicki is not only Marxist-slanted, but also amounts to a quite unjustified debunking exercise.[23] Fountain has produced a useful study of Dmowski, but is limited to the pre-1907 period, while most other biographies fail to do justice to the full complexity of the subject.[24] Wapiński, however, adds several interesting perspectives, despite his Marxist approach, and in a separate study succeeds in capturing something of the essence of *Endek* ideology.[25] Where Polish historians have rendered a better service is in regard to histories of individual political parties and organisations of the inter-war era, with the exception of the Communist Party, which is still a somewhat problematic subject and attracts biased coverage.[26] Works published in the West by Dziewanowski, de Weydenthal, Schatz and Szafer are superior, at least in terms of reliability and objectivity.[27] But the Polish Socialist Party (PPS), the several peasant groups and some smaller parties have been the subject of accomplished research in Poland,[28] as have organizations such as the Non-Party Bloc for Co-operation with the Government (BBWR) and radical right-wing groups.[29]

The history of the ethnic minorities in the Second Republic has proved highly contentious. In 'People's Poland', too many accounts, while offering previously little-known facts, were politically conditioned.[30] Chojnowski's study, which at least reveals some appreciation of the difficulties faced by the Polish state in dealing with the minorities, is probably the best of a generally dubious collection.[31] For many years, the 'Jewish Question' was simply ignored altogether. That has now changed following a dramatic revival of interest in the West, especially from historians who are Jewish or of Jewish background. Almost all have adopted a deeply censorious attitude towards the official and popular treatment of the more than three million Jews in the Second Republic, as shown in the work of, for example, Heller, Korzec, Fishman, Abramsky, Mendelsohn and Gutman.[32] Polish anti-Semitism is their fundamental point of reference, with little thought being given to even the possibility of the role of Jewish anti-Polonism. This remains an area of debate which has some way to go before even-handedness is universally respected.

Finally, although there is already a vast corpus of information about the Second Republic, there is no single, satisfactory general history of it. Zieliński's volume may be said to rise above the usual level of Polish Communist scholarship, but it still manifests an unmistakable political and ideological proclivity.[33] Much the same may also be said of the relevant chapters in a collectively edited general history, while Topolski's more recent volume is rather pedestrian in content and insipid in argument. More informative is the older work of an émigré historian.[34] Davies' brilliant if sometimes provocative works illuminate important aspects of its development, though his generally pessimistic assessment of the Second Republic is disappointing.[35] Watt's book is of a rather different order: while fair-minded and fluently written, it tends to lack analytical depth.[36] The edited works by Wiles and Tomicki provide some penetrating insights, but are more concerned to indicate possible avenues of future research.[37]

What is invariably missing from these and other accounts is sufficient recognition of the Second Republic's achievements, which arguably extended well beyond the cultural and educational spheres. In addition to the valiant struggle to secure its borders and the momentous victory over the Soviet Bolsheviks in 1920, the promotion of integration and national identity, at least among the ethnic Poles, the creation of a progressive welfare system, the emphasis placed on family values and civility, the respect fostered for religion and religious institutions, and the relatively low incidence of serious crime are only a few of the usually unacknowledged or underestimated factors which went into the making of the fabric and integrity of Polish society and the state in these years. It is easy enough to be critical of Poland's transparent failings, but this has surely to be counterbalanced with reference to its many undeniable successes. With Warsaw taking its place as a leading European capital city, boasting a restored Royal Castle as a unifying patriotic symbol,[38] the country often exuded a new mood of confidence and vitality, wrapped in an inimitable Polish sense of style. In the space of a single generation[39] Poland overcame the disaster of partition and many of her most challenging domestic and external problems to re-emerge as an important, justifiably proud nation at the heart of European affairs.

As the millennium approaches, there is every prospect of a brighter future for the study of Polish history. A new cohort of Polish scholars is beginning to appear in the post-Communist era which will have no restrictions on developing and enjoying close contact with colleagues in the West, who, in turn, will derive significant benefit from them and their work.[40] Access to archives in Poland is now freely permitted, and the process of publishing valuable documentary collections is well under way. In British universities the number of undergraduate courses in Polish history is increasing in response to a natural curiosity about the unknown and a broadening European vision. Consequently, if the study of Poland in the last half-century has too often been clouded by disreputable political and ideological influences, the present and future should hold no such fears, and the Second Republic will have its best-ever chance of being accorded a properly considered place in the country's history.

The present volume aims to make a contribution in this respect by providing new insights and reassessments of a number of significant and contentious themes. Thus, the fraught situation between Poland and Germany in the disputed area of Upper Silesia at the end of the First World War is the focus for Peter Leśniewski's discussion, while the equally sensitive topic of the Polish state's relationship with its large ethnic minorities in the early years of independence is analysed by Peter Stachura, who also assesses the significance for the subsequent history of the Second Republic of the Polish victory over the Red Army at the Battle of Warsaw in 1920. John Bates scrutinizes the conditions under which the press operated in inter-war Poland, and Andrzej Suchcitz provides a fresh and important perspective on Poland's military preparations in the fateful year of 1939.

NOTES

1. R. L. Buell, *Poland: Key to Europe* (Knopf, New York, 1939); Robert Machray, *The Poland of Pilsudski* (London, 1926); Charles Sarolea, *Letters on Polish Affairs* (Oliver & Boyd, Edinburgh, 1922).
2. Paul Bartel, *Le Maréchal Pilsudski* (Paris, 1935); Grace Humphrey, *Pilsudski. Builder of Poland* (New York, 1936); Wacław Lipiński, *Wielki Marszałek (1867–1935)* (Warsaw, 1926); W. E. Reddaway, *Marshal Pilsudski* (London, 1939); Jan Starzewski, *Józef Pilsudski, Zarys Psychologiczny* (Warsaw, 1930).
3. William J. Rose, *Poland* (Penguin, Harmondsworth, 1939), and his *The Rise of Polish Democracy* (Bell, London, 1944).

4. Edward Elgoth-Ligocki, *Poland* (London, 1940); Zbigniew Grabowski, *Twenty Years of Polish Independence* (Glasgow, 1944); J. Weyers, *Poland and Russia* (London, 1943); Olgierd Górka, *Outline of Polish History, Past and Present* (Kolin, London, 1942); G. Slocombe, *A History of Poland* (Nelson, London, 1940); Henryk Frankel, *Poland, The Struggle for Power, 1772–1939* (Lindsay Drummond, London, 1945); B. E. Schmitt, *Poland* (University of California Press, Berkeley, 1945); Leszek Kirkien, *Russia, Poland and the Curzon Line* (Caldra House, Duns, 1945). A notable exception to the general rule is the critical assessment of Poland in Simon Segal, *The New Poland and the Jews* (Lee Furman, New York, 1938).

5. Manfred Kridl, Józef Wittlin, Władysław Malinowski, *The Democratic Heritage of Poland* (Allen & Unwin, London, 1944). A more recent appraisal of the same theme is Anita K. Shelton, *The Democratic Idea in Polish History and Historiography* (New York, 1989).

6. A good introduction is Keith Sword (ed.), *Sikorski. Soldier and Statesman* (Orbis, London, 1990).

7. For example, A Gwiżdż, *Burżuazyjno-Obszarnicza Konstytucja z 1921 roku w praktyce* (Warsaw, 1956).

8. *KPP. W obronie niepodległości Polski. Materiały i Dokumenty* (Warsaw, 1954).

9. Janusz Żarnowski, *Struktura społeczna inteligencji w Polsce w latach 1918–39* (Warsaw, 1964), and his *Społeczeństwo Drugiej Rzeczypospolitej 1918–39* (Warsaw, 1973).

10. For example, J. Pajewski (ed.), *Problem Polsko-niemiecki w traktacie wersalskim* (Poznań, 1963); S. Kubiak, *Niemcy a Wielkopolska* (Poznań, 1969); Z. Kaczmarczyk (ed.), *Studia z historii powstania wielkopolskiego 1918–1919* (Poznań, 1962). The national minorities are discussed later in the present volume.

11. Unusually, two major surveys were published in English: Bolesław Klimaszewski (ed.), *An Outline History of Polish Culture* (Interpress, Warsaw, 1964), and Józef Krzyżanowski, *A History of Polish Literature* (Interpress, Warsaw, 1978). The best account, however, is by the emigré Czesław Miłosz, *A History of Polish Literature* (London, 1969).

12. Andrzej Micewski, *Z geografii politycznej II Rzeczypospolitej* (Warsaw, 1964).

13. Bogumił Grott, *Nacjonalizm i religia. Proces zespalania nacjonalizmu z katolicyzmem w jedną całość ideową w myśli Narodowej Demokracji 1926–1939* (Kraków, 1984).

14. G. C. Malcher, *Blank Pages. Soviet Genocide against the Polish People* (Pyrford Press, Woking, 1993); Andrzej Ajnenkiel, 'Blank Pages in Polish History', *The Polish Review*, 33/3 (1988), pp. 333–41.

15. Piotr Wandycz, *Soviet–Polish Relations, 1917–1921* (Harvard University Press, Cambridge, Mass., 1969); Józef Korbel, *Poland Between East and West. Soviet and German Diplomacy Towards Poland, 1919–1933* (Princeton University Press, Princeton, NJ, 1963); Norman Davies, *White Eagle, Red Star. The Polish–Soviet War, 1919–20* (Macdonald, London, 1972); Adam Zamoyski, *The Battle for the Marshlands* (East European Monographs, Boulder, Col., 1981).

16. Piotr Wandycz has authored, *inter alia*, *France and Her Eastern Allies, 1919–1925* (University of Minnesota Press, Minneapolis, 1962), *The Twilight of French Eastern Alliances, 1926–1936* (Princeton University Press,

Princeton, NJ, 1988), *The United States and Poland* (Harvard University Press, Cambridge, Mass., 1980), and *Polish Diplomacy 1914–1945. Aims and Achievements* (Orbis, London, 1988); Anna M. Cienciała, *Poland and the Western Powers, 1935–1939* (University of Toronto Press, Toronto, 1968), and with Tytus Komarnicki, *From Versailles to Locarno. Keys to Polish Foreign Policy, 1919–1925* (University Press of Kansas, Lawrence, Kan., 1984); Jan Karski, *The Great Powers and Poland, 1919–1945. From Versailles to Yalta* (University Press of America, New York, 1985).

17. Andrzej Zakrzewski, *Wincenty Witos. Chłopski polityk i mąż stanu* (Warsaw, 1979); Marek Orzechowski, *Wojciech Korfanty. Biografia polityczna* (Wrocław, 1975); Andrzej Micewski, *Roman Dmowski* (Warsaw, 1971); Andrzej Leinwand, *Poseł Herman Lieberman* (Kraków, 1983); Marian M. Drozdowski, *Ignacy Jan Paderewski. A Political Biography* (Interpress, Warsaw, 1981).

18. Jack J. Taylor, *The Economic Development of Poland, 1919–1950* (Cornell University Press, Ithaca, New York, 1952). In *The Polish Economy in the Twentieth Century* (Routledge, London, 1985), Zbigniew Landau and Jerzy Tomaszewski provide a summary of some of their earlier work published in Polish; Wojciech Roszkowski, *Landowners in Poland, 1918–1939* (Cambridge University Press, London, 1991); Jan Kofman, *Lewiatan a podstawowe zagadnienia ekonomiczno-polityczne Drugiej Rzeczypospolitej* (Warsaw, 1986). See also the useful earlier work by Ferdynand Zweig, *Poland Between Two Wars. A Critical Study of Social and Economic Change* (Secker & Warburg, London, 1944), and Paul Latawski (ed.), *The Reconstruction of Poland, 1914–1923* (Macmillan, London, 1992).

19. Some background in Stefan Kieniewicz, *The Emancipation of the Polish Peasantry* (University of Chicago Press, Chicago, 1969), which provides a synthesis of earlier work published in Polish; and in Olga A. Narkiewicz, *The Green Flag. Polish Populist Politics, 1967–1970* (Croom Helm, London, 1976).

20. Taylor, *The Economic Development of Poland*, p.153.

21. Andrzej Ajnenkiel, *Od 'rządow ludowych' do przewrotu majowego. Zarys dziejów politycznych Polski 1918–1926* (Warsaw, 1979), and *Polska po przewrocie majowym. Zarys dziejów politycznych Polski 1926–1939* (Warsaw, 1980); Andrzej Garlicki, *Przewrót majowy* (Warsaw, 1968), and *Od maja do Brześcia* (Warsaw, 1981); Jacek M. Majchrowski, *Silni, zwarci, gotowi. Myśl polityczna Obozu Zjednoczenia Narodowego* (Warsaw, 1985).

22. Norman Davies, *God's Playground. A History of Poland. Volume II: 1795 to the Present* (Clarendon Press, Oxford, 1981); Antony Polonsky, *Politics in Independent Poland, 1921–1939. The Crisis of Constitutional Government* (Oxford University Press, Oxford, 1972); R. F. Leslie (ed.), *The History of Poland since 1863* (Cambridge University Press, Cambridge, 1983); Joseph Rothschild, *Pilsudski's Coup d'Etat* (Columbia University Press, New York, 1966); Edward D. Wynot, *Polish Politics in Transition. The Camp of National Unity and the Struggle for Power, 1935–1939* (University of Georgia Press, Athens, Ga. 1974). A useful recent supplement to our knowledge of Piłsudski's coup is Antoni Czubiński, *Przewrót majowy 1926 roku* (Warsaw, 1989).

23. Wacław Jędrzejewicz, *Kronika życia Józefa Piłsudskiego, 1967–1935*, 2 vols. (London, 1977), which is available in an abbreviated English version as *Piłsudski. A Life for Poland* (Hippocrene Books, New York, 1982); Andrzej

Garlicki, *Jósef Piłsudski, 1867–1935* (Hippocrene Books, New York, 1995). See also M. K. Dziewanowski, *Jósef Piłsudski. A European Federalist, 1918–1922* (Hoover Institution Press, Stanford, 1969).

24. Alvin M. Fountain, *Roman Dmowski. Party, Tactics, Ideology, 1895–1907* (East European Monographs, Boulder, Col., 1980); Micewski, *Roman Dmowski*; Irena Wolikowska, *Roman Dmowski. Człowiek, Polak, Przyjaciel* (Chicago, 1961).

25. Roman Wapiński, *Roman Dmowski* (Lublin, 1988), and *Narodowa Demokracja 1893–1939* (Wrocław, 1980).

26. Examples include Jerzy Kowalski, *Komunistyczna Partia Polski, 1935–1938* (Warsaw, 1975); H. Cimek and L. Kieszczyński, *Komunistyczna Partia Polski, 1918–1938* (Warsaw, 1984); Antoni Czubiński, *Komunistyczna Partia Polski (1918–1938)* (Warsaw, 1985).

27. M. K. Dziewanowski, *The Communist Party of Poland. An Outline of Its History* (Harvard University Press, Cambridge, Mass., 1959); Jan B. de Weydenthal, *The Communists of Poland. An Historical Outline* (Hoover Institution Press, Stanford, 1978); Jaff Schatz, *The Generation. The Rise and Fall of the Jewish Communists of Poland* (University of California Press, Berkeley, 1991); Tadeusz Szafar, 'The Origins of the Communist Party in Poland, 1918–1921', in Ivo Banac (ed.), *The Effects of World War I. The Class War after the Great War. The Rise of Communist Parties in East Central Europe, 1918–1921* (New York, 1983).

28. Two works by Jerzy Holzer form a useful starting-point: *Mozaika polityczna drugiej Rzeczypospolitej* (Warsaw, 1974), and *PPS. Szkic dziejów* (Warsaw, 1977). See also L. Ziaja, *PPS a polityka zagraniczna 1926–39* (Warsaw, 1974); B. Głowacki, *Polityka Polskiej Partii Socjalistycznej w latach 1929–35* (Warsaw, 1970); J. R. Szaflik, *Polskie Stronnictwo Ludowe Piast 1926–31* (Warsaw, 1970); A. Paczkowski, *Prasa polityczna ruchu ludowego 1918–1939* (Warsaw, 1971); B. Krzywobłocka, *Chadecja 1918–1937* (Warsaw, 1974); H. Przybylski, *Chrześcijańska Demokracja i Narodowa Partia Robotnicza w latach 1926–1937* (Warsaw, 1980).

29. Andrzej Chojnowski, *Piłsudczycy u władzy. Dzieje Bezpartyjnego Bloku Współpracy z Rządem* (Warsaw, 1986); Szymon Rudnicki, *Obóz Narodowo Radykalny. Geneza i Działalność* (Warsaw, 1985).

30. For instance, R. Torzecki, *Kwestia ukraińska w polityce III Rzeszy, 1922–1945* (Warsaw, 1972); Jerzy Tomaszewski, *Rzeczpospolita wielu narodów* (Warsaw, 1985), and his *Ojczyzna nie tylko Polaków. Mniejszości narodowe w Polsce w latach 1918–1939* (Warsaw, 1985).

31. Andrzej Chojnowski, *Koncepcje polityki narodowościowej rządow polskich w latach 1921–39* (Wrocław, 1979).

32. Celia S. Heller, *On the Edge of Destruction. Jews of Poland Between the Two World Wars* (Columbia University Press, New York, 1977); Paweł Korzec, *Juifs en Pologne* (Paris, 1980); Joshua A. Fishman (ed.), *Studies on Polish Jewry, 1919–1939* (Yivo Institute for Jewish Research, New York, 1974); Chimen Abramsky, Maciej Jachimczyk and Antony Polonsky (eds.), *The Jews in Poland* (Basil Blackwell, Oxford, 1986); Ezra Mendelsohn, *Zionism in Poland. The Formative Years, 1915–1926* (Yale University Press, New Haven, Conn., 1981); Yisrael Gutman, Ezra Mendelsohn, Jehuda Reinharz, Chone Shmeruk (eds.), *The Jews of Poland Between Two World Wars* (University

Press of New England, Hanover, 1989). See also *Polin*, 8 (1994), special edition on 'Jews in Independent Poland, 1918–39'.

33. Henryk Zieliński, *Historia Polski 1914–1939* (Wrocław, 1983). In his previous works, the Marxist/Communist influence is even more pronounced.

34. Aleksander Gieysztor, Stefan Kieniewicz, E. Rostworowski, J. Tazbir and Henryk Wereszycki (eds.), *A History of Poland* (Warsaw, 1979); Jerzy Topolski, *An Outline History of Poland* (Warsaw, 1986); Władysław Pobóg-Malinowski, *Najnowsza Historia Polski*. 3 vols. (Gryff, London, 1956–60).

35. Davies, *God's Playground*, and his *Heart of Europe. A Short History of Poland* (Clarendon Press, Oxford, 1984). Not quite of the same calibre but still worth consulting is Hans Roos, *A History of Modern Poland* (Eyre & Spottiswoode, London, 1966), and Henri Rollet, *La Pologne au XXe Siecle* (Pedone, Paris, 1985).

36. Richard M. Watt, *Bitter Glory. Poland and Its Fate, 1918 to 1939* (Simon & Schuster, New York, 1979). In more popular vein still is Neal Ascherson, *The Struggles for Poland* (London, 1987), written for a television programme.

37. Timothy Wiles (ed.), *Poland Between the Wars, 1918–1939* (Indiana University Press, Bloomington, 1989); J. Tomicki (ed.), *Polska Odrodzona 1918–1939* (Warsaw, 1982).

38. See Edward D. Wynot, *Warsaw Between the World Wars. Profile of the Capital City in a Developing Land, 1918–1939* (East European Monographs, Boulder, Col., 1983); Marian M. Drozdowski and A. Zahorska, *Historia Warszawy* (Warsaw, 1972); Marian M. Drozdowski, *Warszawiacy i ich miasto w latach Drugiej Rzeczypospolitej* (Warsaw, 1976); Władysław T. Bartoszewski and Antony Polonsky (eds.), *The Jews in Warsaw. A History* (Basil Blackwell, Oxford, 1991).

39. The generational theme is discussed in Roman Wapiński, *Pokolenia Drugiej Rzeczypospolitej* (Wroclaw, 1991).

40. Some examples are: Walentyna Najdus, *Ignacy Daszyński, 1866–1936* (Warsaw, 1992); Janusz Faryś, *Piłsudski i piłsudczycy. Z dziejów koncepcji polityczno-ustrojowej 1918–1939* (Szczecin, 1991); Mieczysław Wrzosek, *Wojny o granice Polski Odrodzonej 1918–1921* (Warsaw, 1992); Jerzy Kochanowski, *Zapomniany prezydent: Życie i działalność Ignacego Boernera, 1875–1933* (Warsaw, 1993); and Andrzej Misiuk, *Policja Państwowa 1919–1939* (Warsaw, 1996).

2 Three Insurrections: Upper Silesia 1919–21*

Peter Leśniewski

For the people of Poland, the Armistice of 11 November 1918 marked the demise of the three great European empires which had repeatedly partitioned their country, finally causing it to vanish from the map of Europe in 1795. As the war ended in Western Europe, Poles in the ex-Austrian and ex-Russian Polish territories were declaring an independent state and establishing a government in Warsaw. But, for the Polish people living in the area of the Prussian partition, and the Upper Silesians of Polish sentiment, continued recognition of German sovereignty over them in the Armistice terms appeared to place a barrier to any similar unilateral action.[1] However, on Boxing Day 1918, a rebellion by Polish nationalists against the German authorities in Poznań escalated into full-scale guerilla-style warfare throughout the Poznań district. When the fighting broke out in Poznań, the German authorities, fearing that it would spread to their valuable industrial districts in Upper Silesia, clamped down on all Polish nationalist activities. With the area under relatively firm military control and Europe in desperate need of the coal it produced, the landowning industrialists, manufacturers and German administrators in Silesia began to hope that, despite Upper Silesia's apparently overwhelming Polish population, the Peace Conference could be persuaded to leave this important industrial region in Germany's hands.[2]

The following discussion examines the Polish Upper Silesians' struggle to prevent this and find their place within the reborn Polish Republic. Major milestones in this struggle include three dramatic insurrections. The first of these occurred in August 1919, resulting from Germany's success in having a plebiscite declared over all the Upper Silesian territory originally destined for direct handover to Poland. This was compounded by their attempts to intimidate the population before the arrival of the Inter-Allied Commission being sent to administer the territory, implement the plebiscite, and make a recommendation on the line of partition. The other two insurrections, in August 1920 and in May the following year, happened under the aegis of this body, but once again the actions were really directed at the German population. In August 1920 Poles living in urban centres were attacked by gangs of Germans. These elements believed

13

Warsaw had just fallen to the Red Army and Poland no longer existed. A defensive operation by Polish paramilitary units surprised the Germans and forced concessions both from them and the Inter-Allied Commission. As Polish Silesian military strength and confidence grew, with the Commission's recommendation to the Peace Conference about to be made, a final insurrection was staged in May 1921. This aimed at demonstrating the Polish population's resolve and right to the territory they claimed, which now appeared about to be sacrificed on the altar of Great Power expediency.

Poland's claim to Upper Silesia rested upon Germany's acceptance of President Wilson's Fourteen Points as the basis for the November Armistice. The Peace Conference's ethnographic map of Silesia was formulated using Prussia's own census statistics of 1910. These had revealed that most of Upper Silesia was 'inhabited by indisputably Polish populations'.[3] And in a series of papers prepared by the Foreign Office for the Peace Conference, it was noted that

> The question has been raised whether the coal-mining districts of Silesia should be included in the new state of Poland. As the inhabitants are without doubt mainly Polish there would seem no good reason for refusing their union with Poland.[4]

But given the scale of reparations that the Allies were talking about imposing on Germany, it was obvious that the removal of the coal mines and their associated manufacturing base would hit the German economy hard. And despite the shock delivered to Germany's governing classes by the sudden and unexpectedly disappointing outcome to the War, their confidence quickly recovered as the extent of the differences between the Allies on the final peace settlement began to be revealed. To almost all Germans, the idea of yielding to Poland land that had not previously been partitioned Polish territory became increasingly unacceptable. The German arguments for their retention of Upper Silesia began reaching the Allies through various routes.[5] Almost all Germany's objections were based on economic or historical grounds. She emphasized the danger to the European economy if the territory fell under Polish control and denied any past or present Polish connection with Upper Silesia.

Prussia had acquired its Silesian provinces from the Habsburg Empire by force of arms in 1742, only 30 years before the first Polish partition. Silesia and the Duchy of Cieszyn had fallen into Habsburg hands in 1526, when the Bohemian estates had elected Ferdinand I as their King. The Polish monarchy had renounced its overlordship of both territories in favour of Bohemia in 1335.[6] In 1919, Germany cited Bohemia's acquisition of the territory as the date from which Germanic control of Silesia extended. This, of course, was dismissed by most Allied experts. Nevertheless, by the time of Frederick the Great's annexation of Silesia in 1742, most of the rich farmland of Lower Silesia was German. Frederick prized Lower Silesia for the taxes he could raise on it, but had no great regard for Upper Silesia, describing it as 'a ruined country, incapable of defence, whose inhabitants would never be loyal'.[7] And although this comment may have been influenced by other factors, it acknowledged the significant differences between the populations of the two districts.[8]

The acquisition of Silesia had been the making of Prussia. First, the state's income from Lower Silesia augmented the meagre amounts derived from the sandy, forested lands of Brandenburg and East Prussia. Secondly, the exploitation of the rich mineral resources of Upper Silesia, rapidly developed during the nineteenth century, provided the 'iron' for Bismarck's 'blood and iron' policies on which the Reich was forged. After the partitions, Prussia shared the great Silesian coalfield with Austria and Russia, and there was a similar sustained investment in and around the Duchy of Cieszyn (which the Habsburgs had retained in 1742). But in Dombrowa (in the Russian area of partition), after much initial development, further investment was progressively witheld for strategic reasons. By 1914 these Russian mines were old-fashioned and inefficient. And here it should also be noted that, by the start of the twentieth century, the Ruhr had overtaken Silesia as Germany's major industrial region. In Upper Silesia German industrialists began looking east for new markets, and when the war in the east turned in their favour in 1915 they became leading advocates for the annexation of Russian Poland.

During their stewardship of Upper Silesia, Prussian land colonization had continued. German-speaking farmers, for example, occupied almost all of the Prince of Hohenlohe's land on the west bank of the Oder. And, to the east, almost all rural and industrial land had remained firmly under the control of the Prince of Pless, the Donnersmarck dynasty, and other wealthy landowning industrialists, all of whom were counted among the wealthiest and most influential magnates of Europe.[9] Thousands of German managers and technicians, administrators, officials, and soldiers had also flooded into Upper Silesia with their families to service the great industrial machine being built. By 1910 the population was almost two million.[10] The German population was concentrated in the urban areas; but many found the region unattractive. Indeed, Prussian civil servants were paid a bonus to serve in Upper Silesia, and many Germans who could, left the district once their tours of duty or contracts were completed. But the Upper Silesian Poles, officially identified by their Catholic faith and

Wasserpolnisch dialect spoken at home, continued to predominate in and around the 'industrial triangle' located between the towns of Tarnowskie Góry, Mysłowice and Gliwice. Their numbers had been reinforced to a certain extent during the industrial expansion by Poles enticed over the frontier to seek work, but from the latter part of the nineteenth century the German authorities had limited such immigration.[11]

In their attempts to refute Poland's ethnographic claims to Upper Silesia, Germans alleged that the Silesian *Wasserpolnisch* dialect (which contained many German words) was so vastly different from written and 'received' Polish that it was not Polish at all. Pointing out that this language had no literature, they also noted that the people who spoke it had never considered themselves Polish nationals in the past.[12] The Germans blamed this spread of pan-Polish ideas amongst the Silesians on an influx of educated Prussian Poles from Poznań. In this latter point there was a good deal of truth. The spill-over of Polish nationalism from Poznań had resulted from a successful 30-year stand that the Poles there had made against the 1871 *Kulturkampf* and Bismarck's 1886 German colonization project.[13] Other factors stimulating Polish nationalism in Upper Silesia were the Germans' own clumsy attempts to assimilate the Polish-speakers, the Catholic Centre Party's move towards a German nationalist stance, the speeches by Polish deputies in the *Landtag* and *Reichstag*, and the Polish labour leaders' resentment of the German Catholic clergy's influence over non-industrial Poles.[14] But the spread of Polish nationalism also owed much to the proximity of Upper Silesia to Austrian Galicia. The Polish universities and other national institutions in Galicia enjoyed substantial cultural autonomy, and provided an educational haven for their fellow nationals living in the other two areas of partition. All of this served to integrate Silesian Polish society with its neighbouring ones. That said, the vast majority of Poles living in Upper Silesia were either peasants, estate workers or the lowest grades of industrial workers. This gave rise to the most consistent German economic argument for retaining the territory. In the manner and in a language to be witnessed later during British decolonization debates in the 1950s, the Germans focused on the complexity of modern industry. They argued that, like the barbarians who destroyed the ancient world, the incapacity of their native Poles to master the intricacies of technology would mean that the mines and factories would fall into disrepair and disuse and be lost as a resource for the recovery of Europe. To avoid this outcome, Poland would have to employ French expertise and capital to run Silesia's industries – something which the British, in particular, would wish to prevent.

This line of argument fitted in well with the way in which the new Polish Republic was being presented in much of the Western press.

For various reasons, not least Poland's attempt to secure its frontiers, radical liberals both in the United States and Britain were mounting a sustained attack on Poland's reputation. They were partly inspired by similar campaigns against Poland run by the Zionists, the Socialists and the Communists. To frighten conservative public opinion, the Germans, like the Czechs who were in dispute with Poland over Cieszyn, repeatedly referred to Polish aspirations or opposition to their plans as 'Bolshevik'. Whilst these allegations attempted to legitimize their military concentration on Poland's borders, again there was an element of truth behind them. In Upper Silesia the Polish struggle did take on a form of class warfare. Richard Timms ascribes Upper Silesian Polish nationalism to the consequences of the industrialization process which had 'inevitably prepared them for a new consciousness as a class and hence as a nation distinct from the German owners'.[15] It was true that the Upper Silesian Poles were very aware that the vast fortunes of these politically influential German landowning industrialists had been amassed on the backs of their labour. In the mood of the time, they wanted a fair share, and it was through this 'capital versus labour' dimension that Polish nationalism came to be so vigorously supported and demonstrated in Upper Silesia.

This was a very different sort of nationalism from that of their Polish counterparts in Poznań. The agricultural region of Poznań was the stronghold of the Polish National Democrats – bitter opponents of the Polish Socialist Parties. Most Upper Silesian industrial workers were members of trade unions organized on nationalist lines – German and Polish – and socialist parties received strong support. Nevertheless, despite the ideological differences between the Silesian Poles and those of Poznań, they worked closely together on shared nationalist aims. In December 1918, during the interregnum between Imperial Germany's collapse and the restoration of central authority, Upper Silesian delegates participated in the election of an 80-strong Supreme Peoples' Council to represent all Prussian Poles.[16] But this body's executive was propelled into the leadership of the spontaneous rebellion that had broken out in Poznań on 26 December. Although the Peace Conference eventually imposed a military demarcation line across the Poznań district, forcing the German Government to tolerate a Polish administration there, the line was scarcely recognized by either the Polish fighters or the amalgam of German forces opposing them.[17] The continued fighting drained the Executive's resources. They were also under pressure from the Polish Government's peace delegation in Paris. Its members were concerned about the damage frontier conflicts were having on Poland's international standing. They feared a reaction from the Powers if Poles in Upper Silesia also began resisting the German authorities. In fact, expecting the territory to be awarded to Poland within a few months, members of the Poznań Executive had assured the Peace Conference's visiting Inter-Allied Commission that they would act to prevent a similar rising in Upper Silesia.[18] On learning that an armed insurrection was due to occur there on 22 April 1919, Upper Silesia's foremost Polish politician and Executive member, Wojciech Korfanty, persuaded its organizers to abandon their plans.[19]

The conspirators appear to have been socialists and leaders of Upper Silesia's embryonic branch of Piłsudski's Polish Military Organization (POW).[20] Partly for the reasons outlined above and because of close ties already existing between their trade unions and Poland's socialists, from 1919 the Silesian Poles started looking towards the reborn Polish state for assistance. The new independent Poland was both physically and politically closer to the Upper Silesian Poles than Poznań and its National Democrat leadership. Nevertheless Piłsudski realized there was little that Poland could usefully do about the German frontier until the Peace Conference reached its decision. Knowing that the Germans would do all in their power to resist the loss of these assets, he nevertheless permitted the POW to start organizing a paramilitary defence force within Upper Silesia and on the Dombrowa side of the border. From an unpromising experience in the first Upper Silesian insurrection in August 1919, the POW emerged as a formidable fighting force.

Amongst the Allies in Paris, unlike elsewhere on Germany's eastern frontiers, an apparent unanimity had prevailed on the amount of Upper Silesia that was to be transferred to Poland.[21] But the experts had been over-generous. Spurred on by the French members who wanted Germany reduced everywhere, the expert committee, after identifying areas with clear Polish majorities, rounded upwards by incorporating transport infrastructure and what was deemed to be strategically essential territory – all from areas that should have remained German.[22] They took too much territory from the north and added land from the west bank of the Oder. This would have moved the new German frontier away from the strategically vulnerable industrial area being awarded to Poland. There was no official Polish participation in the Committee's decision, but since this extra territory was being transferred directly to Poland, the Polish delegation acquiesced in this. This was a mistake. The injustice further fired German resistance within Upper Silesia, giving them more credible arguments in support of demands for the population to be consulted on their future.

German demands for a plebiscite coincided with their attempts to provoke a Polish rising in Upper Silesia. This aimed at rooting out active opposition there, discrediting Poland and intimidating the population. The Polish nationalists were purged. Over 200 were exiled and many more imprisoned. Others fled from the territory to avoid a similar fate. And even before the peace terms had been presented to Germany, the German propaganda campaign had successfully persuaded the Peace Conference's British delegation that should the peace terms prove unacceptable, then the German opposition might be appeased by ordering a plebiscite in Upper Silesia. As soon as the anticipated German rejection was received in Paris on 29 May, Lloyd George set about convincing the French and the Americans of the need to satisfy Germany over Silesia. He was under heavy domestic political pressure to get Germany to sign – even threatening British abstention should a military occupation of Germany be required to force the Peace Terms on her. President Wilson was very sceptical about Lloyd George's motives and arguments, and Clemenceau correctly predicted trouble should this concession be granted to Germany. After some of the Conference's most acrimonious discussions, the others gave way when safeguards for the Polish Silesians were conceded and British participation in the Inter-Allied military force to be sent there promised.[23]

It fell to the Polish Prime Minister, Ignacy Paderewski, to say why Poland objected to a plebiscite. Should this be held, he declared, then as things stood the Poles had little chance of carrying the agricultural areas. The German state-appointed Catholic clergy were hostile to Polish nationalism. Also, like the clergy, the German landlords exerted a direct influence over the Polish peasants and estate workers. That said, Poland would take the industrial region in the East. This was the complete reverse of what the British experts, though not the American ones, were predicting. But because Poland needed the region's mines, plant and resources to help build a viable industrial sector (and because no alternative was on offer), Paderewski was forced to accept Lloyd George's plebiscite. This was on condition that the vote was counted by individual communes.

Counting the votes of almost 1,500 communes individually was, the Poles believed, the only means they had to ensure that a fair demarcation line would be established across Upper Silesia. Paderewski made it plain that, should the vote be counted as one single constituency, then because of their preponderant influence over Polish-speaking peasants to the North and their direct control over them west of the Oder the Germans would win. After assuring Paderewski on this point, Lloyd George quietly instructed the British official negotiating the plebiscite's terms to have the vote taken *en bloc*. Commenting on his back-door instructions later, the official pointed out that if he had stuck to them, the French and the

Americans would simply have demanded a much smaller plebiscite area throughout which the Poles would have had a majority.[24] Confirming the Polish delegation's belief that they had won this point, it may be noted that (for the Peace Conference's administrative convenience) they even agreed to two more overwhelmingly German districts being added to the plebiscite area.[25] The plebiscite itself was to be held within six to eighteen months after the arrival of an Inter-Allied Commission which would organize it and make recommendations to the Supreme Council on the line that the new frontier should take. German troops would leave within two weeks of the Peace Treaty's implementation, to be replaced by an appropriate-sized Inter-Allied force, consisting of American, British, French and Italian troops. The Commission would arrive with them. It would have full executive authority, except powers over tax and legislation, an ambiguous sovereignty which was to lead to confusion later. However, what was unforeseen was that due to delays in ratification and the refusal of the American Senate to approve it, the Peace Treaty would not come into force until January 1920. This would give German forces of resistance six more months to purge and intimidate the population into supporting the German cause; for, whilst Paris had been making up its mind, in Silesia general conditions had deteriorated even further.

As elsewhere in eastern Germany, along Silesia's frontier with Poland the *Reichswehr* and *Freikorps* units and the locally enlisted *Grenzschutz* (border guards) had been reinforced, and were making artillery and air strikes on Polish towns and villages. In the international press, the Germans were claiming that a Polish invasion of Upper Silesia was imminent. Meanwhile, within Silesia physical attacks on Poles continued, and demonstrations supportive of Germany's retention of Upper Silesia were encouraged. The Polish leaders who were able to, preached restraint, but Spartacist-style agitation thrived as mines were closed down and engines, machine tools, locomotives, rail trucks and any form of transportable material were removed from any location likely to become Polish. As strikes and rioting broke out, wild secessionist schemes circulated amongst Germany's senior military commanders.[26] Another uprising by Polish partisans was nipped in the bud by Korfanty on 22 June, but one week later the British Army's *Cologne Post* reported that, as a result of armed retaliation by Poles in Kosel, 'sanguinary reprisals' were being inflicted in Upper Silesia. The news of the plebiscite added to the uncertainty. Acting on behalf of the Upper Silesians from Warsaw, the Polish Government made repeated appeals for Allied intervention. During July and August the strikes escalated. In Paris, some thought the Silesian authorities were attempting to provoke a Polish–German military confrontation.

Conversely, the French believed that the Poles had orchestrated them to force the Allies to intervene.[27] But whatever view was taken, the negative effect of the Silesian mining strikes on European coal production made Upper Silesia an object of international concern.

On 16 August the increasingly violent response by the German authorities towards the strikers finally provoked an insurrection. In addition to more pay and bonuses, the 200,000 strikers demanded the reopening of the closed factories and mines, the reinstatement of discarded workmen, the release of all political prisoners and permission for food deliveries to be received from across the Polish frontier. A rumour that unemployed workmen were about to be deported to France to carry out reconstruction work had also swept through the region. *The Times* reported that in numerous villages all the male population over the age of 17 had been rounded up and marched off.[28] The strikers' families were also under attack. The Poles claimed that the Germans, despite having purged the Polish leaders, had found that Polish workers remained unresponsive to German propaganda and intimidation. Thousands of workers were also forced to flee when the Silesian authorities started arresting them as well. Some were killed or wounded resisting arrest. Others went into hiding, supported by their families. Allegations circulated about how, attempting to find them, German volunteers were torturing the fugitives' wives and children.[29] In Katowice, crowds protesting against high food prices were fired on by German troops. Ten people were killed and many wounded when *Grenzschutz* soldiers fired on Polish miners queueing at Mysłowice to collect outstanding wages: they had refused to form into groups of ten because they feared deportation.[30] The news swept through the region and within hours Poles living in Katowice, Bytom, Tarnowskie Góry and the smaller towns and villages around them rose in spontaneous popular revolt. By its very nature the fighting was fragmentary but widespread, occurring first in the eastern districts, and then spreading out through the Pszczyna (Pless) and Rybnik districts. The Government's Special Commisioner, Otto Hörsing, the virtual dictator of Upper Silesia, ordered all workmen to return to their jobs and announced that any insurgent caught with arms would be shot.[31]

The insurgents had few weapons, but they captured several thousand rifles which they speedily distributed and turned on the soldiers. Amidst the confusion, some POW units were activated. About 9,000 Upper Silesian émigrés who had fled the German persecution joined hastily organized military units and recrossed the frontier. Hörsing's Press Bureau blamed Spartacist agitation, but even the left-wing British *Daily Herald* rejected this, citing the German *Freiheit*'s view that the unrest was simply the fruit of Hörsing's policy of violence.[32] The first official communication concerning the insurrection arrived in Paris from Herbert Hoover, the Supreme Economic Council's Director-General of Relief who had just completed an inspection of the Council's Coal Commission operation in Central Europe. He recommended an Allied military occupation to restore Upper Silesia's coal production, which he reported was 'jeopardizing the life of Europe'. Hoover also recommended that a four-man Inter-Allied commission be despatched to take charge of the region.[33] But the Peace Conference could not intervene until the Peace Treaty was implemented. This was because the Armistice (which remained in force) had left Upper Silesia under German sovereignty until then. Several suggestions were made, ranging from sending Coal Commissioners to administer the Silesian coalfield as one unit to anticipating the Peace Treaty 'by a few weeks'; but they all foundered on the lack of German consent.

Within a few days the German authorities had the military situation back under their control. The reinforcements rushed into the industrial area had brought the total number of armed personnel at their disposal to between 80,000 and 100,000 men. They retaliated with great force, and since the insurgents preferred death to surrender the German troops took few prisoners. Those they did capture were executed. Unarmed Poles were also shot, or killed by other methods. *The Times*'s correspondent thought the military authorities' behaviour 'the ugliest feature of the whole catastrophe'.[34] Finally responding to the Peace Conference's concerns, the Germans invited the heads of the military missions liaising with them in Berlin to send an Inter-Allied Commission composed of a few junior officers to Upper Silesia.[35] However, they restricted the Commission's role to investigating the causes of the insurrection and, on arrival, it found itself ineffective in dealing with the situation. At the Peace Conference's insistence, another more high-powered commission consisting of the heads of the Berlin military missions was despatched to ensure that order had been restored. They were to report their findings to the Conference and make recommendations to the German Government.[36] At Katowice, this second Inter-Allied Commission was joined by its United States representative, Colonel A. C. Goodyear.

A member of Hoover's Coal Commission, Goodyear had been acting as the Peace Conference's local arbitrator in Upper Silesia since the start of the insurrection. His primary objective was the restoration of coal production. To this end he liaised between the warring factions, attempting to identify the causes of the fighting, halt the executions of Poles and obtain the return of over 200 German hostages who had been interned in Poland. They had been carried over the frontier by Poles retreating from the determined military onslaught the Germans had mounted on the towns the

Poles had held.[37] Goodyear's activities brought him into indirect contact with the Warsaw Government, which was under considerable domestic political pressure to intervene in Silesia and considerable diplomatic pressure not to. The sudden arrival of independence had unleashed a great tide of patriotism in Poland. The insurrection shifted the Poles' attention away from their eastern frontiers towards the plight of their Silesian cousins. A 'League for the Union of Upper Silesia with Poland' sprung up, along with many other support groups whose activities grew over the next two years. In Warsaw, the national political organizations' rank and file held rallies and demonstrations demanding that their Government send armed assistance. A governmental crisis was only averted when Paderewski called the leaders of the major political parties to a meeting endorsing the Government's strict adherence to the Peace Treaty.[38] This tension between national sentiment and the restriction placed on it by international pressure would severely test the Polish Government in the months ahead.

In Upper Silesia, with the insurrection crushed and the general strike ending, Goodyear obtained the Polish Government's permission for the German hostages' return. He also began discussions with the German authorities on a general amnesty for the 22,000 Silesian refugees now in Poland.[39] *The Times* noted that the strike had only been broken because, faced with a choice of working or being deported, the strikers had sullenly chosen the former.[40] Goodyear described the industrial area as being outwardly calm, adding only that strong feelings of unrest and dissatisfaction still existed beneath the surface.[41] In their report to Paris, the Inter-Allied Commissioners failed to establish the exact cause of the insurrection. They recommended the setting up of a strong Allied Commission backed by a military presence in Upper Silesia, and that more pressure be applied to the Polish Government to stop the POW organizing itself there.[42] In a separate report the British representative observed that the Commission's greatest difficulty had been in finding impartial advice. He also acknowledged that the combination of national, industrial and religious differences in Upper Silesia had been rendered more acute by the prospect of a plebiscite. As long as Polish and German agents were attempting to influence the plebiscite's outcome, continued discontent had to be expected.[43] Seizing on the Commission's comment about Polish national intrigue being stimulated from outside Silesia, the German Government attempted to put an anti-Polish interpretation on the Commission's findings. Whilst accepting that the German troops had acted with great brutality, by way of mitigation it argued that 'the numerous cases of inhuman treatment of the Germans by the Polish rebels provoked the troops to the utmost'. They did reject the Commission's view that the return of Polish leaders would contribute to general tranquillity, but promised to review their list of 262 persons officially debarred from returning.[44]

With order re-established and Upper Silesian coal being produced once again, the Peace Conference focused on new problems, such as forcing German troops from the Baltic States. A British proposal to use Polish troops there was rejected because it might cause renewed conflict in Upper Silesia.[45] In response to Paderewski's plea that a large number of Allied officers be sent to Upper Silesia as observers, six junior officers still working there were ordered to remain as a permanent Allied sub-commission – though still under the Command of the Entente's military representatives in Berlin.[46] Although the Peace Conference can justifiably be criticized for its failure to protect the Polish Silesians, it should be remembered that the intelligence it received (and would go on receiving) from its various sources was highly partial. In fact, the daily reports contained in *The Times* and *The Morning Post* from correspondents on the spot in Katowice were more informed. And, apart from France, such were the Great Powers' domestic political climates and diminishing military resources that there was a reluctance to confront a problem whose solution (Allied occupation and the plebiscite) was believed to be only weeks away. The Powers were also reluctant to undermine the German Government's weak domestic position by overriding its sovereignty in Upper Silesia. Whatever their shade of political opinion, conceding anything to Poland, especially on Upper Silesia, was anathema to all Germans. It could also be said that by acting severely in Upper Silesia the German Government would enjoy near-unanimous national support. But, in one of his last addresses to the *Sejm*, Paderewski absolved the German Government from blame over the insurrection. Instead, he blamed Upper Silesia's administration and the 'refractory soldiers' who had tormented the Silesian workmen.[47] The authorities' conscription of thousands of local Silesians from this highly dimorphic population into the *Grenzschutz* units also created a bitter legacy. These men were known personally to the 'Polish Silesians' and, in many cases, were related to them. This element of civil war effectively consolidated not only the German volunteers' support but also the commitment of these conscripts to the German cause. These and many more irreconcilable differences were to be the inheritance of the Peace Conference's Inter-Allied Commission which finally arrived in Opole on 11 February 1920.

Despite their persistent arguments in favour of a genuine Inter-Allied presence in Upper Silesia, the French found themselves with almost sole responsibility for administering and policing the Upper Silesian plebiscite area.[48] There were several reasons for this. At the military commanders' urging, it was agreed that the Power providing the plebiscite area's largest military contingent would fill the related commission's executive presidency. But, after the American Senate refused to ratify the Peace Treaty, its Army could not participate in any of the plebiscites.[49] Amongst British politicians there was a growing reluctance to leave British troops under French command. The Chief of the Imperial General Staff (CIGS), Field Marshal Sir Henry Wilson, was also quite opposed to any British Army involvement in Europe.[50] By early January 1920 Wilson had whittled down the British military's German-Polish plebiscite commitments to just a couple of batallions deployed in Gdańsk and around Kwidzyn (Marianwerder) and Olsztyn (Allenstein).[51] The breach caused by the absence of American and British troops was partially compensated by increasing the numbers of French ones. However, when they and the even less numerous Italian troops failed to maintain the Upper Silesia Commission's authority, France was attacked for threatening the Entente's future. By then, critics had come to a near-general belief that the French had contrived a near-monopoly in Upper Silesia in a bid to ensure that the industrial area went to Poland – something seen, correctly, as serving the national interest of France.

From the outset, the Inter-Allied Commission took direct control of every department and service in Upper Silesia. In addition to the economic and financial administration, it ran departments such as the railways, food distribution, postal services, the courts and the police. District controllers were appointed to each *Kreis* to direct local administration and implement the Commission's decrees.[52] The President of the Commission was General Henri Le Rond. Unlike fellow commissioners Lieutenant Colonel Harold Percival and General de Marinis, representing Britain and Italy respectively, Le Rond had an extensive knowledge of Polish affairs. He had served on all of the Peace Conference's Polish Committees, spoken at many Supreme Council and Heads of Delegations' meetings, and was almost the sole author of the plans on which the Commission was organized.[53] The Commissioners were assisted by a small secretariat, and by about 130 mainly civilian officials distributed throughout the departments they were running. Le Rond and the French officials ran most of the key departments and held the most important district controller posts. In the Commission both Percival and Marinis had very restricted non-executive roles, leaving them with time on their hands. Although the Commissioners were technically subordinate to the Peace Conference, Percival quickly allowed himself to be reduced to the role of diplomatic cat's paw for the Foreign Office. Soon relations within the Commission reflected in microcosm the wider diplomatic struggle over the Entente's attitude towards

Germany. Upper Silesia became a pawn in this game. This was manifested in petty jealousies and squabbling amongst officials and controllers over national *amour propre* – something quickly exploited by both the Poles and the Germans.

At first the Commissioners went out of their way to avoid any impression of division, but a British official later observed that, as the Commissioners began being courted by the various factions, the gradual separation of their views accelerated until the gap became a chasm.[54] Lobbying of the individual Commissioners first resulted from the differing hopes and expectations held by the two camps concerning the Commission's role in Upper Silesia. The Germans had thought the Commission would content itself with maintaining the Upper Silesian status quo. But when Commission officials began reorganizing the administration and making their own decisions, leading Germans began offering serious resistance. Conversely, the Poles expected much more from the Commission than they got. Although Polish became an official language, the Commission's failure to replace any German Upper Silesian officials with Polish ones disappointed the Polish population. The Poles also complained about the Commission's maintenance of the 3,000 all-German *Sicherheitspolizei* (police-militia). After the *Reichswehr* had fulfilled the Peace terms by departing from Upper Silesia prior to the arrival of the Commission's Inter-Allied military force, the only official military formation left there was the *Sicherheitspolizei* – the German Government having also complied with Peace Conference requests to disband or evacuate all other paramilitary units.[55] Generally speaking, however, the Poles were happy with French domination of the Commission and the Germans resented it. They aired their complaints to the sympathetic British, themselves increasingly disenchanted with the obvious French partiality for the Poles. Strikes by German organizations broke out, attacks were made on the French troops and inter-communal tensions rose. After visiting Upper Silesia, E. H. Carr wrote in a report to the Foreign Office that the Commission failed to inspire confidence, either from the point of view of maintaining order or the holding of an impartial plebiscite.[56] But the most significant developments at this time were occurring outside Upper Silesia: that is, the Polish Army's retreat from the Ukraine during June and July 1920. With the Red Army threatening the very existence of the Polish Republic, for many German Upper Silesians the equation was simple: no Poland – no plebiscite.

The German Government had declared territorial neutrality in the conflict, but its attempts to extend this neutrality to Upper Silesia foundered on the questionable sovereignty awarded to the Inter-Allied Commission.[57]

German fears that the region might be turned into a battlefield did have a basis. Discussing the Soviet advance and the possibility of a German–Soviet military alliance, Marshal Foch stated that, if Poland were defeated, the Poles could 'crystallize' around the Allied force in Upper Silesia and 'hold on for time'.[58] The Soviets' advance had brought calculated declarations of neutrality from all of Poland's neighbours except Rumania, which halted the transit of Allied troops or military supplies to Poland. As an expression of solidarity with the Soviets, at railways and ports across Europe trade unions and socialist organizations were already operating a European-wide embargo on military equipment to Poland. Allegations about infringements to neutrality made headlines in the press. Three French soldiers were killed in an accident caused by German railway employees attempting to hinder the movement of two Allied batallions travelling from Cieszyn to reinforce Upper Silesia.[59] German Silesian newspapers whipped up the political temperature by supporting calls for a general strike. By 17 August reports were circulating about the Red Army having taken Warsaw. That same day German strikes and demonstrations degenerated into violent attacks on French troops and Polish civilians. At Katowice rifles and hand grenades were used to attack the District Controller's office. Four more French soldiers were killed and a doctor sympathetic to the Polish cause was lynched in the street. The violence continued the next day. Polish shops were looted, Polish newspaper printing machines were smashed and the headquarters of the official Polish Plebiscite Committee was set on fire. Percival reported that French troops had failed to take any steps to protect these establishments. Korfanty, who had been appointed by the Warsaw Government to head the official Polish Plebiscite Committee, informed the Commission that he was mobilizing the Polish population for self-protection. As the scale of the Red Army's defeat at Warsaw became clearer, a 20,000-strong army of ragged Polish-speaking youths appeared the next day, and an accompanying strike by Polish miners shut down three-quarters of the region's 45 coal mines. Within a few days nearly all of the industrial area and the predominantly Polish districts around it were in their possession. Wherever they established control, the Polish bands disarmed and expelled the *Sicherheitspolizei*. Other German functionaries were also dismissed.[60] A two-way traffic in prisoners, hostages and supplies was conducted across the Polish border with the insurgents' headquarters at Sosnowice. With industry at a standstill, the Commission's troops pulled back to the towns and urban centres and, with the Poles now controlling the eastern part of the plebiscite area, Korfanty launched a political initiative to end the conflict.

After a series of meetings which Le Rond later claimed credit for arranging, Korfanty, Silesian Polish political party leaders and Polish trade union representatives reached an agreement with Dr Urbanek, the Director of the official German Plebiscite Committee, and leaders of the corresponding German organizations.[61] Arms would be laid down, calm restored and work in the mines resumed in exchange for, amongst other things, the formation of a joint committee to implement measures against outsiders unlawfully influencing the plebiscite; the prohibition of discriminatory or intimidatory behaviour towards other persons in private or industrial life; and the replacement of the *Sicherheitspolizei* by a new Upper Silesian police force composed in equal proportion of Upper Silesians of German and Polish sympathies.[62] The Poles now began to feel a movement towards equality of status, but the manner of their attaining it aroused fierce resentment amongst some British members of the Commission.

On the international stage the impending decision on Upper Silesia's future began to acquire a strategic significance. Agreements between the Entente partners and Germany had turned continued delivery of German Ruhr-mined coal to France and Belgium into a condition for European economic stability – any default on Germany's part initiating a legitimate occupation of the Ruhr's industrial districts. Britain and France were well aware (as events in January 1923 illustrated) that an occupation of the Ruhr could prove disastrous for the German economy, even threatening the integrity of the Reich itself. This action would suit the French and Belgian Governments because it would vastly reduce the power of their ever-threatening German neighbour. But the British Government, which was desperate by now for the return of pre-war trading conditions, had retreated to its traditional European 'balance-of-power' strategy. In practical terms, this meant preventing the French from becoming too powerful on the Continent and helping the fledgling German democracy to survive as the motor for European economic recovery. Lloyd George believed that Germany needed Silesian industry to pay its reparations, and that Germany's continued possession of Upper Silesia would help negate the economic, political and strategic consequences of a Franco-Belgian occupation of the Ruhr. Thus, from pragmatic ambivalence over Upper Silesia's future, British policy gradually shifted to one that backed German retention of the industrial area. Never slow to exploit discord in the Entente's ranks, German negotiators tacitly linked continuation of reparation coal deliveries for Belgium and France with the fate of Upper Silesia; and soon the Polish press was reporting that the German Government was withholding support for Germans living in the Southern Tyrol in exchange for Italian support in Upper Silesia.[63] In subsequent diplomatic encounters, the British defence of German interests in Upper Silesia became quite overt. The first British demand was for a reorganization of the Commission.

Percival had reported that the Commission's handling of the August crisis had engendered a great loss of confidence in its function amongst the respective Upper Silesian communities. The British Foreign Secretary, Lord Curzon, believed that its prestige could only be restored by replacing Le Rond and the Commission's military commander, General Jules Gratier. Percival, who had offered to resign on grounds of ill-health, could also be dismissed.[64] This suggestion, and Curzon's other proposed improvements, were designed to increase British control over the Commission's activities without having to make a corresponding British military commitment. Curzon regarded the revision as being so necessary that he threatened to withdraw the British contingent from the Commission if his demands were not met.[65] The French would not sanction either Le Rond's or Gratier's dismissal, but conceded that the Commission required more accountable administrative procedures. Around the highly politicized industrial area, the district controllers were reshuffled to increase British representation there. The intelligence services were opened up to the British and the Italians, and 12 British officers were appointed to the new ethnically mixed Upper Silesian police force.[66] The Foreign Office was pleased with the outcome, and Lord Hardinge minuted that British control had been considerably increased by the new scheme.[67] The revitalized Commission now attempted to fix a date for the plebiscite and refine its regulations. The Poles wanted an early date but the Germans did not.[68] However, a great debate was sparked by a Polish request to have the non-resident (outvoter) articles in the Peace Treaty abolished. These permitted anyone who had been born in Upper Silesia but who now lived elsewhere to vote in the plebiscite.

At the request of the Poles, outvoting provisions had been introduced for the plebiscites at Kwidzyn and Olsztyn. These articles had been included in the Peace Treaty before the Peace Conference had decided upon a plebiscite for Upper Silesia. In the rush to amend the Treaty, the Olsztyn plebiscite articles were simply transferred over to the Upper Silesia plebiscite articles *in toto*.[69] But the result of these two plebiscites held in East Prussia during July 1920 had revealed that the vast majority of outvoters were not Poles but Germans. Writing to Curzon, Percival estimated that, since German outvoters could form at least 20 per cent of the total vote, they could 'turn the scale in favour of Germany in communes where there might otherwise be a small majority in favour of Poland'.[70] The diplomatic wrangles over outvoters ebbed and flowed. Any change to the Versailles Treaty would require the consent of Germany and Poland. This was thought so unlikely that none of the Powers contested the out-voters' right to vote. Diplomatic exchanges centred around where and when they would vote, and the security implications posed by possibly up to 350,000 German outvoters arriving in Upper Silesia simultaneously.[71] Within Upper Silesia, Korfanty led a campaign to deter outvoters from registering in Germany. He was aided in this by the horror stories about Polish atrocities carried each day in the German national press. In a speech at Oleśno (Rosenberg), he allegedly 'called upon his audience to treat German outvoters as traitors and to help him drive them away by force'.[72] Korfanty's demagogic personality dominated the plebiscite debate. In German eyes, there was no crime he was incapable of committing. But, although he was melodramatic, we have already seen that he preferred diplomatic to military action. Some of the younger Polish leaders were very headstrong and blamed him for not seizing Upper Silesia early in 1919.[73] Korfanty attempted to maintain a fine balancing act with them. In a bid to retain moderate support, he had to restrain the POW, the Sokół (Falcon) groups, and the Bojowska–Polska terror squads. Shortly after his Oleśno speech had achieved its desired effect, Korfanty urged the Polish Silesians to keep quiet and offered the Germans a mutual understanding guaranteeing order.[74] An uneasy peace prevailed whilst joint committees compiled voting registers. In Germany, the anti-Polish press campaign had started to backfire. Instead of an anticipated 300,000 outvoter registra-tions by early February, only 170,000 applications had been received. On top of a daily diet of Polish terrorism and press editorials speculating about Silesian coups and invasions, perhaps the last straw for many poten-tial outvoters was the German plebiscite organizer's offer of free life insurance. The news that British troops were being sent to Upper Silesia coincided with an increase in the number of outvoter registrations to 190,000 – still a considerable number, but many fewer than expected.[75]

In Poland neither the press nor the voluntary organizations that had sprung up in the wake of the 1919 insurrection would permit the public's interest in the plebiscite to subside. Newspaper articles, public posters and cinema films fanned public opinion in an effort to collect funds for the plebiscite campaign. Heightened national awareness meant that almost every decision taken by the Commissioners or the Conference was imme-diately condemned as having been a concession to Germany – and Britain had pushed for them on Germany's behalf. The final details were ham-mered out at a meeting held in London on February 21.[76] The plebiscite would be held on March 20, 1921 and outvoters would vote in their respective communes alongside the residents that same day.

The arrival of 3,000 British troops had provided the Commission's military force with much-needed credibility amongst the Germans. But the Commission was dogged with foreboding in the days preceding the vote. Rumours of coups and counter-coups circulated. Reacting to rumours of an invasion, members of the Allied Military Missions in Warsaw monitored the size and movements of the Polish Army units on the Silesian border. There were exaggerated reports of violence, including cross-border terrorist raids. And on 8 March, the day before mobilization of German outvoters began, Allied troops occupied three Rhineland towns. This action was in response to further German intransigence over reparations and their continued attempts to link payments with German retention of Upper Silesia – a condition that France had never accepted.[77] The wave of patriotism this action generated in Germany spurred the outvoters to action, and their arrival in Upper Silesia greatly aided German morale. Over the next ten days some 280 trains brought 180,000 outvoters from Germany and 10,000 from Poland. The Germans were well-organized. Many had received free rail tickets, and the German *Schutzbund* (protective league) provided up to ten days' free board. Sarah Wambaugh notes that some had not been to Upper Silesia for decades, while many of them were old, crippled, or in the later stages of pregnancy. The rail journeys became 'a triumphal progress, bands playing and flags waving at every station'.[78] Thanks to the presence of the extra troops and the efforts of the Upper Silesian leaders to keep their factions in check, to everyone's relief it all passed off without incident. Percival recorded that 20 March was one of the quietest days Upper Silesia had experienced since August 1920. In some areas an almost holiday atmosphere prevailed, and the only crowds that *The Times*'s special correspondent encountered 'were round some French tanks and at Post Offices in search of plebiscite stamps'.[79]

As the votes began to be counted, both sides started claiming victory, but it soon became clear that (as Paderewski had predicted) the communes to the west of the Oder had clearly voted for Germany, with the communes around the industrial triangle generally for Poland. However, there was no clear outcome across the industrial area's patchwork of communes. Out of the 1,474 commune polling areas, approximately 792 voted for Germany and 682 for Poland.[80] But in the battle of statistics that followed the commune vote and its location were disregarded by Britain and Germany. It was the total of 706,820 votes cast for Germany and 479,418 for Poland that was seized upon. Reich President Friedrich Ebert immediately published a proclamation in Berlin claiming the whole of Upper Silesia for Germany. In London the British Cabinet decided that, in view of the high total of votes cast for Germany in the plebiscite, Curzon should inform the

British Commissioner that he should resist attempts by the Commission (which was responsible for making the recommendation) to award any part of Upper Silesia to Poland.[81] Marinis informed the Italian Foreign Ministry that he personally supported his British colleague on this, but failing an instruction to this effect he would be disposed to let Poland have certain narrowly circumscribed districts on the south and east of the plebiscite area.[82] Needless to say the Poles did not view the result in the same light. They focused not on the huge German majorities in the west, but on the number of communes won in the agricultural south-east and amongst the mixed communities in and around the industrial area. There can be little doubt which interpretation was correct, and Sir Eyre Crowe warned Curzon that

> We must remember, as regards the territorial arrangements to be made as a result of the plebiscite in Upper Silesia, that the French will be in a strong position if they maintain that the Treaty, by expressly stipulating for a frontier line to be laid down in pursuance of the vote by communes, clearly contemplates a division of territory.[83]

This clearly meant the establishment of a frontier, not the award of the whole plebiscite area on the basis of a simple majority. But the correct interpretation did not suit either the German or the British aims. Their politicians and officials continued to quote the overall majority. If contemporary newspaper reports and analysis are the first draft of history, this perhaps explains why English-language historiography still perpetuates the myth that Germany 'won' the plebiscite.[84] Lloyd George told the House of Commons that roughly seven-elevenths of the electorate voted to remain in Germany. The question now remained: what was to become of the four-elevenths who had not?

In a post-plebiscite message to his fellow countrymen, Korfanty praised their endurance, courage and self-sacrifice but warned that the fight had not ended: 'we are now entering a period of diplomatic struggles and international negotiations which are to decide the fate of our home'. Their unity and strength had to be maintained 'in order that our boundaries may be pushed far to the West'.[85] In the arguments and exchanges between the Commissioners, the Government officials and all other interested parties following the plebiscite, every conceivable factor justifying their favoured solutions was explored. For their own reasons, neither Britain nor France wished to partition the industrial area. The frontiers their Commissioners proposed therefore differed greatly. The French favoured the line that the Poles had wanted before the plebiscite. This included the whole industrial area and had the merit of a small Polish majority. The British line sacrificed many thousands of Poles to Germany but few Germans to Poland. It grudgingly conceded the Rybnik and Pszczyna districts to the Poles but denied them any territory in the industrial area. The Italian Commissioner's line was very similar to the British one.[86] Count Sforza, the Italian Foreign Minister, later suggested a more generous settlement for Poland which conceded bits of the industrial area to them. Unsurprisingly, news of what the Italian and British were recommending to the Conference in Paris was leaked and published by Korfanty's newspaper, the *Grenzzeitung*, on Sunday 1 May.[87] Fearing their wishes were about to be disregarded, the Polish miners immediately responded to calls for a general strike and 24 hours later a third Polish insurrection had broken out.[88]

The Silesian Poles had planned carefully for this insurrection. They were well-organized and, in their own fashion, well-led. Their major command and supply lines again extended back over the Polish frontier. They were reinforced by the Polish half of the Commission's 6,000-strong mixed police militia who, after disarming their German colleagues, had deserted *en masse* to the Poles. Fully alive to the gravity of the situation the insurrection created, the Warsaw Government distanced itself from the conflict. It dismissed Korfanty from the Plebiscite Committee, banned the recruitment of volunteers in Poland and ordered the frontier to be closed.[89] Korfanty stopped claiming how spontaneous the uprising had been and confirmed that to prevent anarchy occurring he had taken charge of it. All territory interpreted as Polish from the plebiscite results would be occupied and administered by him until the emergency ended.[90] The western boundary of this territory became known as the 'Korfanty line'. It followed the river Oder to below Opole, then north-east past Dobrodzień (Gutentag) and joined the Polish frontier south of Oleśno. With an estimated 60,000 Polish irregulars sweeping westwards towards the 'Korfanty line', world attention once again focused upon Upper Silesia.

The absence of the Commission's President in Paris convinced Percival that Le Rond had known that the insurrection had been about to occur. With the British troops having returned to Cologne, wholesale slaughter was probably only prevented by the decision to concentrate the vastly outnumbered French and Italian troops in the towns. This was where most of the German-voting population resided. French tanks engaged Polish armed bands attempting to enter Katowice, and the Poles killed 34 Italian troops at Rybnik. Outside the towns, the French remained passive and co-operated with Korfanty's administration. The Germans activated their *Selbstschutz* (self-defence) forces. Berlin appointed General Hoeffer to command them and the many *Freikorps* units rushing to Silesia. In a bid to re-establish Allied authority, some of the Commission's British officers started rebuilding the police force, recruiting local Germans from amongst over 30,000 German volunteers who were flooding into the area.[91] British officers became involved in a critical battle with the Poles for the high ground at Góra Św. Anny (Annaberg), where the Polish westerly advance was halted.[92] With the *Reichswehr* on standby, confrontation between French soldiers and German irregulars, and the possibility of a German–Polish war, governments were galvanized into action. An ex-Rhineland Commissioner and experienced administrator, Sir Harold Stuart, arrived to replace Percival and early in June 6,000 British troops arrived to reinforce the French and Italian soldiers.[93]

The arrival of a military force acceptable to the Germans and the strong diplomatic pressure applied in Warsaw and Berlin saved the situation. It was also very timely for the Poles. The German opposition was becoming increasingly formidable and Korfanty was having great difficulty in keeping control of his forces and maintaining a united political front. The reinvigorated Inter-Allied force established a neutral zone between the opposing armies, occupied it and negotiated a staged withdrawal of the respective forces over two weeks. By the end of July most of the incoming Germans and *Freikorps* units had withdrawn, and the Polish insurgents and local members of the *Selbstschutz* had melted back into the community. With the military situation partially defused and the Commission's authority restored, attention switched back to the international political arena.[94]

Recently available documents indicate that officials from the newly established League of Nations believed that a League solution to Upper Silesia's problems would help to establish the organization's authority and perhaps encourage Germany to apply for membership later.[95] They schemed to get the Italian Government to propose this, and when Britain and France failed to reach a compromise in Paris early in August 1921, Lloyd George seized on the suggestion.[95] The provisional frontier was drawn up in Geneva by the League Council's non-permanent members (Spain, Brazil, China and Belgium). After studying the statistics, consulting their experts and even taking the views of German and Polish Silesians into account, they concluded that the territory should be allocated on a ratio based on the total votes cast for each country. At the same time, they hoped to do everything possible to minimize the number of minorities in each block. The League Council members added provisions establishing joint administrative structures and measures to facilitate economic readjustment. Officials from the League were also to be located there to adjudicate on disputes between the parties as they occurred. Poland received the districts of Rybnik, Pszczyna, Mysłowice, Chorzów, Tarnowskie Góry and Lubliniec. Germany received the rest.[96]

When the League Council's decision was announced in October it was the Germans who were more disappointed with the outcome than the Poles, and the German Government fell. For several months direct Polish–German negotiations took place under the auspices of the League to hammer out the Upper Silesia Convention.[97] When this came into effect on June 3 1922, the respective territories were handed over and the Inter-Allied Commission withdrew. Although the territorial conflict had ended, the dispute continued through every available political, economic and diplomatic channel until the whole of Upper Silesia was reincorporated into the Reich by force of arms in 1939.

For the Polish Upper Silesians it appeared to be a rather pyrrhic victory. Far more Poles were left in Germany than Germans in Poland. The 1919 Minorities' Treaty signed by Poland gave 'Polish Germans' rights not awarded to Poles living in Germany. Manufacturing industries generally remained in German hands, and the condition of the Poles left working on farms and on the estates on the German side of the new frontier failed to improve. Because of the privations and the political upheavals Poland experienced in the early 1920s many Silesians who had fought for reunion with Poland quickly became disillusioned with the deal. German propaganda made great use of these disaffected elements. However, from May 1926, the market gap caused by a year-long strike by British miners enabled Poland to start exploiting to the full Upper Silesia's coal resources. This was aided by the completion of a direct rail link to the new Polish port at Gdynia – enabling easier access to the Baltic market, which the Poles retained after the strike.

Today the whole of Upper and Lower Silesia is incorporated in the Polish Republic and the industrial region's production of coal still remains one of Poland's most important industries. As has been the fate of heavy industries elsewhere in Europe, however, since the early 1990s Upper Silesia has been increasingly experiencing the pain of economic reconstruction sparked by the recent political changes in Poland. But looking more hopefully towards Poland's increased economic and political ties with Western Europe and Germany in particular, perhaps the memories of the 1919–22 Upper Silesian conflict which presaged even more terrible events and regimes will finally be laid to rest.

NOTES

* The financial assistance of The Carnegie Trust for the Universities of Scotland for my work is gratefully acknowledged.

1. In contrast to the treatment of the Polish population in the area of the Prussian partition, the Armistice returned Alsace and Lorraine to France with immediate effect.
2. See *The Peace Handbooks*, prepared for the Peace Conference by the Foreign Office Political Intelligence Department, No. 40, Upper Silesia, No. 52, Prussian Poland and Ethnographic Maps, for detailed information on this subject.
3. Link, Arthur S. (ed.), *The Papers of Woodrow Wilson* [PWW] (Princeton, 1987), vol. 45, pp. 534–9. 'Point XIII. An independent Polish state should be erected which would include the territories inhabited by indisputably Polish populations.'
4. *Documents on British Foreign Policy* [DBFP], first ser. vol. xvi, Pt. 1, Chap. 1, p. 20. Annex to No. 13. Memorandum by Mr James Headlam-Morley respecting Upper Silesia at the Peace Conference.
5. Germany was not permitted to make any submission to the Peace Conference until receipt of Peace Terms in May 1919. But the manner of the war's ending had left Germany's intelligence and propoganda networks intact. These, together with the press in Germany and neutral countries as well as personal contacts with the many Allied military intelligence missions investigating conditions in Germany, were used to channel German views to the Allied delegations in Paris.
6. Wambaugh, Sarah, *Plebiscites Since the War* (Washington, 1933) vol. 1, pp. 144, 207/8. The Treaty of Trencin 1335 recognized that the territories had been a *de facto* fiefdom of the Bohemian crown since the previous century.
7. Gooch, G. P., *Frederick the Great* (London 1990), p. 19.
8. Bowles, T. Gibson, *Sea Law and Sea Tower* (London, 1910), pp. 6/7. In the Treaty of Breslau Frederick took over from Maria Theresa a mortgage on Silesia's silver mines with an annual interest payment of £75,000 to English merchants. He attempted to evade this payment, but was unsuccessful.
9. Pounds, J. G., *The Upper Silesian Industrial Region* (Indiana, 1958), pp. 11/12. This work gives a full account of the geology of Upper Silesia and its industrial development.
10. Wambaugh, *Plebiscites*, p. 211. The 1910 Prussian census recorded the population in the territory forming the 1921 Plebiscite as 1,921,000. Of this, a total 1,248,000 were recorded as being Polish and 673,000 German.
11. Non-resident workmen were nevertheless a very attractive commodity for the industrialists, especially after employers' social insurance contributions were introduced in Germany. Pools of foreign workers were sometimes maintained in camps over the borders.
12. Because of their schooling, most Upper Silesians spoke and were literate in German language. It was the language of the authorities, used in the workplace and in official life. There had been schooling in the Polish language after the 1848 revolution, but this had ended with the 1871 *Kulturkampf*. The subsequent colonization programme and the H-K-T Movement ensured that the Polish language remained confined to domestic life.
13. Nelson, Harold D. (ed.), *Poland – A Country Study* (Washington, 1984), p. 42. Bismarck obtained a 100-million-mark grant from the *Reichstag* to fund this colonization project.
14. Trzeciakowski, Lech, *The Kulturkampf in Prussian Poland* (New York, 1993), pp. 181/3. The German Catholic clergy's hold was undermined somewhat by

the peasants' regular pilgrimages over the Russian frontier to the nearby Polish shrine at Częstochowa.

15. Timms, Richard, *Germanizing Prussian Poland – The H-K-T Society and Struggle for the Eastern Marchland in the German Empire 1894–1914* (1941, New York), pp. 11/16.

16. Hawranek, Kwiatek, *et al.* (eds.), *Encyklopedia powstań śląskich* (Opole, 1982), pp. 90/1 gives details of the political composition of the Upper Silesian delegation to the *Sejm Dzielnicowy w Poznaniu* held on 3–5 December 1918. Upper Silesia sent the largest contingent of the 1,500 representatives attending. The Council's establishment in Poznań was eased by Poles also holding a majority on the Soldiers and Workers' Councils.

17. This is known as the Convention of Trier, and was forced on the Germans by Marshal Foch on 16 February 1919. The German Army's Supreme Council would not recognize it.

18. Public Record Office [PRO] FO608/57 5191. Howard (Warsaw) to Balfour (Paris), 25 March 1919.

19. *Encyklopedia*, p. 707.

20. *Polska Organizacja Wojskowa* (POW).

21. Lundgreen-Nielson, Kay *The Polish Problem at the Paris Peace Conference* (Odense, 1979), *passim*. This is the most comprehensive account of Polish affairs at the Peace Conference.

22. H. D. Nelson, *Land and Power* (London, 1963), pp. 152–3.

23. Link, A. *PWW*, 60, pp. 22–563 *passim*: the Supreme Council debates on holding an Upper Silesian plebiscite.

24. Scottish Record Office [SRO], Lothian Papers GD40/17/901, 7th June 1919, James Headlam-Morley to Philip Kerr. In this letter Headlam Morley, the British official concerned, notes that Lloyd George was attempting to 'deprive the Germans of any possible reason for maintaining that the decision [Peace Treaty] was unfair to them'.

25. These were districts of the Głubczyce (Leobschutz) south of the towns of Kietrz (Katscher) and Głubczyce itself. This had been provisionally allocated to the Czechoslovak state. A small part of the Namslow (Namslau) district was added to the Kluczbork (Kreuzburg) district which was already in the plebiscite area.

26. Carston, F. L., *The Reichswehr and Politics 1918–1932* (Oxford, 1966), pp. 38–45.

27. *DBFP*, 1st ser. 1, ch. 1, 36. Heads of Delegations Meeting, Paris, 18 August 1919, pp. 421/2. Ibid., 38. Heads of Delegations Meeting, Paris, 20 August 1919.

28. *The Times*, Monday 25 August 1919.

29. Challener, Richard, D., *U.S. Military Intelligence – Weekly Summaries* (New York, 1978), 9, No. 119 W/E 6 September 1919. This repeats an appeal sent to the Peace Conference by a Silesian Polish representative prior to the outbreak of the insurrection. It predicted an explosion at any minute.

30. PRO F0608/140 18533A, 1 September 1919. Wyndham (Warsaw) to Curzon (London). This includes an *aide memoire* of 28 August sent by the Polish Foreign Office to the British Legation in Warsaw, giving an analysis of the cause of the insurrection and immediate events.

31. *The Times*, Wednesday 20 August 1919.

32. *Daily Herald*, Friday 22 August 1919.

33. *DBFP*, 1st ser., vol. 1, ch. 1, No. 36, App. 1, pp. 430/1. Heads of the Delegation Meeting of 18 August 1919.
34. *The Times*, Monday 25 August 1919.
35. PRO WO106/971 84080, Annex 1, 24 August 1919. General Malcolm (Berlin) to Director of Military Intelligence (London and Paris).
36. *DBFP*, 1st ser., 1, ch. 1, No. 43, pp. 541/2. Heads of Delegations Meeting, 26 August 1919. The Generals left Berlin for Katowice on 3 September, returning on the 9th.
　　PRO FO608/140 18533: 27 August 1919. Balfour (Paris) to Wyndham (Warsaw).
　　Bane and Luntz, *Organization of American Relief in Europe 1918–1919*, p. 713.
37. Bane and Luntz, *Organization of American Relief*, p. 713. Goodyear estimated that between 15,000 and 30,000 Poles had sought refuge in Poland.
38. PRO FO371/3899 122821, 25 August 1919. Wyndham (Warsaw) to Curzon (London).
39. Correspondence with Professor Wacław Ryzewski of Warsaw University, author of *Trzecie Powstanie Śląskie* (Warsaw 1977), a recognized authority on the military aspects of the Upper Silesian insurrections. Estimates of the Polish dead in the 1919 insurrection vary between 477 and 2,500.
40. *The Times*, Wednesday 27 August 1919.
41. Bane and Luntz, *Organization of American Relief*, pp. 712/13.
42. PRO FO371/3899 134416, 9 September 1919. 2nd Report of Inter-Allied Commission on Upper Silesian Insurrection.
43. PRO WO144/29 Desp. 307, 13 September 1919. General Malcolm's Weekly Report No. 21 to DMI (London).
44. PRO FO371/3849 134416, 13 September 1919 (enclosure). Muller to General Dupont (Berlin).
45. *DBFP* 1st ser., vol. 1, ch. 1, No. 57, pp. 693/7. Heads of Delegation Meeting, 15 September 1919.
46. Ibid. No. 70, pp. 865/6. Heads of Delegation Meeting, 7 October 1919.
47. PRO FO371/3900 154588, 15 November 1919. Rumbold (Warsaw) to Curzon (London). Translation of speech made by Paderewski 12 November 1919, reviewing domestic and foreign affairs.
48. *DBFP*, 1st ser., vol. 1, ch. 1, No. 62, pp. 756/60, 22 September 1919. Ibid No. 73 pp. 931/4 13 October 1919 for examples of debate on subject in Heads of Delegation meetings.
49. Nelson, Keith L. *Victors Divided – America and the Allies in Germany 1918–1923* (Los Angeles, 1975), pp. 148/9. An American 'Silesian Brigade' specifically allocated to the Upper Silesian inter-Allied military force remained in the American Rhineland occupation zone at Koblenz until December 1921.
50. PRO FO608/161 19181, 24 September 1919. Astoria (Paris) to Curzon (London).
　　The unsettled international situation, the commitments of an overextended empire, troubles in Ireland and industrial unrest at home, all combined to place an excessive burden on the British Army at a time of reorganization for its peacetime role.
51. Edmonds, Sir James E. *The Occupation of the Rhineland 1918–1929* (HMSO, 1987), pp. 175/7.

52. Gajda, Patricia A. *Postscript to Victory – British policy and the German–Polish borderlands 1919–1925* (Washington, 1982), pp. 48/9.
53. Lieutenant Colonel Percival was one of several British Army representatives seconded to the Commission directly from the British Army liaison team in Berlin.
54. PRO FO371/5909 C115809/92/18, 14 May 1921. Private letter Craig (Opole) to Lindsay (F.O. London).
55. Waite, Robert G. L., *Vanguard of Nazism – The Free Corps Movement in Post War Germany 1918–1925 (Massachusetts, 1952)*, pp. 137/8. Many *Grenzschutz, Landschutz* and *Freikorps* personnel from outside Upper Silesia were hidden away from the Commission by Silesia's landowning industrialists. They employed them as labourers on the estates or as security guards in the mines and factories. The German Government continued to maintain and finance them. They re-emerged most notably as part of General Hoeffer's *Selbstschutz* during the 1921 insurrection.
56. *DBFP*, 1st ser., vol. XI, ch. 1, No. 18, pp. 23–7. Extract from notes by Mr. E. H. Carr, 12 June 1920. After leaving the Foreign Office E. H. Carr became a noted historian.
57. PRO FO371/4815 C4326/1621/18, 18 August 1920. Percival (Opole) to Curzon (London).
58. *DBFP*, 1st ser., vol. VIII, ch. X, No. 71, p. 598. The other part of the plan was for the Allies to seize the Ruhr. With the French and the Poles preventing them from using the Silesian industries, the Germans would be unable to manufacture arms or munitions.
59. PRO FO371/4815 C5616/1621/18, 24 August 1920. General Le Rond's Report to the Peace Conference.
   DBFP, 1st ser., vol. XI ch. 1 No. 26, pp. 36/7, 18 August 1920. Percival (Opole) to Curzon (London).
60. Ibid. No. 31, pp. 39/44, 25 August 1920. Percival (Opole) to Curzon (London).
61. Ibid. No. 55, pp. 74/5, 21 September 1920. Derby (Paris) to Curzon (London). Summary of Le Rond's statement to the Peace Conference. This is often referred to as the Bytom (Beuthen) Agreement.
62. PRO FO371/4816 C5661/1621/18, 31 August 1920. Percival (Opole) to Curzon (London).
   PRO FO371/4816 C5700/1621/18, 1 September 1920. Private letter Percival (Opole) to Wigram (F.O. London).
63. PRO FO371/5398 N3380/191/55, 25 November 1920. Loraine (Warsaw) to Curzon (London) quoting the *Rzeczpospolita*.
   DBFP, 1st ser., vol. XI ch. 1 No. 33 p. 45, 31 August 1920. Kilmarnock (Berlin) to Curzon (London).
64. Ibid. No. 54, p. 73, 20 September 1920. Derby (Paris) to Curzon (London). The competence of Percival and his deputy, Francis Bourdillon, was a matter of concern in the Foreign Office. Encouraged by Curzon, Percival's unrelenting search for evidence of Franco–Polish collaboration had started to mar his judgement and affect his health.
65. Ibid. No. 42, p. 54, 14 September 1920. Curzon (London) to Derby (Paris).
66. Ibid. No. 50, pp. 70/1, 18 September 1920. Curzon (London) to Derby (Paris). The appointment of the British officers was neutralized by having the new police force transferred to the French-controlled Interior Department.

67. Ibid. No. 61, pp. 80/1, 9 October 1920. Derby (Paris) to Curzon (London). Minute by the Permanent Under Secretary, Lord Hardinge.
68. Germany's financial and economic position could not be established until the extent of its losses, if any, in Upper Silesia were known. The Germans negotiating the amount of reparations that Germany had to pay were using this aspect of the Upper Silesian plebiscite to delay reaching a final settlement.
69. *DBFP*, 1st ser., vol. XVI, Pt. 1, ch. 1, p. 20. Annex to No. 13, 6 April 1921. Memorandum by Mr. J. Headlam-Morley on the Upper Silesian Plebiscite.
70. Ibid. vol. XI, ch. 1, No. 65, pp. 83/6, 28 October 1920. Percival (Opole) to Curzon (London).
71 Ibid. No. 77, pp. 96/7, 29 October 1920. Derby (Paris) to Curzon (London). The French Government were claiming that if over 350,000 German out-voters were to return to Upper Silesia then the present 13,500-strong Inter-Allied garrison would have to be reinforced to bring its strength up to 60,000.
72. Ibid. No. 94, pp. 116/8, 1 December 1920. Percival (Opole) to Curzon (London). Percival also reported that Korfanty had referred to Lloyd George as being 'Poland's greatest enemy and Germany's greatest friend'.
73. Rose, W. J. *The Drama of Upper Silesia – A Regional Study* (London, 1936), pp. 173/7. Many Polish scholars still regard this as the best English-language study of Upper Silesia.
74. PRO FO371/5889 C3229/92/18, 9 February 1921. Max Muller (Warsaw) to Curzon (London), enclosure *Times Warsaw* correspondent draft article, *Korfanty and the Germans – a Modern Cleon*.
75. Ibid. C3126/92/18, 9 February 1921. D'Abernon (Berlin) to Curzon (London).
76. *DBFP*, 1st ser., vol. XV, ch. 2, No. 16, pp. 141/7. Proceedings of Third Conference.
77. Garthorne-Hardy, G. M. *A Short History of International Affairs 1920–1934* (Oxford, 1934), p. 34.
78. Wambough, *Plebiscites Since the War,* vol. 2, pp. 248/9.
79. *DBFP*, 1st ser., vol. XI, ch. 1, No. 171, pp. 196/7.
80. Wambaugh *Plebiscites Since the War*, vol. 1, p. 249, notes that the Polish party did not even bother contesting the Głubczyce (Leobschutz) district on the Oder's West bank.
    For the Commission's published result of plebiscite (giving each commune's Polish and German names) see the Silesian Institute's *Encyklopedia Powstań Śląskich*, Annex 1, pp. 677/705.
81. *DBFP*, 1st ser., vol. XVI, ch. 1, No.1, 22 March 1921. Curzon (London) to Percival (Opole).
82. PRO FO371/5892 C6902/92/18, 29 March 1921. Foreign Office Minute by Sir E. A. Crowe re. conversation that day with the Italian Ambassador.
83. Ibid. C6194/92/18, 23 March 1921. Memorandum, *Foreign Office View on Plebiscite Result*. Minute by Sir Eyre Crowe.
84. Carr, William, *A History of Germany 1815–1985* (London, 1987), p. 260, is but one example of this tendency amongst Anglo-Saxon historians to view the plebiscite as a single constituency.
    But countering this argument *The Times* 4, 5, and 6 April. *After the Plebiscite* by Lt. Col. Repington did give a clear picture, carefully noting that the issue was not by majority vote – the Peace Treaty having prepared the way for a partition of Upper Silesia.

85. PRO FO371/5892 C6969/92/18, 24 March 1921. Percival (Opole) to Curzon (London) enclosure translation *Korfanty Message to Polish Voters 21 March 1921.*
86. PRO FO371/5896 C9210/92/18, 30 April 1921. Le Rond to president of Allied Conference, London. Explains why Commissioners cannot reach an agreement.
87. Wambaugh, *Plebiscites Since the War*, vol. 1, p. 253.
88. PRO FO371/5896 C9054/92/18, 2 May 1921. Percival (Opole) to Curzon (London).
89. PRO FO371/5897 C9223/92/18, 4 May 1921. Max Muller (Warsaw) to Curzon (London).
    PRO FO371/5898 C9366/92/18, 7 May 1921. Max Muller (Warsaw) to Curzon (London).
90. Ibid. C9413/92/18, 4 May 1921. Translation of Korfanty Proclamation.
91. Ibid. C9372/92/18, 7 May 1921. Kilmarnock (Berlin) to Curzon (London).
    PRO FO371/5900 C9902/92/18, 15 May 1921. Percival (Opole) to Curzon (London).
92. PRO FO371/5904 C10745/92/18, 23 May 1921. Foreign Office Minute re. alleged organization of German *Freikorps* by British officers. *The Guardian*, 24 May 1921.
    DBFP, 1st ser., vol. XVI, ch. 1, No. 117, p. 144, 25 May 1921. Percival (Opole) to Curzon (London).
93. PRO FO371/5905 C10827/92/18, 25 May 1921. Bourdillon (Opole) to Curzon (London). Percival had suffered a nervous breakdown and had been taken to a sanatorium located over the Czech border. Several staff members were also reported to be 'under severe strain'.
94. The fighting between Polish and German armed bands, some of which had always been related to smuggling and other criminal behaviour, continued. The Commission's attempts to recover weapons was matched by an escalation in German lawlessness; detained Germans were forcibly released from prisons by their paramilitary forces and the French troops became the target of German ambushes and bombings.
95. Churchill College Archive, Cambridge. Noel Baker Papers, NBKR 4/463, 20 July 1921. Baker to Lord Robert Cecil.
    NBKR 4/454, 21 July 1921. Baker to Professor Attolico. Baker could not envisage either the French or British giving way. Lloyd George had mortally offended both the Poles and the French by suggesting in the House of Commons that it might be necessary to let the German Army end the insurgency.
    NBKR 4/454, 22 July 1921. Baker to Professor Attolica enclosing copy of minute on subject sent to the League Secretary Sir Eric Drummond a month earlier.
    NBKR 4/454, 12 August 1921. Professor Attolica: telephone message to Sir Eric Drummond. Told by Italian Foreign Minister Toretto that 'in the private conversations which took place yesterday the known suggestion about the League of Nations has been ventilated'.
96. McEwen, J. M. (ed.), *The Riddell Diaries 1908–1923* (London, 1986), pp. 349/50, entry for 11 and 12 August 1921.
    Middlemas, Keith (ed.), *Diaries of Thomas Jones – Volume III, Ireland 1918–1925.* Entry 12 August 1921 records meeting Lloyd George at Victoria Railway Station on return from Paris: 'He was in great form describing the

way he had pulled off the reference of Upper Silesia to the League of Nations – the PM had kept it up his sleeve until the last moment. He was immensely pleased with the dramatic character of the whole procedure.'

97. Harrington, Joseph F., Jr., *The League of Nations and the Upper Silesian Boundary Dispute 1921–1922*, in the *Polish Review*, 23 (1978), No. 3, pp. 86–101 *passim*.

3 The Battle of Warsaw, August 1920, and the Development of the Second Polish Republic

Peter D. Stachura

When Poland was re-established in November 1918 as an independent sovereign state after over a century of partition and oppression by her more powerful neighbours, Russia, Germany and Austria-Hungary, she faced an uphill struggle for survival. Domestically, she had to rebuild virtually everything from scratch: the economy, bureaucracy, the judiciary, a social and educational infrastructure, even the Army, all had to be forged anew amidst the detritus of the First World War. Moreover, Poland had to try to ensure the smooth working of a system of Western-style parliamentary democracy for which she had no training or experience. The Germans call 1945 'Year Zero', when just about everything of a physical, traditional, moral and spiritual nature had collapsed in ignominy with Hitler's Third Reich and had to be rebuilt. In like manner, Poland in 1918 had to contemplate and overcome her 'Year Zero', even though she had wholesome values to aid the process.[1]

This unprecedented challenge had to be met with virtually no help from abroad, not even from the Entente Powers, the United States, Britain and France, which formally confirmed Poland's independence at the Paris Peace Conference in 1919, and later that year in the Treaty of Versailles. More ominously, defeated Germany and nascent Soviet Russia were already bitterly opposed to the existence of an independent Poland, for both historical and immediate reasons, particularly because of their substantial losses of territory to Poland. In other words, Poland's survival, it was already clear, would depend almost exclusively on the endeavours of the Poles themselves.

The early post-war years in Europe as a whole could hardly have been less conducive to the task the newly born countries faced in attempting to launch themselves with success. Turbulence was ubiquitous, with shaky governments under intense economic and social strain often experiencing revolutionary assault from within, from both the radical Left and Right.

In Poland's case, these years saw her obliged to fight concurrently no fewer than six wars, whose sole aim was to secure her territorial integrity within firm, legitimate borders. While her western frontier had been delineated in large measure by the peace settlement, those in the east, north-west and south-east, in particular, had been left undefined. In the absence of agreements with neighbouring states concerning these boundaries, Poland soon became embroiled in extensive warfare at a time when she had still not had a reasonable opportunity to address her most fundamental economic, social, institutional and political problems.

Consequently, the early history of the Polish Republic was characterized to a considerable extent by the war against the Germans for Poznania, commencing with the arrival in that area of Ignacy Paderewski on Boxing Day, 1918; the war, also against the Germans, in Upper Silesia from 1919 until 1921, which involved three Polish uprisings; the bitter struggle with militant Ukrainian nationalists for Lwów and Eastern Galicia in 1918–19; the battle with Czechoslovakia for control of Cieszyn/Teschen (Austrian Silesia) in 1919–20; the war with Lithuania for Wilno, the city which was so dear to Józef Piłsudski, who was born close by; and finally, and most important of all, the war against Soviet Russia in 1919–20. This was for Poland a baptism of fire *par excellence*, constituting a unique experience in European history of that epoch.[2]

The Battle of Warsaw, in mid-August 1920, was the decisive encounter of the Polish–Soviet war, which had begun in early 1919 in a desultory fashion following the withdrawal of German forces from the Eastern Front at the end of the First World War, when both Russian and Polish forces sought to fill the resulting vacuum and assert their territorial claims.[3] The Soviets and their supporters always claimed that the war was caused by an imperialist and bourgeois Poland being used by the West for an anti-Bolshevik crusade, effectively to counter, if not destroy, the Bolshevik Revolution and the wide-ranging threat it seemed to pose to Europe.[4] This argument is fallacious. Piłsudski was nobody's agent, not least of the Entente Powers, whom he deeply distrusted, with justification. He pursued an independent policy that he believed served the best interests of Poland – nothing more, nothing less. In the early post-war era he sought to recreate in the east something akin to the old Polish–Lithuanian Commonwealth, a confederation of the smaller eastern states under Poland's overall leadership as the most efficacious barrier against the threat to their independence from Russia. In any case, in the absence of international delimitation of Poland's eastern borders, Piłsudski merely sought to re-establish his country's interest and influence in areas which had been historically Polish, or at least with a long-standing and substantial

Polish cultural and political presence. In the event, circumstances did not permit the realization of Piłsudski's federalist concepts.[5]

In reality, the essential causes of the war were twofold. The first was the burning desire of Lenin and his Bolsheviks to extend, as a matter of crucial importance to the long-term survival and success of the Revolution, into Poland, and thereafter into the heart of Europe. Germany, where a large, well-organized and active Communist party (KPD) already existed, had been earmarked as the strategic centre of this ambitious enterprise. For many contemporaries, especially the Poles, however, Lenin's plan was simply another, if the latest, manifestation of Tsarist imperialism, dressed up in the class rhetoric of revolutionary Bolshevism, claiming Poland as part of the Russian Empire. The Poles understood the situation as a direct threat to their fragile independence, which neither the Bolsheviks nor their 'White' opponents were prepared to accept. Secondly, the war was brought about by Poland's natural requirement to fix without delay her frontiers in the East. Britain had wanted to have the so-called 'Curzon Line' recognized, but Poland rejected this outright because it would have left huge tracts of historically Polish territory in Russia. The British, reluctant and late converts to the notion of an independent Poland in the first place, were generally unsympathetic to the Polish interest, and far more concerned with countering French influence in the region and not offending either German or Russian sensibilities too much.[6]

The war initially went rather well for Poland. Polish forces, appreciating the strategic importance of the Ukraine, and exploiting the internal preoccupations at that time of the Bolsheviks, successfully mounted a pre-emptive strike, penetrating as far as Kiev by May 1920.[7] Shortly afterwards, however, the Bolsheviks had just about completed the rout of the Whites in the Russian Civil War, and were then able to turn their full attention to the Polish front. Within a few months their counter-offensive, spearheaded by Semyon Budyonny's notorious *Konarmiya*, the élite 'Red Cavalry' formations,[8] had expelled the Poles from the Ukraine altogether and had begun to advance on several fronts towards Warsaw. By the beginning of August 1920, no fewer than five Soviet armies, 20 divisions in all, well-equipped, battle-hardened and well-motivated ideologically, stood only a few miles from the Polish capital, under the command of General Mikhail Nikolayevich Tukhachevsky. Tagged on, and accentuating the political-ideological imperative of the Bolshevik campaign, was a Provisional Revolutionary Committee, led by two renegade Poles, Feliks Dzierżyński, the already notorious head of the Cheka, the Bolshevik secret police, and Julian Marchlewski, a veteran radical Socialist, now a Communist. Their objective was to set up a Soviet Poland in the wake of the Red Army's military campaign.[9]

From a Polish point of view the situation could hardly have been more desperate. Lenin had made it clear that the utter destruction of what he called 'bourgeois, white Poland' was an urgent necessity if revolutionary Bolshevism were to be able to sweep into central and western Europe. Tukhachevsky's infamous Order of the Day on 2 July 1920 declared: 'Over the dead body of White Poland lies the road to world-wide conflagration.' Poland stood in mortal danger of once more being wiped off the map of Europe and becoming a Soviet satellite. And, for all practical purposes, she stood virtually alone in this moment of profound crisis.

In Britain a vigorous propaganda campaign with the slogan 'Hands-off-Russia' had been introduced by left-wing members of the Labour Party and Trade Unions, Communists and liberal intellectuals, in broad political circles, the press and academia.[10] Dockers refused to load munitions destined for Poland and, of course, Prime Minister David Lloyd George had never made any secret anyway of his contempt for and dislike of Poland. [11] The French, always alert to their interests in converting Eastern Europe into an anti-German bulwark, made diplomatic noises about helping Poland, despite their own acute economic and political problems. As it happened, only a small Inter-Allied Mission, including General Maxime Weygand, was sent somewhat grudgingly and belatedly to Warsaw.[12] The Germans, especially in prominent government circles and the high command of the *Reichswehr*, looked forward to Poland's destruction with ill-concealed glee. Their desire to win back the 'lost' land in the East and their perception of a Polish military threat guaranteed their hostility. There was apparently a faint possibility for a time of the *Reichswehr* and the right-wing, nationalist *Freikorps* units joining up with the Red Army to crush Poland. Leon Trotsky, Minister of War and leader of the Red Army, tentatively advanced a plan to his opposite number in the *Reichswehr*, General Hans von Seeckt, to repartition Poland – a forerunner of the Hitler–Stalin Pact in 1939. However, Germany decided at a late stage to remain neutral in the conflict.[13] Finally, the Czechoslovaks, fearful of adverse Russian reaction, and equally keen to weaken Poland, blocked the transit of armaments from Hungary for which the Poles had already paid. Thus, Poland fought alone.

This mortal threat, which was underlined by the fall in July to the advancing Bolsheviks of the north-eastern Polish cities of Wilno, Grodno and Białystok, was met by an unprecedented display of national unity and patriotism by wide sections of ethnic Polish society. Although compulsory conscription had been introduced, volunteers flooded into the Army. None the less, the Bolsheviks enjoyed a clear advantage in manpower and equipment. Political differences, which had dramatically surfaced as soon as the euphoria of independence had passed, were pushed to one side again as a Council for the Defence of the State (*Rada Obrony Państwa*) was set up in July, spawning an emergency coalition government under the premiership of the Peasant Party leader, Wincenty Witos. But there was no panic among either the Army or the civilian population of the capital, much to the amazement of contemporary observers.[14] And in a breathtaking display of Polish nonchalance, Witos took a few days off to go and help bring in the harvest![15]

The Bolshevik onslaught that began in early August and reached a climax within a few days was met by a daring counter-offensive conceived by Marshal Piłsudski and executed with the aid, sometimes in improvised fashion, of his staff, including Generals Kazimierz Sosnkowski, Tadeusz Rozwadowski and Władysław Sikorski. Within a short time, three Soviet armies had been split, encircled and then destroyed. Another fled into internment in East Prussia, and a fifth, which included the *Konarmiya*, suffered huge losses at the hands of Sikorski a few weeks later at the battle of Komarów, near Zamość, the last cavalry battle in European history. In early September the Polish victory at the Battle of the Niemen completed the rout and ended the war. Bolshevik casualties were catastrophic in terms of numbers killed, wounded and taken prisoner. Hundreds of thousands more of them fled in complete disarray back to Russia, pursued by the rampant Polish forces. Indeed, the road to Moscow lay wide open to Piłsudski; but, of course, he was far too wise to seriously consider taking that step.[16] Lenin, his grand plan in ruins, had no option but to sue for peace.

The Battle of Warsaw was as stunning a victory for the Polish Army as it has ever achieved in modern times, and this is not to forget Monte Cassino, Falaise, Breda and other triumphs during the Second World War. For most military analysts, only King Jan Sobieski's triumph over the Turks in the Battle of Vienna in 1683 bears comparison. By the same token, Warsaw was the most devastating defeat suffered by the Red Army until Afghanistan at the end of the 1980s. That was the magnitude of the Polish victory, and the Russians neither forgot nor forgave it.

How the victory was achieved has exercised historians ever since. Some have pointed to a lack of coordination on the Bolshevik side, or to a fatal clash between the military and the political imperatives of the Bolshevik Party. Certain individual leaders, notably Trotsky, Stalin and Tukhachevsky, have been severely castigated for alleged errors of judgement or conduct. In other words, Russian mistakes, it has been argued, provide the most convincing explanation of the outcome.[17] Others, at the time and since, have attributed the victory to Divine Providence. It was

Piłsudski's bitter political enemies, the right-wing National Democrats (*Endecja*), who coined the phrase 'Miracle on the Vistula' as a way of denigrating his achievement, and they also sought to stress the importance of the contribution of General Weygand and a few French officers of the Inter-Allied Mission. To his credit, however, Weygand refused to claim any credit, remarking that 'this victory ... is a Polish victory ... carried out by Polish generals in accordance with the Polish operational plan'.[18]

The real and fundamental reasons for victory lay in the sense of national purpose and patriotism that was generated in Poland. Lenin freely acknowledged the weight of this factor. The Poles' inherent susceptibility to internecine quarreling was, for once, transcended by the realization that their very survival and destiny as a nation was at stake. This was complemented by the superb fighting qualities and spirit of the Polish Army, and by the inspirational leadership of the Commander-in-Chief, Marshal Piłsudski, ably supported by several outstanding generals. Altogether, the episode brought forth a truly unsurpassed effort from the ethnic Polish population. To this extent, it provided a poignant commentary on the character of the infant Second Republic, underlining the vital interaction of war and wider society. It may also be argued that the victory was so seminal that its significance for the longer-term development of Poland before the Second World War was unmatched by any other single event, with the possible exception of the May coup in 1926. Piłsudski was in no doubt about its importance. While describing the battle as a 'brawl' (*bijatyka*), he wrote that it 'none the less launched the destinies of two states and 150 million people ... and all but shook the fate of the entire civilized world'.[19]

The victory over the traditional enemy avenged, in a sense, the Russians' brutal suppression of the insurrections of 1830–1 and 1863–4, which was profoundly satisfying to the historically minded Poles. More crucially, it allowed Poland to preserve her newly won independence, giving it a remarkable and much-needed injection of self-confidence and self-belief at a time when nothing else seemed to be going right for it, at home or abroad. Poland's subsequent progress as a relatively successful and important nation in the mainstream of European life between the World Wars was thus initiated in rather spectacular fashion. At the same time, the victory repulsed the forces of revolutionary Bolshevism from western Europe, at least until the end of the Second World War. In 1920 Poland fulfilled her traditionally self-perceived role as Europe's last bastion of civilized, Christian values against the barbaric, Asiatic east – meaning Russia. Moreover, the international order that had been created by the Treaty of Versailles had successfully withstood its first major test, even if the principal architects of that treaty had hardly lifted a finger to defend their work. The genesis of the appeasement policy of the 1930s is surely to be found, therefore, at the very outset of the inter-war period, in the West's reaction to this crisis. Ominously, the West was inadvertently giving notice, particularly to countries such as Poland, Austria and Czechoslovakia, that they were on their own in the face of totalitarian aggression, whether of the Bolshevik, Fascist or National Socialist variety.

The experience of the war against the Soviets taught the overwhelming majority of Poles that Bolshevism meant only repression, destruction and subjugation. Few Polish workers or peasants had rallied to the class slogans of 'bourgeois capitalism' or 'landlordism' of the invading Red Army and its political commissars, much to Lenin's consternation. The unthinkable had happened: they put country before class. Subsequently, the Communist Party of Poland (KPP) enjoyed only minimal support, and then invariably from sections of the ethnic minorities, notably the Jews, who became especially prominent in the leadership cadres.[20] Bolshevism, in other words, was widely perceived as an alien ideology and political system, associated with the detested Russians and an increasingly despised ethnic group within Poland. The connection between Bolshevism and Jews – 'Jewish Bolshevism' – which was to become the stock-in-trade jibe of the radical Right across Europe, was made conclusively in Poland in 1920, and mercilessly propagated by the *Endecja* and its allies.[21] The formation of this outlook was facilitated, of course, by the powerful influence exerted by the Catholic Church, many of whose hierarchy and clergy strongly identified with the *Endecja*: their ranks included a number of prominent and outspoken anti-Semites, such as August Cardinal Hlond, Primate of Poland, and Archbishop Adam Sapieha of Kraków.[22] The mass of Poles, therefore, especially the large majority who were practising Catholics, had little difficulty in repudiating Bolshevism during the lifetime of the Second Republic.

The outcome of the war resulted, inevitably perhaps, in generally bitter and suspicious relations between Poland and the Soviet Union throughout the inter-war years. The Soviets, affronted by the independence of a country they had come to regard as a natural part of their empire, never had the slightest intention of renouncing their ambition to subjugate Poland, the Non-Aggression Pact they concluded with it in 1932 notwithstanding. Tension remained high in the border regions, where the Russians encouraged incursions by raiding bands into the small Polish towns and estates, necessitating the establishment in 1923/4 of a Border Patrol Corps by the government of General Władysław Sikorski. Moral and material support was also given by Moscow to Byelorussian agitation against the Polish state. More seriously, no sooner had the Treaty of Riga been concluded than the

Soviets were actively conspiring with Germany against Poland, with whom 'peace' was obviously regarded as merely a temporary inconvenience.[23]

Defeat had important consequences for the development of the revolutionary regime in Russia itself. Other factors, such as the dire economic situation at the end of the Civil War, the reconstruction of the Bolshevik Party at the Xth Congress in March 1921, and the Kronstadt revolt, played a part, but in face of the reality that Bolshevism could not be exported after 1920, at least not in the way envisaged by Lenin and his party comrades, they were forced instead to turn inwards in order to consolidate the Revolution in Russia. The introduction of the New Economic Policy (NEP), the emphasis on 'Socialism in One Country', and even the emergence of the Stalinist dictatorship, all emanated in part from the war's impact on the Soviet side.[24]

In contrast, the victorious Poles were given an immediate impetus to complete on a note of triumph the other wars she had been forced into since 1918. The Ukrainians had already been defeated over Eastern Galicia, but now the Lithuanians and Germans were also dealt with successfully, so that, for example, parts of Upper Silesia and the historic cities of Lwów and Wilno were fully integrated into the Republic. International recognition of all its frontiers was finalized in March 1923, when the Ambassadors' Conference gave its stamp of approval.[25] The only reversal came over Teschen in 1919–20, where the Czechs broke off diplomatic discussion to take advantage of Poland's preoccupation with a variety of other pressing matters to seize the area, which contained a predominantly Polish population. The injustice was rectified during the international crisis over the Sudetenland in 1938, however, when Polish forces regained this part of the national territory.

Any lingering doubts which Poland may have entertained about her future being in her own hands alone were swiftly dispelled by the events of 1920. With no help from anyone, the natural and understandable reaction was the conception of the Piłsudski-inspired 'Doctrine of the Two Enemies', identifying Germany and the Soviet Union, in equal measure, as her inveterate adversaries. Germany's continuing antagonism was demonstrated shortly after the war by the pronouncements of leading figures in government and the army. Chancellor Jozef Wirth, a member of the left-wing of the Centre Party and a firm upholder of the democratic Weimar Republic, had no qualms in calling in 1922 for Poland's destruction, while General Hans von Seeckt, the *Reichswehr* chief, produced an infamous memorandum on 11 September 1922 in which he averred that 'Poland's existence is intolerable, incompatible with the survival of Germany. It must disappear.'[26] The Franco-Polish alliance of 1921 was not taken very seriously by either side, particularly by the 1930s, when the United States had withdrawn into isolationism and Britain had made it all too clear that she had no real interest in Poland's fate.

It cannot be said that victory brought anything other than ephemeral political harmony to Poland. No sooner was the war over than old animosities were resurrected and intensified, for example, over the terms of the Treaty of Riga with the Bolsheviks that formally ended the war in March 1921, and also over the introduction of the new Constitution the same month, which was designed by the nationalist Right to limit presidential powers, with its enemy, Piłsudski, in mind. The *Endecja* was unforgiving. From the beginning, Polish political life had been characterized by vicious intra-party argument, which not only poisoned the social and political atmosphere in the country at large, but often also transformed the *Sejm* into a place of tumult. Personal insults were freely exchanged, petty procedural points were introduced with the express purpose of disrupting debate, ministers were frequently less than frank about what they said, and it was almost a daily occurrence for parliamentary sittings to be suspended in order to allow tempers to cool. The proportional system of representation had given rise to a plethora of parties, many of which were small, so that, as in contemporaneous Weimar Germany, stable cabinet government proved impossible. As many as two dozen or so parties had seats in parliament in the early 1920s. To many observers, Poland had reverted to the 'Republic of Anarchy' of the eighteenth century, concluding that the failure to achieve consensus on almost anything was bound to jeopardize the country's very existence, as it had in the past. The Germans' notion of Poland being a *Saisonstaat*, a country incapable of governing itself, had an uncomfortable ring of truth about it.[27]

Even the apportioning of credit for the victory over the Bolsheviks soon emerged as a bone of acute contention. The *Endecja* continued to disparage vehemently Piłsudski's achievement in favour of emphasizing the French contribution, and the rancour showed few signs of abating during the lifetime of the Republic. For instance, in the early 1930s, when Piłsudski's regime (*Sanacja*) moved forcefully against its political opponents in all sectors, including the universities, one well-known university academic, Professor Wacław Sobieski, who held the Chair of Medieval History at the Jagiellonian University, Kraków, and who was an active member of the *Endecja*, was sacked when he tried to publish in France an account of the Battle of Warsaw which highlighted the indispensability of General Weygand's role.[28]

What mattered most of all, however, was that the victory allowed Piłsudski to shift the balance of political power within Poland in his favour, at the expense of his great rival, Roman Dmowski, leader of the *Endecja*, who really never recovered the initiative.[29] The two personalities who, in their different ways, had done more than any other to forge the specifically Polish input to the making of independence, had been bitter personal rivals since before the First World War. In the crisis-laden early post-war years their rivalry had further intensified to the point where, arguably, the national interest was compromised.

Piłsudski had watched with growing dismay the course of political life as it reached new depths of depravity in December 1922, when the recently elected President of the Republic, Gabriel Narutowicz, the Marshal's nominee, was assassinated in Warsaw by an ultra-nationalist. Civil war seemed possible. This tragedy, coupled with his objections to certain parts of the Constitution, disgusted Piłsudski so much that he decided the following year to retire from politics altogether. It was a short-lived retirement, however, for in May 1926, having concluded that he could stand aside no longer as political and economic problems appeared once again to threaten Poland's independent existence, he intervened with a *coup d'état*. Ultimately, he and his followers had invested too much in the cause of independence to allow it to fail amidst political ineptitude, corruption and economic crisis. Above all, the Marshal was adamant that the fruits of victory in 1920 should not be forfeited by the Poles themselves. Once more, he took centre stage in the life of the country.[30]

The Polish–Soviet War had thrown into sharp relief the problems Poland had with her large non-Polish minorities, who made up approximately one-third of the population: there were over five million Ukrainians, three million Jews, one and a half million Byelorussians and 750,000 Germans, and in addition, much smaller numbers of Russians, Lithuanians, Tartars and Czechs. Among many in the Ukrainian, German and Jewish communities, in particular, a rejectionist attitude *vis-à-vis* the Polish state prevailed from the outset. The Ukrainians had fought for their own state in 1919–20 against the Poles, and had lost. Bitterness between the two sides continued, and in due course some extreme Ukrainian nationalists took to terrorism as a means of advancing their cause. Similarly, although many Germans had migrated to the Reich after the peace settlement rather than live under Polish rule, most of the large number that remained hoped for Poland's collapse and their reintegration into Germany. The national unity in the war against the Bolsheviks, therefore, had not been total by any means, being restricted by and large to ethnic Poles. Substantial numbers of non-Polish citizens had been hoping for a Bolshevik victory as a means of advancing their particular separatist agenda.[31]

The position of the Jews at that time and throughout inter-war Poland is still a most sensitive topic. In addition to tensions that had arisen between Poles and Jews by the end of the nineteenth century, and Polish resentment at some of the wartime activities of Jews, notably in relation to their role in the policies of the occupying Germans, the Poles had not forgotten that the well-organized and influential 'Jewish lobby' at the Paris Peace Conference in 1919 had vigorously sought to prevent the creation of an independent Poland, and that when this effort failed, had succeeded in having the Minorities Charter foisted on Poland.[32] Anti-Semitism, but also, equally importantly, Jewish anti-Polonism, scarred relations between the two communities from 1918 onwards. The Jewish minority was not homogeneous in any sense, of course, given the different religious, social, economic, educational, linguistic and political levels within it, and it has to be acknowledged that there were Jews who performed their patriotic duty in the war, some even by giving their lives. Piłsudski himself was moved to acknowledge their sacrifices.[33] But in Eastern Poland in particular, with its substantial Jewish population, relatively large numbers of Jews, especially younger ones, articulated their unhappiness at being citizens of the new Polish state by openly or tacitly supporting the Bolsheviks. Parts of the extensive Jewish press in major cities, publishing in Yiddish as well as Polish, were noticeably reticient in reporting developments at the front; while too many Jewish leaders, other than the small group of assimilationists in the *Agudat Israel*, kept such a low profile as to raise legitimate questions about where their sympathies lay.[34]

The Polish victory did nothing to improve relations with the Jews. Indeed, Polish resentment at the alleged traitorous behaviour of many Jews, the surge in nationalist pride that accompanied victory, and the disappointment of many Jews at the outcome of the war, only served to intensify animosities from both directions. The *Endecja*, which exerted the most influence in government until 1926, was especially concerned to assert the rights of what it wanted to be a nationalist, Catholic Poland against those considered to be of dubious loyalty, while Jews, particularly the Zionists, Socialists and Communists among them, felt compelled to offer fierce resistance. After 1920, therefore, the Polish–Jewish symbiosis moved along an increasingly fraught course, until some marginal, transient relief was forthcoming in the early aftermath of Piłsudski's coup.[35] In time, however, and especially during and after the Depression era, relations between Poles and Jews, and also between Poles and the other ethnic minorities, sharply deteriorated.

Finally, the victory emphasized, above all, the crucial importance of the Army to Poland. Hurriedly constituted from the multitude of Polish soldiers who had fought on all sides and on most fronts during the First World War, but inspired by the example of Piłsudski's Legions, the Army showed outstanding powers of improvisation to become a formidable fighting force, epitomizing the nation's indomitable will to live in freedom. Following its historic defeat of the Bolsheviks and success in the other wars of 1919–21, the Army was rightly accorded a status and prestige second to none in Polish society, its influence extending well beyond the military sphere. Entry to the officer corps was especially something eagerly to be aspired to, though it was virtually the exclusive preserve of the educated ethnic Polish middle class and landed gentry (*szlachta*). The Army also emerged as the main institution through the system of compulsory conscription for forging national unity, above class and ethnic divisions.[36] Following Piłsudski's coup in 1926, it became the most important agency of political influence in government, with many top officials and ministers drawn from officer ranks. The discredited parliamentary system was reduced in scope within an increasingly authoritarian regime, though it was not eliminated, as happened in many other European countries in the 1930s. It is fair to refer, therefore, to the progressive militarization of Polish political and institutional life under Piłsudski until his death in 1935. This led directly to the era of the 'Colonels' Rule', 1935–9.[37]

In commemoration of victory over the Bolsheviks, and of the 48,000 who had laid down their lives for Poland, the 15 August was designated 'Polish Soldiers' Day', an annual event that was celebrated with much military ceremonial and patriotic pride until 1939. Unobserved during the wartime German and Soviet occupations, of course, and studiously ignored during the post-war Communist era for fear of upsetting fraternal relations between 'People's Poland' and its Soviet masters, who were concerned not to have the putative invincibility of the Red Army exposed as spurious, the event was not resurrected until the early 1990s, in a Poland once more democratic and independent. Marshal Piłsudski, whatever view may be taken of his subsequent political role in Polish affairs, had rightly earned an exalted place in the pantheon of modern Polish military heroes, on a footing with King Jan Sobieski III and Tadeusz Kościuszko, thereby underlining the significance of the victory for all time.

The present analysis should not overlook, however, at least one obvious and important negative consequence for the Army, which is that the victory of 1920 lulled the military establishment into an erroneous belief in the continuing validity of the methods which had brought that victory. Despite the Second Republic's relatively large expenditure on her armed forces, when measured as a percentage of national income, the Army failed to mechanize on anything like the scale of the *Wehrmacht* and

Red Army in the 1930s. General Sikorski, a national hero for his part in defeating the Bolsheviks, well understood the virtues of mechanized warfare and the tank, as he demonstrated in his perceptive writings during the 1930s.[38] But, having fallen foul of Piłsudski in the aftermath of the coup of May 1926, his views were ignored. While belated recognition of the value of armour began to emerge in the Polish military high command in the late 1930s, far too much ground had still to be made up. The deficiency, which was crucially linked to the question of mobility, was a vital factor in deciding the outcome of the September Campaign, especially with regard to the German *Blitzkrieg* tactics.

The Polish–Soviet War, and the Battle of Warsaw in particular, represented a quintessential triumph of David over Goliath that was exhilarating, the more so as it was unexpected. Its importance was appreciated at once by the Poles themselves, and indeed by Lenin and his Bolsheviks, but was properly understood in the West by only a few informed onlookers. For most people outside Poland, it was an event that happened in 'a far-away country', whose outcome was not considered to be all that significant. In the fullness of time and from a wider historical perspective, however, it can now be more readily seen that what took place in August 1920 was a crucial turning-point not only for Poland but also for the rest of Europe, which was spared domination by, or at least confrontation with, revolutionary Soviet Bolshevism for another quarter of a century.[39] There were very good reasons, therefore, for more than the Poles to be grateful to Marshal Piłsudski and the Polish Army for their heroic triumph.

NOTES

1. The economic and financial details are in Zbigniew Landau and Jerzy Tomaszewski, *The Polish Economy in the Twentieth Century* (London, Routledge, 1985), pp. 27–55; Jack J. Taylor, *The Economic Development of Poland, 1919–1950* (Ithaca, Cornell University Press, 1952), pp. 29–33; Ferdynand Zweig, *Poland Between Two Wars. A Critical Study of Social and Economic Changes* (London, Secker & Warburg, 1944), pp. 27–38. A more recent, general survey is Paul Latawski (ed.), *The Reconstruction of Poland, 1914–1923* (London, Macmillan, 1992).
2. Comprehensive details of the various campaigns and the military units involved are in Mieczysław Wrzosek, *Wojny o granice Polski Odrodzonej 1918–1921* (*The Wars over the Frontiers of Reborn Poland, 1918–1921*) (Warsaw, Biblioteka Wiedzy Historycznej, 1992).

3. It is claimed by John Wheeler-Bennett, *The Nemesis of Power. The German Army in Politics, 1918–1945* (London, Macmillan, 1953), p. 123, that by allowing the Bolsheviks to occupy the evacuated areas, the Germans were making their first attempt to undermine the Polish state.

4. Elizabeth Kridl Valkenier, 'Stalinizing Polish Historiography: What Soviet Archives Disclose', *East European Politics and Societies*, 7 (1993), No. 1, pp. 109–34, here p. 117.

5. Detailed discussion in M. K. Dziewanowski, *Josef Piłsudski. A European Federalist, 1918–1922* (Stanford, Hoover Institution Press, 1969). See also Przemysław Hauser, 'Josef Pilsudski's Views on the Territorial Shape of the Polish State and His Endeavours to put them into Effect in 1918–1921' *Polish Western Affairs*, 33 (1992), No. 2, pp. 235–49; and Piotr Wandycz, 'Poland's Place in Europe in the Concepts of Piłsudski and Dmowski', *East European Politics and Societies*, 4 (1990), No. 3, pp. 451–68.

6. H. J. Elcock, 'Britain and the Russo-Polish Frontier, 1919–1921', *Historical Journal*, 12 (1969), No. 1, pp. 137–54.

7. Norman Davies, *White Eagle, Red Star. The Polish-Soviet War, 1919–20* (London, Macdonald, 1972), pp. 105–29; Adam Zamoyski, *The Battle for the Marshlands* (New York, Columbia University Press, 1981), pp. 36–57.

8. Zamoyski, *Marshlands*, pp. 58–110; Stephen Brown, 'Communists and the Red Cavalry: the Political Education of the Konarmiia in the Russian Civil War, 1918–20', *The Slavonic and East European Review*, 73 (1995), No. 1, pp. 82–99.

9. Norman Davies, *Heart of Europe. A Short History of Poland* (Oxford, Clarendon Press, 1984), p. 118; Adam Westoby and Robin Blick, 'Early Soviet Designs on Poland', *Survey*, 34 (1982), Part 2, p. 114.

10. L. J. Macfarlane, 'Hands Off Russia. British Labour and the Russo-Polish War, 1920', *Past & Present*, 38 (1967), pp. 126–52.

11. Norman Davies, 'Lloyd George and Poland, 1919–20', *Journal of Contemporary History*, 6 (1971), No. 2, pp. 132–54. The British Prime Minister had been most keen for the Poles to accept the Soviet 'peace offers' in July 1920 which, in reality, were patently unacceptable because they were tantamount to demanding a complete Polish capitulation. See *Documents on British Foreign Policy, 1918–45*, 1st ser. (London, 1947–), Volume XI, Document Nos. 345, 411, 418.

12. F. Russell Bryant, 'Lord D'Abernon, the Anglo-French Mission, and the Battle of Warsaw, 1920', *Jahrbücher für Geschichte Osteuropas*, 38 (1990), No. 4, pp. 526–47; Norman Davies, 'Sir Maurice Hankey and the Inter-Allied Mission to Poland, July–August 1920', *Historical Journal*, 15 (1972), No. 3, pp. 553–61.

13. Wheeler-Bennett, *Nemesis*, pp. 125 f.; Gordon A. Craig, *The Politics of the Prussian Army, 1640–1945* (Oxford, Clarendon Press, 1955), pp. 389–93. Some generals, including Wilhelm Groener, First Quartermaster General, were sympathetic to the notion of mounting a campaign against Poland as early as summer 1919, but they were inhibited by their fears of Entente intervention. General Hans von Seeckt, Head of the *Reichswehr* 1920–26, declared shortly after assuming office that Poland was Germany's 'mortal enemy': see Francis L. Carsten, *The Reichswehr and Politics, 1918–1933* (Oxford, Oxford University Press, 1966), pp. 30, 39–42, 68. For coverage of overall German

attitudes in 1920, Gerhard Wagner, *Deutschland und der polnisch-sowjetische Krieg 1920* (Wiesbaden, Steiner, 1979). On German-Soviet military links, see Manfred Zeidler, *Reichswehr und Rote Armee 1920–1933. Wege und Stationen einer ungewöhnlichen Zusammenarbeit* (Munich, Oldenbourg, 1993).

14. The leader of the Inter-Allied Mission and British Ambassador to Berlin, Lord Edgar V. D'Abernon, provides the most dramatic account of the situation in the Polish capital in *The Eighteenth Decisive Battle of the World* (London, Hodder & Stoughton, 1931). Of interest also is the description of developments in the field leading up to the Battle of Warsaw by J. Piłsudski, *Pisma Zbiorowe* (Warsaw, 1937–38), VII, pp. 95 ff.

15. Norman Davies, *God's Playground. A History of Poland. Volume II. 1795 to the Present* (Oxford, Clarendon Press, 1981), p. 273; M. B. Biskupski, 'Paderewski, Polish Politics, and the Battle of Warsaw, 1920', *Slavic Review*, 46 (1987), no. 3/4, pp. 503–12; Andrzej Zakrzewski, *Wincenty Witos. Chłopski polityk i mąż stanu* (Warsaw, 1977); Wincenty Witos, *Moje Wspomnienia*, Vols. I–III (Paris, 1964–5).

16. Davies, *White Eagle*, pp. 188–225; Zamoyski, *Marshlands*, pp. 125–87, for general details. More specific is Grzegorz Łukomski, 'Od Zamościa do Zamościa. Pułkownik Juliusz Rómmel w działaniach kawaleryjskch wojny polsko-bolszewickiej', *MARS*, I (1993), pp. 47–53.

17. Davies, *God's Playground*, p. 273.

18. Wacław Jędrzejewicz, *Piłsudski. A Life for Poland* (New York, Hippocrene Books, 1982), p. 123. Weygand stressed the modesty of his role in 'La Bataille de Varsovie', *Revue des deux mondes*, 8 (1957), No. 6, pp. 193–215, and in his *Memoires*, Vol. II (Paris, 1957). Rather more is made of his part, however, by Z. Musialik, *General Weygand and the Battle of the Vistula*, 1920 (London, 1987).

19. Józef Piłsudski, *Rok 1920* (London, 1941), p. 165. Another interesting account by a distinguished participant is Władysław Sikorski, *Nad Wisłą i Wkrą. Studium z polsko-rosyjskiej wojny 1920 roku* (Lwów, Zakład Narodowy im. Ossolińskich, 1928): the French version was published as *La Campagne Polono-Russe de 1920* (Paris, 1928).

20. Tadeusz Szafar, 'The Origins of the Communist Party in Poland, 1918–1921', in Ivo Banac (ed.) *The Effects of World War I. The Class War after the Great War. The Rise of Communist Parties in East Central Europe, 1918–1921* (Brooklyn, New York, 1983), pp. 5–52, especially 7–38; Jaff Schatz, *The Generation. The Rise and Fall of the Jewish Communists of Poland* (Berkeley, Calif., University of California Press, 1991), pp. 75–91; Jan B. de Weydenthal, *The Communists of Poland. An Historical Outline* (Stanford, Hoover Institution Press, 1978), pp. 11–12, 18–21, 26–27.

21. Anna Landau-Czajka, '"The Ubiquitous Enemy". The Jew in the Political Thought of Radical Right-Wing Nationalists in Poland, 1926–39', *Polin*, 4 (1989), pp. 169–203.

22. Edward D. Wynot, 'The Catholic Church and the Polish State, 1935–1939', *Journal of Church and State*, 15 (1973), pp. 223–40; Franciszek Adamski, 'The Jewish Question in Polish Religious Periodicals in the Second Republic: the Case of the *Przegląd Katolicki*', *Polin*, 8 (1994), pp. 129–45; Anna Landau-Czajka, 'The Image of the Jew in the Catholic Press during the Second Republic', *Polin*, 8 (1994), pp. 146–75.

23. Carsten, *Reichswehr*, pp. 137 f.; Kai von Jenam, *Polnische Ostpolitik nach dem Ersten Weltkrieg. Das Problem der Beziehungen zu Sowjetrussland nach dem Rigaer Frieden von 1921* (Wiesbaden, Steiner, 1980); Piotr S. Wandycz, *Soviet–Polish Relations, 1917–1921* (Cambridge, Mass., Harvard University Press, 1969), pp. 250–78.
24. Martin McCauley, *The Soviet Union since 1917* (London, Longman, 1981), pp. 39–40; Thomas C. Fiddick, *Russia's Retreat from Poland, 1920. From Permanent Revolution to Peaceful Coexistence* (London, Macmillan, 1990), provides some sharp perspectives.
25. R. F. Leslie (ed.), *The History of Poland since 1863* (Cambridge, Cambridge University Press, 1983), p. 134.
26. Carsten, *Reichswehr*, pp. 138–40.
27. Anthony Polonsky, *Politics in Independent Poland, 1921–1939. The Crisis of Constitutional Government* (Oxford, Oxford University Press, 1972), early chapters; Leslie, *History of Poland*, pp. 139–58; Davies, *God's Playground*, pp. 393–410.
28. Information from private family sources. The Franco-Polish connection in the early 1930s is analysed in Piotr S. Wandycz, *The Twilight of French Eastern Alliances, 1926–1936* (Princeton, NJ, Princeton University Press, 1988). For a former student's view of Professor Sobieski, see Szyja Bronsztejn, 'Polish–Jewish Relations as Reflected in Memoirs of the Interwar Period', *Polin*, 8 (1994), p. 79.
29. Some analysis of this point, albeit with a definite Marxist angle, is given in Roman Wapiński, *Naradowa Demokracja 1893–1939* (Wrocław, 1980), and in his biography, *Roman Dmowski* (Lublin, 1988), which is far from definitive. Andrzej Micewski, *Roman Dmowski* (Warsaw, 1971) is also relatively disappointing.
30. Joseph Rothschild, *Pilsudski's Coup d'Etat* (New York, Columbia University Press, 1966) is still the standard text in English, but see also Antoni Czubiński, *Przewrót majowy 1926 roku* (Warsaw, Młodzieżowa Agencja Wydawnicza, 1989), especially pp. 145–244.
31. The position of the minorities in inter-war Poland has attracted a substantial, often contentious literature, for example Stephan Horak, *Poland and Her National Minorities, 1919–1939* (New York, Vantage Press, 1961), 61 ff., 80 ff., 101–80. Also somewhat controversial is Jerzy Tomaszewski, *Ojczyzna nie tylko Polaków. Mniejszości narodowa w polsce w latach 1918–1939* (Warsaw, 1985), pp. 343 ff. More balanced from a Polish point of view, if now dated in terms of sources, is Adam Żółtowski, *Border of Europe. A Study of the Polish Eastern Provinces* (London, Hollis & Carter, 1950), pp. 240–58, 284–310. On specific groups, see for example Alexander J. Motyl, *The Turn to the Right. The Ideological Origins and Development of Ukrainian Nationalism, 1919–1929* (Boulder, Col., East European Monographs, 1980); Richard Blanke, *Orphans of Versailles. The Germans in Western Poland, 1918–1939* (Lexington, University Press of Kentucky, 1993); Thomas Urban, *Deutsche in Polen. Geschichte und Gegenwart einer Minderheit* (Munich, Beck, 1993).
32. Tytus Komarnicki, *The Rebirth of the Polish Republic. A Study in the Diplomatic History of Europe, 1914–1920* (London, Heinemann, 1957), pp. 291–303; Mark Levene, *War, Jews and the New Europe. The Diplomacy of*

Lucien Wolf, 1914–1919 (Oxford, Oxford University Press, 1992); Mark Levene, 'Britain, a British Jew, and Jewish Relations with the New Poland: the Making of the Polish Minorities Treaty of 1919', *Polin*, 8 (1994), pp. 14–41; Andrzej Kapiszewski (ed.), *Hugh Gibson and a Controversy over Polish–Jewish Relations after World War I. A Documentary History* (Kraków, Jagiellonian University Press, 1991), which examines the role of this first American Minister to Poland; Patrick B. Finney, ' "An Evil for All Concerned": Great Britain and Minority Protection after 1919', *Journal of Contemporary History*, 30 (1995), No. 3, pp. 533–51. Emphasizing the Jewish contribution to Polish independence is Marian Fuks, 'Żydzi w Zaraniu Niepodległości Polski', *Biuletyn Żydowskiego Instytutu Historycznego w Polsce*, 2 (1989), No. 1, pp. 35–44.

33. Józef Piłsudski in *Kurjer Poranny*, August 1920, quoted in A. Groth, 'Dmowski, Piłsudski and Ethnic Conflicts in pre-1939 Poland', *Canadian Slavic Studies*, 3 (1969), No. 1, pp. 87–8. A good introduction to the topic is Y. Gutman *et al.* (eds), *The Jews of Poland Between Two World Wars* (Hanover, New England, University of New England Press, 1989).

34. Michael C. Steinlauf, 'The Polish-Jewish Daily Press', *Polin*, 2 (1987), pp. 219–45; Andrzej Paczkowski, 'The Jewish Press in the Political Life of the Second Republic', *Polin*, 8 (1994), pp. 176–93. The most important Polish-Jewish daily was 'Nasz Przegląd': see Marian Fuks, *Prasa żydowska w Warszawie, 1823–1939* (Warsaw, PWN, 1979), pp. 159–293; Ezra Mendelsohn, *Zionism in Poland. The Formative Years, 1915–1926* (New Haven, Conn., Yale University Press, 1981).

35. Jędrzejewicz, *Piłsudski*, p. 248.

36. Davies, *God's Playground*, p. 419.

37. Edward D. Wynot, *Polish Politics in Transition. The Camp of National Unity and the Struggle for Power, 1935–1939* (Athens, Georgia, University of Georgia Press, 1974) is an informative survey.

38. Władysław Sikorski, *Przyszła Wojna. Jej możliwości i charakter oraz związane z nim zagadnienia obrony kraju* (Warsaw, 1934). The English version is *Modern Warfare. Its Character, Its Problems* (London, Hutchison, 1942).

39. For a comprehensive listing of relevant literature, see John A. Drobnicki, 'The Russo-Polish War, 1919–1920: A Bibliography of Materials in English', *The Polish Review*, 42 (1997), No. 1, pp. 95–104.

4 National Identity and the Ethnic Minorities in Early Inter-War Poland

Peter D. Stachura

One of the principal reasons why the Second Polish Republic has been severely criticized over the years relates to its perceived treatment of ethnic minorities, who comprised about one-third of her population at any one time. With few exceptions, historians and other commentators have roundly condemned Poland for practising widespread discrimination and persecution of its minorities, thereby consigning them to the status of second-class citizens. In the West, Horak set the tone when he referred to 'Polish terroristic policies against the national minorities',[1] while Korzec later wrote that Poland installed 'a reign of terror and oppression' against the minorities.[2] More specifically, the Poles have been accused of opposing the legitimate nationalist aspirations of the Ukrainian minority and failing to devise 'a consistent programme which might have reconciled them to the Republic',[3] and also of subjecting the Germans to just about every conceivable injustice behind a so-called 'bleeding frontier' (*blutende Grenze*) between Poland and the Reich.[4]

The most persistent and vehement criticism, however, has come from historians of Polish–Jewish relations, most of whom are of Jewish origin,[5] who are virtually unanimous in denouncing inter-war Poland as a virulently anti-Semitic country,[6] or even worse, as an 'extremely, perhaps even uniquely, anti-Semitic country',[7] thus putting Poland more or less in the same category in this respect as Hitler's Germany.[8] One prominent writer states bluntly that Poland 'stood out' in Eastern Europe on account of its 'aggressive and intolerant nationalism ... that discriminated against the national minorities ..., primarily ... the Jews'.[9] Another describes the Jews of inter-war Poland as 'a conquered population' suffering 'terrible oppression',[10] and Mendelsohn castigates the Second Republic as 'a state pervaded by Polish nationalism and anti-Semitism'.[11] Critics cite as further evidence for their case the numerous complaints about Poland's conduct which the minorities, especially the Germans and Jews, submitted to the League of Nations.[12] Accepting without question the validity of the arguments adduced by these historians, a well-known source has suggested that the repressive policies can be attributed to 'the pervasive air of national insecurity' in inter-war Poland.[13]

An additional body of criticism was provided by a number of Polish historians writing during the lifetime of the now-defunct Communist 'People's Republic of Poland', particularly during the Stalinist era of the early 1950s. Mindful of the tenets of Marxist-Leninism and the shadow of their Soviet masters, they wrote off inter-war Poland as a 'bourgeois', 'reactionary', even 'fascist' state, in the grip of rapacious capitalists and landlords, and oppressing just about everyone, including the minorities.[14] The twist here, however, was that while the Ukrainians and Byelorussians were unreservedly depicted as victims, no mention was made, for crudely political reasons, of the German and Jewish minorities.[15] This type of criticism of the Second Republic often appeared to be a carbon copy, albeit on a grander scale, of the anti-Polish propaganda disseminated by the Moscow-dominated and otherwise quite insignificant Communist Party of Poland (KPP) before the war. Even when this criticism abated somewhat in the 1960s and 1970s, and some developments in inter-war Poland were discussed more positively, this was usually explained by a desire on the part of the Communist regime to legitimize certain political trends.[16] Only in the 1980s, against a backdrop of the rise of *Solidarność* (Solidarity) as a genuinely patriotic movement of anti-Communist protest and the influence of a Polish Pope, John Paul II, and, more noticeably, in the post-Communist period of the 1990s, has the inter-war era really begun to be assessed in Poland in a manner that is free of political and ideological baggage, though the commentary remains generally critical on the subject of the minorities. For instance, Tomaszewski concludes that the minorities 'found themselves in an appalling and unbearable situation'.[17]

The comprehensive disparagement of Poland's attitude towards the minorities might well suggest that it is entirely justified. Indeed, it is even thought that Poland's conduct in this regard 'does not deserve to be defended from either a moral or pragmatic point of view'.[18] However, in the aftermath of the collapse of Communism and the current reapproximation of Poland to the West, the time seems apposite to reconsider aspects of Poland's history, including the controversial and complex problem of her inter-war minorities, which many would agree is vital to a properly informed and objective understanding of that period.[19] The present paper focuses on developments during the formative years of the Second Republic which, it is argued, determined the fundamental pattern of relations between it and the minorities for the remainder of the inter-war era.

The Polish Republic established in 1918 was immediately multi-ethnic and multicultural in character. According to the National Census of

September 1921, which was based on individuals' declared nationality, only 69.2 per cent of the 27.2 million population stated that they were Polish, while 14.3 per cent (or about four million) said that they were Ukrainian, 3.9 per cent German, 3.9 per cent Byelorussian (or White Russian) and 7.8 per cent Jewish (or 2.1 million): 707,400 Jews gave their nationality as Polish, thus giving a final Jewish population of 2,853,318, or 10.5 per cent of the total. There were also very small numbers of Russians, Tartars, Czechoslovaks and Lithuanians.[20] Thus, around one-third of the population was non-Polish, though there are unsubstantiated claims that the Polish authorities deliberately underestimated the size of the minorities and that the real figure was nearer 40 per cent.[21] A second National Census in December 1931, where the mother tongue was the criterion for determining ethnic origin, broadly confirmed this composition in a population that had increased to some 31.9 million, except that the German element had fallen to 2.3 per cent of the whole, or 741,000, while the Jews had increased to over three million and the Ukrainians to five million. By 1939, the population was 35.1 million.[22] Some of the minorities were located mainly in one particular part of the country, such as the Ukrainians in the south-east (Eastern Galicia, Volhynia and southern Polesie) and the Byelorussians in the east and north-east (Polesie and Nowogródek); while others, notably the Germans and Jews, were scattered over a much wider area of the country.

This configuration was also manifested in relation to the ethnic character of Poland's urban landscape. Almost all the major cities had populations that were anything from 25 to over 40 per cent Jewish. The capital, Warsaw, known to Jews as 'the mother city of Israel', had a Jewish population in 1921 of 310,000, or 33.1 per cent.[23] Kraków's population of 245,304 in 1935 was 28.6 per cent Jewish,[24] while in Łódź in 1921 the corresponding figure was 32 per cent.[25] Wilno and Lwów had a similar pattern. In the small towns (*shtetl*) of eastern Poland (the *kresy*), the Jews often formed an overwhelming majority: for instance, over 90 per cent in Pińsk.

By number and location alone, therefore, the major minorities were conspicuous elements in inter-war Poland, which at once raised the question in 1918 of whether she was to be a nation-state, as was the vogue in Europe as a whole at that time, or a state of nationalities. In any case, it seemed obvious that the longer-term stability of the state depended on how well these disparate ethnic groups would be able to achieve a level of harmony and coexistence with the majority ethnic Polish population. Above all, the circumstances brought to the fore the crucial theme of national identity in the new Poland.

Before 1918, a variety of conflicting views had been expressed about what shape and character a re-established, independent Poland should take. With the failure of the 1863 insurrection against the Russians, thus ending, for the time being at least, the era of Romantic nationalism in Poland, most Poles invested their energies and hopes in a process that came to be known as 'Organic Work'. Notions of armed rebellion as a way of regaining Poland's freedom and independence were abandoned in favour of a strategy which, shaped by the Positivist school of thought in Warsaw, emphasized the virtues of developing the economy, education, language and culture through hard work and thrift within the partitionist political and constitutional order. 'Organic Work' was understood as a more rewarding and effective means, in the new age of industrialization, of preserving the Polish identity, even if this meant accepting the oppressive reality of partition and postponing the idea of regaining independence far into the future. In terms of practical politics, it obliged an everyday accommodation with the partitioning powers, Russia, Germany and Austro-Hungary, despite the concomitant programmes of intensive Russification and Germanization that were launched in the post-1863 era with the aim of destroying everything which could be designated 'Polish'.[26] Some Poles were more enthusiastic than others about accepting compromise and subordination, of course, though few of them remained in active opposition to the Tsar or the Kaisers. The situation was easier perhaps in Austrian Poland, in Galicia, where, following the *Ausgleich* of 1867, the Polish aristocratic landowners were gradually accorded considerable autonomy in return for their loyalty and political support for the Hapsburgs.[27] None the less, from all parts of partitioned Poland, it seemed that, in reality, any prospect of recovering independence had vanished.

This depressing scenario had not materially altered before the outbreak of the First World War. For the major powers there had not been a 'Polish Question' for decades, for they all had more pressing concerns, often in competition with one another. Among some Poles, however, the period of political passivity within the framework of 'Organic Work' had given way from the 1880s onwards to a renewed quest for political direction which, in turn, stimulated debate about leading questions, especially 'Who is a Pole?' and 'What is Poland?'[28] The debate, focusing on the themes of ethnicity, religion, geography and culture, as well as Poland's economic and strategic needs, was sharpened by several important social trends in the second half of the nineteenth century.

First, the peasantry, who had been emancipated in the Russian partition shortly after the collapse of the 1863 insurrection, and earlier in the Prussian and Austrian-occupied areas of Poland, developed a new sense of national and class consciousness, of being 'Polish', which provided a potential mass base for a resurgent Polish nationalist movement. Some of them also, after moving to the towns, formed the core of an industrial working class.[29] Second, while Polish–Jewish relations had been fairly stable prior to the 1863 insurrection, they had begun to deteriorate in the latter decades of the century. Relatively large numbers of Jews had become active and successful in the development of industry and commerce, arousing some resentment among Poles. But the Jews were also perceived increasingly as being over-zealous in collaborating with the partitionist authorities, particularly in Russian Poland. In the popular mind, they got the name of being Tsarist agents, acting against the Polish interest. The influx before 1914 of about 250,000 Jewish refugees from Tsarist persecution exacerbated the problem, not least because these so-called 'Litvaks' spoke Yiddish, dressed distinctively and displayed an affinity with Russian cultural norms.[30] The foundation and growth from the late 1890s of Zionism, which might broadly be described as an expression of Jewish nationalism with the aim of establishing a separate Jewish state in Palestine, accentuated for many Poles the perception that the Jews in their midst were an alien group whose intrinsic interests ran counter to their own.[31] Long-standing religious prejudice played a role here, as did the view held by both Poles and Jews that the other was 'strange', 'different' and incomprehensible. Both were locked into traditional stereotypes, each having a sense of superiority over the other.[32]

Third, the landed nobility and gentry (*szlachta*), many of whom had suffered confiscation of their estates, deportation and exile for their leading role in the 1863 insurrection, were a much reduced social, economic and political force, largely resigned to partition. This paved the way for the subsequent emergence of an embryonic middle-class intelligentsia, with its genesis in sections of the déclassé *szlachta*, as the putative leaders of the nation.[33]

Despite the repressive nature of Partition, Poles were not immune to the ferment of new ideas and attitudes, including that of a neo-Romantic nationalism, which swept across Europe after about 1890. Literary figures such as Henryk Sienkiewicz (1864–1916) and Stefan Wyspiański (1869–1907) caught the mood and the imagination in their widely acclaimed works. The small Polish middle class, believing that the era of 'Organic Work' had finally run its course and was no longer capable, therefore, of furthering the national cause, sought to give a new political lead. The National League (*Liga Narodowa*), set up in 1893, spawned four years later the National Democratic Party (*Stronnictwo Narodowo-Demokratyczne*), whose leader, Roman Dmowski (1864–1939), took the initiative in defining the nature of Polish nationality and identity in a series of writings, including *Thoughts of a Modern Pole* (*Myśli nowoczesnego Polaka*) in 1903 and *La Question Polonnaise* in 1909. For Dmowski, a future Poland was to be a centralized, unitary state, extending eastwards to the borders prior to the First Partition of 1772, and dominated by ethnic Poles: a Poland for the Poles, expressive of an integral nationalism. The non-Polish minorities who would inevitably be encompassed within such a Polish state were to be assimilated and polonized. The Germans and Jews, however, were to be the exception, for Dmowski believed that they were totally alien and hostile to the Polish body politic.[34] Moreover, the National Democratic Party, though initially critical of what it regarded as the excessively compliant, even loyalist attitude of the Vatican and the Catholic Church in Poland towards the partitionist powers, also developed the view that only Roman Catholics could be genuine Poles. The Catholic Church had, after all, though within limits, been the sole national institution left standing after 1863, and had emerged as the authentic standard-bearer of 'Polishness'.[35]

Dmowski, together with several other colleagues such as Zygmunt Balicki, author of *National Egoism and Ethics* (1903), thus fashioned an exclusivist ideology of the *Endecja* (National Democrats, or *Endeks*) which became more and more influential as Poland approached the day of independence, and thereafter during the inter-war years. It adopted an evolutionary approach to the matter of independence, believing that although this was the long-term goal, it was more realistic to work gradually towards it by attempting to extract concessions in an *ad hoc* manner from the Tsar, and after the 1905 Revolution in Russia, through the newly created parliamentary (*Duma*) system.[36] To this extent, the *Endecja* was before 1914 an updated, if somewhat attenuated version of the positivist-collaborationist school of thought. With its stridently anti-German and anti-Semitic outlook, this right-wing, ultra-nationalist and conservative ideology and movement offered a striking contrast to a second major school of thought in Poland that was represented, above all, by Józef Piłsudski (1867–1935).

With his roots in the nascent revolutionary Socialist movement in the Tsarist Empire,[37] Piłsudski rejected the philosophy and practice of collaboration in any form, in favour of a continuation of the insurrectionist tradition. The essence of his outlook was that Russia, rather than Germany, was Poland's main enemy. He believed consistently that a free and independent Poland would arise only by dint of her own military endeavours, and as a one-time leader of the Polish Socialist Party (PPS), founded in 1893, he led sporadic assaults on the Tsarist authorities, for which he was banished to Siberia in 1887–92. Always more of a nationalist than a socialist, particularly as time wore on, in the years before the First World War Piłsudski developed a federalist concept which aimed to place a future independent Polish state at the head of a federation of states in Eastern Europe.[38] Unlike the *Endecja*, he acknowledged the rights to nationhood of other peoples languishing in the Tsarist Empire, including the Ukrainians, Byelorussians and Lithuanians.[39] Based on the premise that Russia was the perennial enemy of all of them, he formed the view that their long-term security and independence could be assured only within a federal structure, which carried distinct echoes of the old Polish–Lithuanian Commonwealth of earlier centuries. Within a Polish state, Piłsudski affirmed the equality of all ethnic groups, including the Jews, some of whom were his close associates in the PPS, provided that they showed loyalty to Poland.[40] Repudiating the self-consciously Catholic ethos of the *Endecja*, he preferred a far more tolerant, flexible and secular approach. He himself was a somewhat ambivalent Catholic: he converted to Protestantism in 1899 to marry a divorcée, and did not rejoin the Church until 1916.[41] Thereafter, he maintained a correct but hardly warm relationship with the Church, particularly as most of the hierarchy and priesthood supported his arch-rival, the *Endecja*.[42]

On the eve of the First World War, therefore, various strands of Polish nationalism and interpretations of what constituted the Polish national identity were discernible, even if the prospect of an independent Poland still seemed at best a remote possibility, especially as the Poles themselves completely lacked political unity. Nationalist sentiment had permeated all major social classes in partitioned Poland, though to different degrees. Nevertheless, a platform had been created from the Polish language, culture and historical tradition which would prove useful if circumstances during the course of the war restored the 'Polish Question' to the agenda of international diplomacy. On the other hand, it was unavoidable that Polish nationalism would be in competition with the developing national awareness of other ethnic groups, including of those whose political aspirations might not be easily reconciled with those of the Poles. The choice for Poland, if it came to it, lay between a national unitary state or a supranational federal state.

Even though Piłsudski had forecast before 1914 not only the outbreak of a major European war but also a series of significant developments during it affecting the fortunes of the belligerents, including those of the three partitionist powers, it remained uncertain for several years how the conflict might influence the 'Polish Question'. Certainly, Piłsudski, true to his belief in a muscular approach, had formed the Polish Legions in 1914 as a way of advancing the Polish cause by military means, and Dmowski had set up a Polish National Committee (KNP) in Warsaw as a forum for pressurizing the Russians into granting concessions which, in Dmowski's mind, meant some degree of autonomy under Tsarist tutelage. Later, following the collapse of the Tsarist regime in early spring 1917, the Polish National Committee was moved to Lausanne, then Paris, to seek Allied support and recognition as the authentic representative of Polish interests.[43] But none of these endeavours by themselves had any real chance of achieving substantive gains in the corridors of power. Between 1914 and 1917 each of the partitionist states had issued declarations to the Poles, promising in vague terms certain reforms and gestures to the principle of autonomy.[44] These were merely measures of temporary expediency, however, reflective of the changing balance of military and diplomatic power in the war. What they all wanted, in fact, was Polish manpower for their armies, factories and fields. It must also be noted that neither Britain nor France expressed any desire to restore an independent Poland, until their attitude was transformed in the latter stages of the war by developments over which they exercised little or no control.

In the first instance, the commitment to an independent Poland that was intimated by President Woodrow Wilson of the United States in his State of the Union Address in January 1917, and a year later in his famous Fourteen Points, finally and firmly put the 'Polish Question' before the eyes of the international community. Only because of this American initiative and subsequent pressure did the other principal Western Allies come to accept the proposition that Poland should once again be free and independent, even though there was no consensus until after the end of the war about what territorial shape Poland should take. Secondly, the Bolshevik Revolution in Russia, in Autumn 1917, complemented in a sense President Wilson's moves, in that it was the first unequivocal sign that the old order in Europe could be successfully challenged. The defeat and collapse of the Central Powers the following Autumn ensured that a new map of Europe would arise from the detritus of war, and that on this map, after an absence of 123 years, there would be a sovereign Polish state. What kind of Poland was to be created, however, remained a matter of intense discussion.

Wartime developments in Poland itself had brought fresh perspectives and a greater impetus to bear on the connecting themes of Polish national identity and nationalism, particularly regarding the position of the Jews. Before and during the war, the overwhelming majority of them had been opposed to the idea of independence for Poland. No sooner had the conflict started than a so-called Committee for the East was created by German and Austrian Zionists, with the aim of persuading the Central

Powers to make concessions to the Jews and reorganize Central Europe in a way that omitted any suggestion of an independent Polish state.[45] More specifically, the Committee proposed a German-controlled multinational state across Central Europe (*Mitteleuropakonzept*) in which the Poles would be but one ethnic group among many others. Although the Germans rejected this plan and refused to recognize the Jews as a separate national minority, the Committee's activity outraged Polish opinion and strengthened the belief that the Jews constituted a formidable obstacle to the realization of Poles' legitimate longing for independent nationhood. Furthermore, when the Germans expelled the Russians from Warsaw in September 1915, and subsequently from the rest of what had been Russian Poland, they pursued a policy of occupation which relied heavily on the willing assistance of many Jews, some of whom were later alleged to have been implicated in war-profiteering and other low-life activity.[46] For many Poles, particularly those who sympathized with the *Endecja*, the Jews were thus confirmed as their implacable enemy.[47]

This unfortunate perception was apparently vindicated fully by the conduct of a powerful, well-organized 'Jewish Lobby' at the Peace Conference in Paris, commencing in January 1919. In October 1918 the World Zionist Organization, based in Copenhagen, had already issued a list of demands on Jewish rights, including the demand for Jewish national autonomy in Poland.[48] The creation of the Committee of Jewish Delegations representing American, British and French Jewry followed in March 1919, in which personalities such as Lucien Wolf (1857–1930) and Leon Reich (1875–1929) made known in no uncertain terms their opposition to the establishment of an independent Poland, arguing essentially that the Poles were incorrigibly anti-Semitic and incapable, therefore, of treating the Jewish minority with fairness and respect.[49] Dmowski, more than any other Pole, had attracted the hostility of Jewish opinion, notably during his visit to the United States in 1918, when he made little effort to conceal his anti-Semitism, despite the strenuous entreaties of Ignacy Paderewski (1860–1941), the world-famous Polish pianist, who was busy trying to court support for Poland in the highest echelons of the American government.[50]

The growing anti-Polish campaign mounted by prominent Jews and Jewish organizations at the Peace Conference involved also, on the British side, Lewis Namier, born into a wealthy, assimilated Jewish family in Warsaw, who was employed by the Foreign Office to advise on Polish affairs.[51] Namier was as passionately pro-Zionist as he was anti-Polish, and he found strong support for his views from the British Prime Minister, David Lloyd George, the eminent economist, John Maynard Keynes, and E. H. Carr, the later well-known left-wing historian of Soviet Russia, who, as a government official, was Secretary of the Committee at the Peace Conference charged with considering provision for minorities in the post-war states in Eastern Europe. The Chairman of that Committee, the British diplomat Sir James Headlam-Morley, was openly sympathetic to the 'Jewish Lobby'.[52] Furthermore, *The Times* became notorious for publishing articles by Israel Cohen, a Special Commissioner with the World Zionist Organization, which amounted to polonophobic diatribes.[53] Among other prominent British Jews and their supporters who actively sought to advance the Jewish interest in Poland by denigrating the Poles were the financier and businessman Sir Herbert Samuel and the Labour politician George Lansbury.[54]

When it emerged that the Peace Conference was not to be prevented from applying the principle of national self-determination enunciated by President Wilson, and that an independent Polish state was to be created after all, the same 'Jewish Lobby' then tried to persuade the international statesmen in Paris to have the Jews in Poland recognized as a separate national minority enjoying extensive autonomy.[55] Before that, a special Jewish Congress in Warsaw on 26–30 December 1918 had sought to con-struct a united forum around a Jewish National Council to assert Jewish demands in Poland.[56] Although internecine Jewish dissension wrecked this enterprise, it was one more unmistakable indication that the Jews were determined to fight against the fledgling Polish state in order to protect what they regarded as their vital interests, and were quite prepared to mobilize world opinion behind their efforts. This explains why in late 1918 and early the following year sensational stories of pogroms against Jews in several Polish cities and towns, notably in Lwów (November 1918), Pińsk (April 1919) and Wilno (April 1919), were propagated in the international press, prompting the American government to despatch a high-level delegation under Henry Morgenthau, himself a Jew, to inves-tigate.[57] As it transpired, he was able to assure his government that the press reports were either grossly exaggerated or simply untrue.[58] In all three cases, Jews had been killed, not simply for being Jewish, as had been claimed, but because they had been assisting the Ukrainian nationalists or the Bolsheviks in military activity against Polish forces.[59]

What Jewish pressure politics did eventually manage to secure at the Peace Conference was the imposition on Poland, as an integral part of the settlement which established the Polish state, of the Minorities' Treaty, whose purpose was to provide formal constitutional and political safe-guards for Poland's ethnic minorities, but especially for the Jews. The Treaty further embittered Polish–Jewish relations in an already fraught atmosphere because, while it was triumphantly hailed as 'a great victory for the Jewish cause',[60] it was regarded by the Poles as both a grievous insult to their long tradition of tolerance, and as an unwarranted encroachment on Poland's national sovereignty at a particularly sensitive time.[61] In the event, the Poles had no option but to accept the Treaty, albeit with undisguised reluctance. Speaking in the *Sejm* on 31 July 1919, the Peasant Party (Piast) leader, Wincenty Witos (1874–1945), denounced the Minorities' Treaty as a deliberate ploy by the Jews to disgrace the Polish people.[62] Clearly, the situation which had already arisen by spring 1919 was hardly conducive to the fostering of good Polish–Jewish relations in the new era of independence.

Poland had no respite either from the other major ethnic groups. As a consequence of Germany's defeat and disintegration into revolution in November 1918 and the mass emigration to the Reich of Germans from areas now forming part of Poland, most of the million or so Germans who remained immediately adopted an overtly hostile posture towards the new Polish state. Only the small minority of German socialists was prepared to grudgingly acknowledge its loyalty. The others, encouraged by various organizations including the *Reichszentrale für Heimatdienst*, *Deutsche Stiftung* and *Verein für das Deutschtum im Ausland*, soon engaged in anti-Polish agitation and propaganda of one kind or another.[63] In south-eastern Poland, commencing in November 1918, Ukrainian nationalists fought the Poles for control of Lwów and Eastern Galicia.[64] Rising tension was also evident between Polish estate-owners and the mainly Orthodox Byelorussian peasantry, thus adding an element of class and religious conflict to the incipient clash of nationality. In short, at the very beginning of Poland's independent existence, her authority and legitimacy as a state were subject to serious, even violent, challenge from her four principal ethnic groups.

To construct a positive relationship with such substantial ethnic minorities would have been daunting even where a state enjoyed a settled and balanced environment. In Poland's case, however, the wider context in which she had to address this issue could hardly have been more inauspicious. To the initial problems arising from an economy stunted by partitionist policies and then devastated by war and post-war hyperinflation, little or no basic infrastructure, a chronic shortage of capital and the inevitable divisions in a nation which had experienced so many years of loss of independence, were added, at least until the Piłsudski coup in 1926, the consequences of a fundamental absence of stable political leadership: between 1918 and 1926 there were no fewer than 14 governments, a record even worse than that of the Weimar Republic in Germany, which is invariably spotlighted as the epitome of political instability in inter-war

Europe. Matters were made worse for Poland by the enduring threat to her independence that was posed by revanchist Germany and the Soviet Union, against which her alliances of 1921 with France and Romania offered increasingly dubious security. There is no denying, therefore, that Poland's struggle for survival against overwhelming odds on all fronts after 1918 is a most important factor to be borne in mind when her approach to the minorities' issue is considered. At the same time, it was arguably during the early post-war years that actions and attitudes on all sides established a framework that remained basically unaltered until 1939, even if the details were often radically changed.

The German minority, which was always likely to continue posing severe problems because it was inevitably caught up in the trauma experienced by Germany as a result of profound economic, social and political upheaval during the early 1920s, conducted itself in a manner that was at once provocative and calculated to give notice that it regarded its status in Poland, and Poland herself, as temporary. For example, it had hoped for Poland's defeat in the war against the Bolsheviks in 1920.[65] Subsequently, in Poznania, Pomerania and what had been before the war West Prussia, the sizeable German communities eagerly accepted funds, propaganda and moral support from the Reich in their struggle to keep their distance as far as possible from the Poles and to prepare for the day when they would regain control of the 'lost territories'. The losses under the 'Diktat' of Versailles, the plebiscites in East Prussia in 1920,[66] and the armed struggles over Poznań in 1918–19 and Upper Silesia 1919–21[67] added to an atmosphere of profound hostility and hatred which was never dispelled, and which merely intensified after Hitler came to power in Germany in 1933. By 1939 a large majority of the Germans in Poland had become enthusiastic Nazis.[68]

It might not have been surprising if the Poles, for their part, had reacted in the same way towards the German minority. But, although there are examples in the early post-war years of some confiscation of land or property belonging to Germans and the dissolution of several German organizations for anti-state activity, such as the *Deutschtumbund* in 1923,[69] it is the relative tolerance on the Polish side that is the most arresting feature of the relationship, despite the considerable influence wielded in government at that time by the avowedly anti-German *Endecja*. Several government ministers, it is true, including Prime Ministers Władysław Grabski (1874–1938) and General Władysław Sikorski (1881–1943), did emphasize the need for tough measures,[70] but there was, in reality, no sustained, coherent programme of polonization or of de-Germanization from any Polish government.[71] The indisputable evidence is that the Germans remained an economically privileged group, retaining a substantial stake in farming, land- and estate-ownership, and in industry and commerce, especially in the textile centres of Łódz and Bielsko-Biała, and mining in Upper Silesia. Their per capita income was consequently noticeably higher than that of the average Pole, and they were allowed extensive freedom to use their own language and organize their own press, cultural associations, libraries, sports clubs, schools, cooperatives, even banks. From time to time the cash-strapped Polish government even provided limited funding for some of these activities.[72] Moreover, the Germans, who were predominantly Protestant, were free to practise their faith in mainly Catholic Poland. Nor were they discriminated against politically: they were allowed to establish their own parties and to contest elections, resulting in German representatives regularly taking their place in the *Sejm* and in the Senate. Once there, regrettably, most of them used the parliamentary platform to challenge Polish statehood.[73]

Despite this wide-ranging freedom to maintain their identity and to pursue their interests, the Germans steadfastly refused to be reconciled to the Polish Republic. Their disloyalty was also informed by the traditional sense of superiority evinced by many Germans towards Poles and Poland, which they dismissed contemptuously as a *Saisonstaat*, an entity that was here today, but gone tomorrow, and thus not to be taken seriously. Such an invidious outlook could only spell trouble.

The much larger numbers of Ukrainians proved to be as intractable as the Germans, except that some of them were prepared from the outset to take up arms against the Polish state, in the shape of the Ukrainian Military Organisation (UVO), and later, the Organization of Ukrainian Nationalists (OUN).[74] Here again was a vital clash of concepts of nationality and class, with the Ukrainians believing that they had as much right as the Poles to independence. Culturally, they had been making advances in the second half of the nineteenth century which gave them something of a basis for their claims. Consequently, Ukrainian nationalism posed an immediate and persistent threat to Poland after 1918, exacerbated by the fact that in Eastern Galicia they were in the majority, even if they were largely poor, ill-educated peasants, while the Poles constituted the dominant landholding class, as well as controlling (with the Jews) the towns. Despite the transient alliance in 1920–1 between Poland and Semon Petliura's so-called 'Ukrainian People's Republic' against the Soviet Bolsheviks,[75] relations in these early post-war years were informed by mutual suspicion, resentment and hatred, and the attempted assassination in Lwów on 25 September 1921 of Marshal Piłsudski by a Ukrainian terrorist set the scene for ongoing conflict.[76]

The Poles did grant concessions to the Ukrainians regarding the use of their religion, language, schooling, press, cooperatives and broadly cultural activities, and afforded them the opportunity of developing their own political parties, but these measures were never enough to satisfy their aspirations.[77] A large majority boycotted the National Census of 1921 and the elections of November 1922 as a gesture of defiance against the Polish state, and harboured resentments over the admittedly slow pace and limitations of agrarian reform. Party political and public opinion in Poland, with the exception of the Communists, ruled out any idea of surrendering hard-won Polish territory; and while there were those on the Left, in sections of the PPS and the radical peasant party 'Liberation' (PSL), who favoured granting a large measure of territorial autonomy,[78] this would have been most unlikely to bring peace given the militancy of the Ukrainian nationalist movement. The balance of power in the country-side could have been changed to some extent through more reform that allowed the Ukrainian peasantry in the longer term a greater stake in landownership, but anything more far-reaching would surely have under-mined the legitimate interests of the Polish state. Those interests were served by the state's understandable exclusion from local government bodies of unreliable Ukrainian staff in the early 1920s, and by the granting of land in Eastern Galicia in the mid-1920s to the victorious and much-admired veterans of the Polish–Soviet War. Further cultural and educa-tional concessions were always possible, and some were granted in later years, though not Ukrainian-language schools, which declined in number, or the promised Ukrainian university in Lwów. Illiteracy rates, however, which were very high in 1918, dropped substantially, thanks to increas-ing Polish school provision – for example, through the school statute of 31 July 1924.[79] None the less, like the German minority, the Ukrainians remained a constant threat to Poland, especially as their militants were often, if intermittently, supported with money, arms and propaganda by Poland's external enemies.[80]

While a significant proportion of the 1.5 million Byelorussians remained disaffected, only a few engaged in direct anti-statist activity and, in any case, they lacked the cultural maturity and capacity for political organization to be ranked alongside the Germans and Ukrainians in terms of the potency of their opposition to Poland. The short-lived Hromada political movement (1925–8), which demanded independence and the confiscation without compensation of Polish estates, caused some anxiety for the Poles before being crushed. Byelorussian opposition was ineffec-tive, also, because increasing numbers of the younger generation were assimilated through military service, schooling and the proselytization of the Catholic Church; as a minority located next door to Russia, the Byelorussians too frequently appeared also to be manipulated or diverted by the dictates of Soviet foreign policy.[81]

Of a quite different order from all the other ethnic groups were the Jews. They did not form a homogeneous minority, of course, being split into Orthodox, Socialist and Zionist, religious and secular, conservative and radical, rich and poor, bourgeois and proletarian, with a plethora of sub-strata in all of these broad categories. Mendelsohn characterizes them socially as 'lower middle class and proletarian, with a numerically small but important intelligentsia and wealthy bourgeoisie'.[82] There was, therefore, no such thing as a united Jewish population in any sense except that, apart from the small assimilationist Orthodox conservatives, they were hostile to the establishment of an independent Poland and continued in this vein after 1918.[83] In the face of two competing negative outlooks, it was always highly questionable whether a meaningful relationship could be forged between them in the early post-war years.[84]

The provocation of the Minorities' Treaty and the apocryphal stories of pogroms were only the beginning of Jewish-inspired opposition to the Polish state. The pro-Soviet Communist Workers' Party of Poland (KPRP), set up in December 1918, soon attracted a substantial Jewish following, especially in its leadership cadres; and the party's most prominent ideologues and personalities were frequently Jewish.[85] The main Jewish socialist party, the *Bund*, exhibited strong sympathy for the Communists, and likewise refused to recognize the legitimacy of the state.[86] Both conducted a vigorous campaign of agitation which reached a climax in the early post-war years in their support for the Red Army's invasion of Poland in 1920. In this these parties, together with elements from the Zionist camp, struck a responsive chord among broad swathes of the Jewish community, particularly in Eastern Poland, where there were numerous local actions of sabotage and spying for the Soviets.[87] Sections of the extensive Jewish press, and leading figures, including Henryk Ehrlich (1882–1941), the *Bund* leader and member of the Warsaw City Council, joined in this treasonous chorus.[88] While some Jews gave their lives for Poland in the Polish–Soviet War and in the other wars Poland had to fight in those early years to secure her borders, a large majority made their loyalties all too clear: they were pro-Soviet or Zionist, and anti-Polish.

The impact on Polish public opinion of such conduct at the moment when Poland was fighting for her very existence as an independent country was arguably definitive. The perception was reinforced for many Poles that the Jews were their enemy. Even Piłsudski, who was considered to be philo-Semitic in some quarters,[89] was moved to remark that 'multitudes of Jews' had behaved unpatriotically during the conflict.[90] In fact, even before 1914, the Marshal, victor at the Battle of Warsaw which was the decisive turning-point in the Polish–Soviet War, had come to impugn the loyalty of many Jews to the Polish cause; and after 1918, when he perceived them to be linked too often to revolutionary Socialism and Bolshevism, he never publicly condemned the anti-Semitism of the *Endecja*.[91] Only on the political Left and among the liberal intelligentsia of Warsaw was this perception of Poland's Jewish minority not generally shared.[92]

If one Jewish leader personified for Poles the distrust and resentment many of them harboured towards the Jews, especially in the aftermath of the war against the Soviet Bolsheviks, it was the General Zionist leader, Yitshak Gruenbaum (1879–1960), described by one writer as 'fundamentally anti-Polish'.[93] A somewhat intemperate, doctrinaire and egocentric individual, who had returned to Warsaw in 1918 after spending many years in Russia as a Zionist activist, he made it his mission in his new life in Poland to agitate incessantly against the state, and to encourage others to follow his uncompromising example.[94] He exploited press freedom to mount his propaganda attacks, and led Jewish opposition in the *Sejm* to the new Constitution from the moment it was introduced for debate until finally approved in March 1921, on the spurious pretext that it did not offer sufficient protection to the Jews. It has to be said that the Constitution, modelled on that of the Third French Republic, was extremely liberal and contained a string of guarantees for all the ethnic minorities, as did the Treaty of Riga (Article VII) between Poland and Soviet Russia the same month.

Gruenbaum's most notorious disservice to Polish–Jewish relations, however, came in Autumn 1922 when, with the assistance of the German senator and subsequent Nazi Erwin Hasbach, he masterminded the organization of the Bloc of National Minorities to fight the parliamentary elections in November.[95] Winning 21.6 per cent of the vote and 89 seats in the *Sejm*,[96] the Bloc sent out the wrong signal to the Poles: it was, as Gruenbaum had intended, a declaration of political warfare against the state, or as Engel puts it, 'a red rag to the Polish people',[97] and a calculated impediment, therefore, to ethnic harmony. The destructive nature of Gruenbaum's creation was revealed all too starkly in December 1922, when it tipped the balance of votes in the presidential election in favour of the leftist candidate Gabriel Narutowicz, who was immediately stigmatized by the Right as a 'Jewish President' and assassinated a few days later by an ultra-Nationalist. The ensuing poisonous atmosphere in Polish political life, which threatened to break out into civil war, owed much, therefore, to the nefarious activity of Gruenbaum and his fellow Zionists, which continued without pause when it denounced the incoming government of General Sikorski as anti-Semitic.[98]

Given the volume and intensity of opposition from Jewish circles, the Polish state might well have been expected to adopt the harshest measures of self-defence, particularly as its energies were being expended in so many different directions in the early 1920s. Such a response might also have been expected on account of the powerful position in government at that time of the *Endecja* and its right-wing allies. On the contrary, however, the response was remarkably restrained. Not only were 600,000 Jewish refugees from the Russian civil war granted Polish citizenship between 1918 and 1921,[99] but the Jews were permitted as much freedom as anyone else to practise their religion, organize an extensive and thriving press publishing daily and weekly newspapers and magazines in Polish, Yiddish and Hebrew,[100] develop their culture in the broadest sense, set up their own secular and religious schools[101] and pursue their political interests through their own parties. Furthermore, Jewish students formed a markedly disproportionate percentage of the university population,[102] and Jewish scholarship flourished from its base in Wilno where the Institute for the Science of Judaism (YIVO) was later set up with the aid of a government grant.[103] Consequently, the Jewish community in inter-war Poland was not only the largest in Europe, it was also the most dynamic and creative, as is widely acknowledged.[104]

Jews certainly met with resentment because of their predominant role in industry, commerce, banking and several liberal professions, including the law and medicine; and they were largely excluded from certain areas of public employment, such as the civil service, state-run industry, schools and the Army officer corps (except for the medical and legal sections).[105] But their numerous other benefits were not seriously challenged during this early period, either by the popular will or by governmental decree. Government legislation, such as the Sunday Rest Law of 18 December 1919, which the Jews bitterly resented, was invariably implemented in a haphazard fashion, thus causing the Jews far less inconvenience in everyday practice than they claimed.[106] Although some Jews were poor, especially in the eastern *shtetl*, and a Jewish proletariat was to be found in towns and cities, they enjoyed as a whole a higher standard of living than the vast majority of Poles, and had the wider freedoms to enjoy it.[107] The objective picture that emerges of their overall situation in the early 1920s makes a mockery of the tales of abject destitution, discrimination and persecution that Gruenbaum and his circle so gratuitously propagated, especially for foreign consumption, thus frequently putting Poland in the worst possible light with little effective means of reply. Nothing the Poles did was ever right, as far as they were concerned. Thus, when in July 1925 the Grabski government concluded an agreement with the Jewish Club in the *Sejm*, the so-called *Ugoda*, on a wide range of issues, it was loudly dismissed by many Jews, including Gruenbaum, as a cynical ploy by the Poles to attract foreign investment.[108] This claim was unjustified. What had become very clear was that Jewish polonophobia was as powerfully on display as Polish anti-Semitism. Most Jews did not want to mix with their Polish neighbours, preferring for all practical purposes a ghetto-type independent existence within which they increasingly nurtured their own national, Jewish consciousness and identity.[109] For them, the state and the Poles were objects of contempt and antipathy.

It has been argued that Poland from the beginning should have adopted other courses of action which might have carried more hope of reconciling the minorities to her. For example, a federal structure allowing substantial autonomy has been advocated as a more appropriate policy for a multi-ethnic country such as inter-war Poland was. This seems to presuppose, however, that even a liberal degree of autonomy, such as that enshrined in a statute passed by the *Sejm* in September 1922 for Eastern Galicia,[110] would have been acceptable to, say, the Ukrainians and Germans, when it is fairly clear otherwise that they wanted nothing less than separation, either to rejoin the Reich on the one hand, or to establish their own independent state on the other. The Poles rightly concluded, in any case, that concessions had to stop somewhere, for more and more would be demanded until the sovereignty of the state was irrevocably compromised. The renunciation of Polish territory, therefore, was out of the question for all but a marginalized few on the political Left. Similarly, a policy of compulsory population transfer, or 'ethnic cleansing', could never have been entertained by the Poles, and the encouragement given by the post-Piłsudski *Sanacja* regime to the mass emigration ideas of the Revisionist Zionists under Vladimir Jabotinsky (1880–1940)[111] should not be understood as signalling even a tentative step towards anything as repulsive as 'ethnic cleansing'. Through all her vicissitudes since 1918, Poland retained a sense of decency and humanity that may be said to have been sadly lacking in some other neighbouring countries at that time, above all in Soviet Russia during the Leninist era. The Marxist solution adduced by the Communist Party of Poland for a total transformation of the economic, social and political design of the state, in which class and ethnic differences would (in theory at least) be completely abolished, attracted only minimal support from ethnic Poles.[112]

The early post-war history of Poland contains a striking paradox: when, by 1923, she had in a veritable baptism of fire secured her frontiers and independent status, relations with the four principal ethnic minorities continued to be characterized by acrimony and distrust, a sort of internal war. In the years ahead, this situation did not basically change. If anything, it actually deteriorated under the brutalizing impact of the Depression, external threat and heightened nationalism on all sides in the 1930s. Despite the guarantees of civil rights and democratic liberties enshrined in legislation, especially in the Minorities' Treaty and the Constitution of 1921, both of which the Polish state tried to implement as best it could amidst the most unpropitious circumstances in the early 1920s, the minorities were not prepared to help establish a *modus vivendi* which would have been to the benefit of everyone. It is difficult to avoid the conclusion, therefore, that the solution to the minorities' question lay more with the minorities themselves than with the state.[113] A more cooperative attitude by them, involving a more balanced and realistic perspective on their problems, was surely the only answer that Poland's generally constructive and relatively liberal approach deserved.[114] In any case, as citizens of the Republic, they all had a duty and responsibility to respect and work with the state. And, after all, it cannot be denied that the longer-term interests of the minorities would have been better served had there been cooperation and compromise instead of confrontation and denunciation. Later, the Germans of Poland were engulfed in the murderous *débâcle* of the Third Reich, the Ukrainians and Byelorussians oppressed by the Stalinist system in the Soviet Union, and the Jews decimated in the horrors of the Holocaust. From the dismal perspective of 1945, those of them who had survived the catastrophes of the Second World War must have been sorely tempted to look back on their early time in Poland with genuine nostalgia, for they would know, deep down, that their situation had been far better than they had ever been prepared to admit, and that their fate might have been very different had they made the requisite effort to make their peace with the Poles when they had the chance.[115]

As for the Poles themselves, the challenge posed by the problem of the minorities had incontrovertibly helped strengthen their resilience, their resolve to surmount the divisive legacy of partition, and their sense of national identity and pride, which transcended social and political differences. The unifying influence of two major institutions, the Catholic Church and the triumphant Polish Army, added further solidity to the patriotic ethos. In consequence, never again, not least in 1939 *vis-à-vis* the combined Nazi and Soviet onslaught, or in 1945 *vis-à-vis* the Stalinist yoke that was so shamefully imposed with Western connivance, could it be claimed by her enemies that Poland's nationhood was a thing of the past.

NOTES

1. Stephan Horak, *Poland and her National Minorities, 1919–39* (Vantage Press, New York, 1961), p. 158.
2. Paweł Korzec, 'Antisemitism in Poland as an Intellectual, Social and Political Movement', in Joshua A. Fishman (ed.), *Studies on Polish Jewry, 1919–1939* (Yivo Institute for Jewish Research, New York, 1974), p. 12.
3. Oskar Halecki, *A History of Poland* (Routledge & Kegan Paul, London, 1977), p. 298.
4. Richard Blanke, 'The German Minority in Inter-War Poland and German Foreign Policy – Some Reconsiderations', *Journal of Contemporary History*, 25 (1990), No. 1, pp. 87–102. His *Orphans of Versailles. The Germans in Western Poland, 1918–1939* (University Press of Kentucky, Lexington, 1993) is tendentious.
5. Point made by Stefan Kieniewicz, who is himself Jewish, in 'Polish Society and the Jewish Problem in the nineteenth century', in Norman Davies and Antony Polonsky (eds), *The Jews in Eastern Poland and the USSR, 1939–1946* (Macmillan , London, 1991), p. 70.
6. For example, Lucy Dawidowicz, *The War Against the Jews* (Penguin, London, 1975), pp. 472 ff.; Shmuel Almog, *Nationalism and Antisemitism in Modern Europe, 1815–1945* (Pergamon Press, Oxford, 1990), p. 107.
7. Ezra Mendelsohn, 'Jewish Historiography on Polish Jewry in the Interwar Period', *Polin*, 8 (1994), pp. 4–5.
8. Joseph Marcus, *Social and Political History of the Jews in Poland, 1919–1939* (Mouton, New York, 1983), p. 8.
9. Yisrael Gutman, *The Jews of Warsaw, 1939–1943. Ghetto, Underground, Revolt* (Indiana University Press, Bloomington, 1982), p. xvi.
10. Celia S. Heller, *On the Edge of Destruction. Jews of Poland Between the Two World Wars* (Columbia University Press, New York, 1977), pp. 3, 13.
11. Ezra Mendelsohn, *Zionism in Poland. The Formative Years, 1915–1926* (Yale University Press, New Haven, 1981), p. 1.
12. Adam Żółtowski, *Border of Europe. A Study of the Polish Eastern Provinces* (Hollis & Carter, London, 1950), pp. 323–4; Horak, *Poland and her National Minorities*, p. 215.
13. R. F. Leslie (ed.), *The History of Poland since 1863* (Cambridge University Press, Cambridge, 1983), pp. 138, 148.
14. For example, Zanna Kormanowa (ed.), *Historia Polski, 1864–1945* (Warsaw, 1952). Among those who helped write school history textbooks in similar vein were the later well-known historians and Communists Stefan Kieniewicz, Józef Gierowski and Roman Wapiński. See *Polin*, 4 (1989), pp. 409–10, and Antony Polonsky's remarks in Timothy Wiles (ed.), *Poland Between the Wars, 1918–1939* (Indiana University Press, Bloomington, 1989), p. 3 ff.

15. For example, Marian M. Drozdowski, 'The National Minorities in Poland in 1918–1939', *Acta Poloniae Historica*, 22 (1970), pp. 226–51.
16. For example, Andrzej Micewski, *Z geografii politycznej II Rzeczypospolitej* (Warsaw, 1964), and Andrzej Chojnowski, *Koncepcje polityki narodowościowej rządow polskich w latach 1921–39* (Wrocław, 1979).
17. Jerzy Tomaszewski, *Rzeczpospolita wielu narodów* (Warsaw, 1985), and his *Ojczyzna nie tylko Polaków. Mniejszości narodowe w Polsce w latach 1918–1939* (Warsaw, 1985); Andrzej Chojnowski, 'The Jewish Community of the Second Republic in Polish Historiography of the 1980s', *Polin*, 1 (1986), pp. 288–99.
18. Józef Lewandowski, 'History and Myth: Pińsk, April 1919', *Polin*, 2 (1987), p. 67.
19. Henri Rollet, *La Pologne au XXe Siecle* (Pedone, Paris, 1985), p. 146.
20. *Rocznik Statystyki Rzeczypospolitej Polski IV* (Warsaw, 1925–6), p. 26. Useful supplementary data is in Edward Szturm De Sztrem (ed.), *Statistical Atlas of Poland* (The Polish Ministry of Information, London, n.d.). For Jewish figures, see Joseph Lichten, 'Notes on the Assimilation and Acculturation of Jews in Poland, 1863–1943', in Chimen Abramsky, Maciej Jachimczyk and Antony Polonsky (eds), *The Jews in Poland* (Basil Blackwell, Oxford, 1986), p. 21, and Mendelsohn, *Zionism in Poland*, p. 5.
21. Tomaszewski, *Rzeczpospolita*, p. 343; *Horak, Poland and her National Minorities*, pp. 12, 81 ff., 101; Drozdowski, 'National Minorities', pp. 236–67, which quotes a figure of 7 million Ukrainians.
22. Zbigniew Landau and Jerzy Tomaszewski, *The Polish Economy in the Twentieth Century* (Routledge, London, 1985), p. 115. The Jewish population in 1939 was 3,474,000.
23. Władysław T. Bartoszewski and Antony Polonsky (eds), *The Jews in Warsaw. A History* (Basil Blackwell, Oxford, 1991), pp. 2, 35. More statistical information in Edward D. Wynot, *Warsaw Between the World Wars. Profile of a Capital City in a Developing Land, 1918–1939* (East European Monographs, Boulder, Colorado, 1983), pp. 106–7, 307. n. 4. See also Stephen D. Corrsin, *Warsaw Before the First World War. Poles and Jews in the Third City of the Russian Empire, 1880–1914* (East European Monographs, Boulder, Colorado, 1989).
24. Czesław Brzoza, 'The Jewish Press in Kraków (1918–1939)', *Polin*, 7 (1992), p. 134.
25. Wiesław Puś, 'The Development of the City of Łódz (1820–1939)', *Polin*, 6 (1991), p. 16; Julian K. Janczak, 'The National Structure of the Population in Łódz in the Years 1820–1939', *Polin*, 6 (1991), p. 25, gives 35 per cent.
26. Stanislaus A. Blejwas, *Realism in Polish Politics. Warsaw Positivism and National Survival in Nineteenth Century Poland;* Adam Bromke, *Poland's Politics. Idealism versus Realism* (Harvard University Press, Cambridge, Mass., 1967); Adam Bromke, *The Meaning and Uses of Polish History* (East European Monographs, Boulder, Colorado, 1987).
27. Piotr S. Wandycz, *The Lands of Partitioned Poland, 1795–1918* (University of Washington Press, Seattle, 1974), pp. 277 ff., 319 ff.
28. Brian A. Porter, 'Who is a Pole and Where is Poland? Territory and Nation in the Rhetoric of Polish National Democracy before 1905', *Slavic Review*, 51 (1992), No. 4, pp. 639–53; Piotr Wandycz, 'Poland's Place in Europe in the

Concepts of Piłsudski and Dmowski', *East European Politics and Societies*, 4 (1990), No. 3, pp. 451–68.
29. Stefan Kieniewicz, *The Emancipation of the Polish Peasantry* (University of Chicago Press, Chicago, 1969), pp. 174 ff.; Peter Brock, *Nationalism and Populism in Partitioned Poland. Selected Essays* (Orbis Books, London, 1968), p. 17.
30. Kieniewicz in Davies and Polonsky (eds), *Jews*, p. 75; Ezra Mendelsohn, *The Jews of East Central Europe Between the World Wars* (Indiana University Press, Bloomington, 1983), p. 20.
31. Joseph Goldstein, 'The Beginnings of the Zionist Movement in Congress Poland: the victory of the Hasidim over the Zionists?', *Polin*, 5 (1990), pp. 114–30; Piotr Wróbel, 'The First World War: the Twilight of Jewish Warsaw', in Bartoszewski and Polonsky (eds), *Jews of Warsaw*, pp. 252–3.
32. Władysław T. Bartoszewski, 'Poles and Jews as the "other"', *Polin*, 4 (1989), pp. 6–17; and Rafael Scharf's comments in Antony Polonsky (ed.), *'My Brother's Keeper?'. Recent Polish Debates on the Holocaust* (Routledge, London, 1990), pp. 191 ff.
33. Lesile (ed.), *History of Poland*, pp. 53 ff.
34. Alvin M. Fountain, *Roman Dmowski. Party, Tactics, Ideology 1895–1907* (East European Monographs, Boulder, Colorado, 1980), pp. 158–71; Andrzej Micewski, *Roman Dmowski* (Warsaw, 1971); Roman Wapiński, *Roman Dmowski* (Lublin, 1988). Both of the latter are Communist-slanted and otherwise unsatisfactory.
35. Nedim Ögelman, 'Ethnicity, Demography and Migration in the Evolution of the Polish Nation-State', *The Polish Review*, 40 (1995), No. 2, pp. 159–79.
36. Edward Chmielewski, *The Polish Question in the Russian State Duma* (University of Tennessee Press, Knoxville, 1970), pp. 20–32, 33–81, 161–69.
37. Good coverage in Lucjan Blit, *The Origins of Polish Socialism. The History and Ideas of the First Polish Socialist Party, 1875–1886* (Cambridge University Press, Cambridge, 1971); Robert Blobaum, *Feliks Dzierzyński and the SDKPiL. A Study of the Origins of Polish Communism* (East European Monographs, Boulder, Colorado, 1984); Robert Blobaum, *Rewolucja: Russian Poland, 1904–1907* (Cornell University Press, Ithaca, New York, 1995).
38. Piotr Wandycz, 'Polish Federalism 1919–20 and its Historical Antecedents', *East European Quarterly*, 4 (1970), No. 1, pp. 25 ff., 35–6; M. K. Dziewanowski, 'Joseph Piłsudski, 1867–1967', *East European Quarterly*, 2 (1969), No. 1, p. 378. Further details in M. K. Dziewanowski, *Josef Pilsudski. A European Federalist, 1918–1922* (Hoover Institution Press, Stanford, 1969).
39. Piłsudski reaffirmed this outlook on several occasions just after the end of the First World War – for example, before the Byelorussian National Council in Minsk on 19 September 1919, as reported by Wacław Jędrzejewicz, *Piłsudski. A Life for Poland* (Hippocrene Books, New York, 1982), p. 93. See also Przemysław Hauser, 'Józef Piłsudski's Views on the Territorial Shape of the Polish State and His Endeavours to Put them into Effect in 1918–1921', *Polish Western Affairs*, 33 (1992), No. 2, pp. 235–49.
40. Alexander J. Groth, 'Dmowski, Piłsudski and Ethnic Conflict in pre-1939 Poland', *Canadian Slavic Studies*, 3 (1969), No. 1, pp. 85–8.
41. Jędrzejewicz, *Piłsudski*, pp. 27, 60.

42. As made clear in Neal Pease, 'The "Unpardonable Insult": the Wawel Incident of 1937 and Church–State Relations in Poland', *Catholic Historical Review*, 77 (1991), No. 3, pp. 423–34; and Edward D. Wynot, 'The Catholic Church and the Polish State, 1935–1939', *Journal of Church and State*, 15 (1973), pp. 223–40.

43. Tytus Komarnicki, *The Rebirth of the Polish Republic. A Study in the Diplomatic History of Europe, 1914–1920* (Heinemann, London, 1957), pp. 41–8, 91–7, 147–52, 156 ff., 201–14; Hans Roos, *A History of Modern Poland* (Eyre & Spottiswoode, London, 1966), pp. 15–46.

44. See the Chronology in the Appendix for details.

45. Egmont Zechlin, *Die deutsche Politik und die Juden im Ersten Weltkrieg* (Vandenhoeck & Ruprecht, 1969), pp. 119–33; Frank Golczewski, *Polnisch-Jüdische Beziehungen 1881–1922. Eine Studie zur Geschichte des Antisemitismus in Osteuropa* (Steiner, Wiesbaden, 1981), pp. 121–80.

46. Wróbel in Bartoszewski and Polonsky (eds), *Jews of Warsaw*, p. 282.

47. Jerzy Holzer, 'Polish Political Parties and Antisemitism', *Polin*, 8 (1994), p. 196.

48. Marcus, *Social and Political History*, pp. 296–7.

49. Eugene C. Black, 'Lucien Wolf and the Making of Poland: Paris, 1919', *Polin*, 2 (1987), pp. 5–36; Mark Levene, *War, Jews and the New Europe. The Diplomacy of Lucien Wolf, 1914–1919* (Oxford University Press, Oxford, 1992); Mark Levene, 'Britain, a British Jew, and Jewish Relations with the New Poland: the Making of the Polish Minorities Treaty of 1919', *Polin*, 8 (1994), pp. 14–41.

50. Wiktor Sukiennicki, *East-Central Europe during World War I. From Foreign Domination to National Independence* (East European Monographs, Boulder, Colorado, 1984), vol. 2, p. 895; George J. Lerski, 'Dmowski, Paderewski and American Jews', *Polin*, 2 (1987), p. 95.

51. Paul Latawski, 'The Dmowski–Namier Feud, 1915–1918', *Polin*, 2 (1987), pp. 38 ff. Namier was born Bernstein vel Niemirowski, which in 1910 he changed to Bernstein-Naymier, and to Namier in 1913, when he became a British citizen (*Polin*, 5, 1990, p. 304). Further details in Julia Namier, *Louis Namier. A Biography* (London, 1971).

52. Black, 'Lucien Wolf', p. 23; J. Headlam-Morley, *A Memoir of the Paris Peace Conference 1919* (London, 1972).

53. '*The Times*', 8 February 1919, article entitled, 'The Pogroms in Poland', provides but one example. Cohen's reports, which were widely circulated in the American press, seriously damaged Poland's reputation, as noted in Piotr S. Wandycz, *The United States and Poland* (Harvard University Press, Cambridge, Mass., 1980), pp. 160–5. See also Israel Cohen, 'My Mission to Poland, 1918–19', *Jewish Social Studies*, 3 (1951), No. 3, pp. 149–72, and his *Travels in Jewry* (London, 1952).

54. Levene, 'Britain, a British Jew', pp. 15–16, 30; Patrick B. Finney, ' "An Evil for All Concerned": Great Britain and Minority Protection after 1919', *Journal of Contemporary History*, 30 (1995), No. 3, pp. 533–51.

55. Interesting insights in Andrzej Kapiszewski (ed.), *Hugh Gibson and a Controversy over Polish-Jewish Relations after World War I. A Documentary History* (Jagiellonian University Press, Kraków, 1991). Gibson was the first American minister appointed to the new Polish Republic, in April 1919.

56. Harry M. Rabinowicz, *The Legacy of Polish Jewry. A History of Polish Jews in the Inter-war Years, 1919–1939* (Thomas Yoseloff, New York, 1965), p. 31.

57. Lewandowski, 'History and Myth', pp. 50–72; Jerzy Tomaszewski, 'Pińsk, Saturday 5 April 1919', *Polin*, 1 (1986), pp. 227–51. Rabinowicz, *Legacy of Polish Jewry*, p. 38, refers to 110 pogroms in November 1918 alone, but without supporting evidence.

58. Wandycz, *United States and Poland*, pp. 166 ff.; Norman Davies, 'Ethnic Diversity in Twentieth Century Poland', *Polin*, 4 (1989), p. 149.

59. Norman Davies, *White Eagle, Red Star. The Polish-Soviet War, 1919–20* (Macdonald, London, 1972), pp. 47–8.

60. Levene, 'Britain, a British Jew', p. 35.

61. W. F. Reddaway, J. H. Penson, O. Halecki, R. Dyboski (eds), *The Cambridge History of Poland. Volume 2: From Augustus II to Pilsudski (1697–1935)* (Cambridge University Press, Cambridge, 1951), pp. 505 ff.; Richard M. Watt, *Bitter Glory. Poland and Its Fate, 1918 to 1919* (Simon & Schuster, New York, 1979), p. 78.

62. David Engel, *In the Shadow of Auschwitz. The Polish Government-in-Exile and the Jews, 1939–1942* (University of North Carolina Press, Chapel Hill, 1987), p. 20.

63. Przemysław Hauser, 'The German Minority in Poland in the Years 1918–1939', *Polish Western Affairs*, 32 (1991), No. 2, pp. 13–14, 24; Watt, *Bitter Glory*, p. 174; Karol Fiedor, 'The Attitude of German Right-Wing Organisations to Poland in the Years 1918–33', *Polish Western Affairs*, 14 (1973), No. 2, pp. 247–69.

64. Horak, *Poland and her National Minorities*, pp. 50–5; Rose Bailly, *A City Fights for Freedom. The Rising of Lvov in 1918–1919* (London, 1956).

65. Jerzy Krasuski, 'The Key Points of Polish–German Relations up to 1939', *Polish Western Affairs*, 33 (1992), No. 2, pp. 302 ff.; and Gerhard Wagner, *Deutschland und der polnisch-sowjetische Krieg 1920* (Steiner, Wiesbaden, 1979).

66. Jerzy Sobczak, 'The Weimar Republic's Propaganda Concerning the Plebiscites in Warnia and Mazuria', *Polish Western Affairs*, 13 (1972), No. 2, pp. 334–55.

67. Some background in Joachim Rogall, *Die Deutschen im Posener Land und in Mittelpolen* (Langen Müller, Munich, 1993); Thomas Urban, *Deutsche in Polen. Geschichte und Gegenwart einer Minderheit* (Beck, Munich, 1993).

68. Drozdowski, 'National Minorities', pp. 231 f.

69. Hauser, 'The German Minority', p. 23.

70. Krasuski, 'Key points', p. 302.

71. Blanke, 'The German Minority', pp. 89 ff., takes the opposite view.

72. Janczak, 'The National Structure', pp. 25 f.; Danuta Berlińska, 'The German Minority in Opole, Silesia', *Polish Western Affairs*, 32 (1991), No. 2, pp. 39–52.

73. Hauser, 'The German Minority', p. 22. In the November 1922 elections, for example, the German parties won 17 *Sejm* and 5 Senate (Upper House) seats.

74. Alexander J. Motyl, 'Ukrainian Nationalist Political Violence in Inter-War Poland (1921–1939)', *East European Quarterly*, 19 (1985), No. 1, pp. 45–55; fuller coverage in Alexander J. Motyl, *The Turn to the Right. The Ideological*

Origins and Development of Ukrainian Nationalism, 1919–1929 (East European Monographs, Boulder, Colorado, 1980).

75. Somewhat bitterly discussed in Michael Palij, *The Ukrainian-Polish Defensive Alliance, 1919–1921. An Aspect of the Ukrainian Revolution* (Canadian Institute of Ukrainian Studies Press, Toronto, 1995), *passim*.

76. Bohdan Budurowycz, 'Poland and the Ukrainian Problem, 1921–1939', *Canadian Slavic Papers*, 25 (1983), No. 4, pp. 477 ff. See also Stanisław Skrzypek, *The Problem of Eastern Galicia* (Polish Association for the South-Eastern Provinces, London, 1948), and Taras Hunczak (ed.), *The Ukrainian Revolution. Documents, 1919–1921* (Ukrainian Academy of Arts and Sciences in the United States, New York, 1984).

77. Żółtowski, *Border of Europe*, pp. 284–310.

78. Drozdowski, 'National Minorities', p. 233. Further details in Eugeniusz Koko, *Wolni z wolnymi. PPS wobec kwestii ukraińskiej w latach 1918–1925*. (Gdańsk University Press, Gdańsk, 1991).

79. Horak, *Poland and her National Minorities*, pp. 78 f., 143 ff.

80. Budurowycz, 'Poland and the Ukrainian Problem', p. 478.

81. Drozdowski, 'National Minorities', pp. 242 ff.; Horak, *Poland and her National Minorities*, pp. 171 ff.; Nicholas P. Vakar, *Belorussia. The Making of a Nation* (Harvard University Press, Cambridge, Mass., 1956). Highly critical of Polish policy is the study by the Polish Communist, Aleksander Bergman, *Sprawy białoruskie w II Rzeczpospolitej* (PWN, Warsaw, 1984).

82. Mendelsohn, *Jews of East Central Europe*, p. 27.

83. Despite overhelming evidence to the contrary, Korzec in 'Antisemitism as an Intellectual', p. 15 writes that 'the bulk of Polish Jewry ... welcomed the creation of an independent Polish state with joy and hope'!

84. Chojnowski, 'The Jewish Community of the Second Republic', pp. 288–99.

85. Jaff Schatz, *The Generation. The Rise and Fall of the Jewish Communists of Poland* (University of California Press, Berkeley, 1991), pp. 95–103; Tadeusz Szafar, 'The Origins of the Communist Party in Poland, 1918–1921', in Ivo Banac (ed.), *The Effects of World War I. The Class War after the Great War. The Rise of Communist Parties in East Central Europe, 1918–1921* (East European Monographs, Boulder, Colorado, 1983), pp. 35 f.; Jan B. de Weydenthal, *The Communists of Poland. An Historical Outline* (Hoover Institution Press, Stanford, 1978), pp. 18 f., 25; Moshe Mishkinsky, 'The Communist Party of Poland and the Jews', in Yisrael Gutman, Ezra Mendelsohn, Jehuda Reinharz and Chone Shmeruk (eds), *The Jews of Poland Between Two World Wars* (University Press of New England, Hanover and London, 1989), pp. 56–74.

86. Good analysis in Bernard K. Johnpoll, *The Politics of Futility. The General Jewish Workers' Bund of Poland, 1917–1943* (Cornell University Press, Ithaca, New York, 1967). See also Jerzy Holzer, 'Relations between Polish and Jewish Left-wing Groups in interwar Poland', in Abramsky et al., *Jews in Poland*, pp. 144 f.

87. Szafar, 'The Origins of the Communist Party in Poland', pp. 9 f., 18 ff.; Adam Zamoyski, *The Polish Way. A Thousand-Year History of the Poles and their Culture* (John Murray, London, 1987), pp. 345–7; M. K. Dziewanowski, *The Communist Party of Poland. An Outline of History* (Harvard University Press, Cambridge, Mass., 1976), pp. 88–95.

88. Rabinowicz, *Legacy of Polish Jewry*, pp. 217 f. See also Davies, *White Eagle*, pp. 163, 188–225, and Adam Zamoyski, T*he Battle for the Marshlands* (East European Monographs, Boulder, Colorado, 1981), pp. 125–40.

89. Heller, *Edge of Destruction*, p. 82; Norman Davies, *Heart of Europe. A Short History of Poland* (Clarendon Press, Oxford, 1984), p. 144.

90. W. F. Reddaway, *Marshal Pilsudski* (Routledge & Kegan Paul, London, 1939), p. 140.

91. Groth, 'Dmowski, Piłsudski', pp. 83–7. See also Anna Landau-Czajka, 'The Image of the Jew in the Catholic Press during the Second Republic', *Polin*, 8 (1994), pp. 146–75, especially pp. 155 ff., and Franciszek Adamski, 'The Jewish Question in Polish Religious Periodicals in the Second Republic. The Case of the Przegląd katolicki', *Polin*, 8 (1994), p. 137.

92. Holzer in Abramsky *et al.*, *Jews in Poland*, p. 202; Norman Davies, *God's Playground. A History of Poland. Volume II: 1795 to the Present* (Clarendon Press, Oxford, 1981), p. 262.

93. Daniel Stone, 'Polish Diplomacy and the American Jewish Community between the Wars', *Polin*, 2 (1987), p. 76; Antony Polonsky, *Politics in Independent Poland, 1921–1939. The Crisis of Constitutional Government* (Oxford University Press, Oxford, 1972), p. 92.

94. Mendelsohn, *Zionism in Poland*, p. 74, warmly praises Gruenbaum, who is also described as 'the most popular Jewish leader of the 1920s' by Michael C. Steinlauf, 'The Polish-Jewish Press', *Polin*, 2 (1987), p. 228. See also Marcus, *Social and Political History of the Jews*, pp. 267, 293 for further comment on Gruenbaum.

95. Holzer, 'Polish Political Parties and Antisemitism', p. 197.

96. The Jews won 35 *Sejm* and 12 Senate seats. Not all Jewish parties joined the Bloc, including the *Bund* and the Folkists.

97. David Engel, 'Works in Hebrew on the History of the Jews in inter-war Poland', *Polin*, 4 (1989), p. 429.

98. Mendelsohn, *Zionism in Poland*, p. 219 ff.

99. M. K. Dziewanowski, *Poland in the 20th Century* (Columbia University Press, New York, 1977), p. 266, n. 7.

100. Marian Fuks, *Prasa Żydowska w Warszawie 1823–1939* (PWN, Warsaw, 1979), pp. 159–293; Andrzej Paczkowski, 'The Jewish Press in the Political Life of the Second Republic', *Polin*, 8 (1994), pp. 176–93.

101. N. Eck, 'The Educational Institutions of Polish Jewry (1921–1934)', *Jewish Social Studies*, 9 (1947), No. 1, pp. 3–32.

102. Szymon Rudnicki, 'From "Numerus Clausus" to "Numerus Nullus"', *Polin*, 2 (1987), pp. 248 ff. For example, 42.5 per cent of students at the Jan Kazimierz University in Lwów in session 1922–3 were Jewish.

103. Rabinowicz, *Legacy of Polish Jewry*, p. 97; Lucjan Dobroszycki, 'YIVO in Interwar Poland: Work in the Historical Sciences', in Gutman *et al.* (eds), *The Jews of Poland*, pp. 494–518.

104. Ezra Mendelsohn, 'Interwar Poland: good for the Jews or bad for the Jews?', in Abramsky *et al.*, *Jews in Poland*, p. 139; Davies, *God's Playground*, pp. 407 f.

105. Raphael Mahler, 'Jews in Public Service and the Liberal Professions in Poland, 1918–1939', *Jewish Social Studies*, 6 (1944), No. 4, pp. 291, 294–305. In 1921 the number of Jews employed in the public services and the liberal professions was 40,560.

106. Mendelsohn in Abramsky *et al.*, *Jews in Poland*, pp. 130 ff., who acknowl-
edges that Jewish suffering has been exaggerated. He makes the same point
in his *Jews in East Central Europe*, p. 323.
107. Jacek M. Majchrowski, 'Some Observations on the Situation of the Jewish
Minority in Poland during the Years 1918–1939', *Polin*, 3 (1988), p. 307;
B. Garncarska-Kadary, 'Some Aspects of the Life of the Jewish Proletariat in
Poland during the Interwar Period', *Polin*, 8 (1994), pp. 238–55.
108. Paweł Korzec, 'Das Abkommen zwischen der Regierung Grabski und der
jüdischen Parlamentsvertretung', *Jahrbücher für Geschichte Osteuropas*,
20 (1972), No. 3, pp. 331–66; Mendelsohn, *Zionism in Poland*, pp. 300–8;
Edward D. Wynot, 'Polish–Jewish Relations, 1918–1939: An Overview', in
Dennis J. Dunn (ed.), *Religion and Nationalism in Eastern Europe and the
Soviet Union* (Lynne Rienner, Boulder, Colorado, 1987), pp. 24 f.
109. Watt, *Bitter Glory*, pp. 359 ff.; Polonsky (ed.), '*My Brother's Keeper*?', p. 63.
Jewish self-imposed isolation in Poland is a recurrent theme in Theo
Richmond, *Konin. A Quest* (Cape, London, 1995).
110. The Statute was never implemented for a variety of reasons, but mainly
because of Ukrainian violence and intransigence.
111. Laurence Weinbaum, *A Marriage of Convenience. The New Zionist
Organisation and the Polish Government, 1936–1939* (Columbia University
Press, New York, 1993); Howard Rosenblum, 'Promoting an International
Conference to Solve the Jewish Problem: the New Zionist Organisation's
Alliance with Poland, 1938–1939', *The Slavonic and East European Review*,
69 (1991), No. 3, pp. 478–501; Jerzy Tomaszewski, 'Vladimir Jabotinsky's
Talks with Representatives of the Polish Government', *Polin*, 3 (1988),
pp. 276–93.
112. The Marxist/Communist view is expressed in J. Tomicki (ed.), *Polska
Odrodzona, 1918–1939* (Warsaw, 1982).
113. An argument that the Polish state, as the stronger partner, had a duty to take
the lead in creating better relations with the Jews is given (unconvincingly)
by Andrzej Bryk, 'The Hidden Complex of the Polish Mind: Polish–Jewish
Relations during the Holocaust', in Polonsky (ed.), '*My Brother's Keeper*?',
pp. 162–65.
114. Davies, *God's Playground*, p. 405 refers to Poland's generally compromising
policy towards the minorities in the 1920s.
115. Ibid, p. 263.

5 Freedom of the Press in Inter-War Poland: The System of Control

John M. Bates

Freedom of speech is part of the general freedom. And freedom is the basis of the republican system.

Stanisław Thugutt[1]

Freedom of the press, as was once remarked, is not an end in itself but a means to the end of a free society. After 123 years of partition a Polish state did, in many respects, axiomatically entail a free Polish society, yet its rulers were continually inclined to limit press freedoms in an increasingly authoritarian manner whenever they perceived either the security of the state or their own position (which they sometimes saw as synonymous) to be under attack. Press liberty, like civil liberties, whilst in theory greatly to be desired, proved in practise to be so inconvenient to those running the country that they often seemed to treat them as dispensable. The benchmark of a truly democratic society is perhaps the ability to countenance dissent – whether in the form of social protest or press criticism – but it is practised, not inherent. The psychological legacy of living under a partitionist regime left an impact on the society and its rulers whose magnitude was revealed only in the fledgling democracy.

Up to 1989, most post-war accounts of the suppression of newspapers in inter-war Poland had of necessity to give pride of place to the privations suffered by the radical left-wing and particularly the Communist press. This was both a reflection of the fact that these papers were indeed stringently repressed by the authorities and also indicative of a degree of tendentiousness imposed by the Communist authorities, who frequently contrasted the 'success' of the postwar state with the alleged failings of interwar Poland.[2] It is certainly true that the only spell of complete publishing freedom which the Communist press enjoyed occurred in the first few weeks following the liberation. By early 1919, if not sooner, the new authorities began to contemplate a clampdown on the Communist press which was to last until the demise of the Second Republic. However, if it is remembered that one of the principal and unchanging tenets of institutional control is to

87

defend the existing political system, this is not altogether surprising: the inter-war authorities could hardly fail to zealously confiscate, ban and censor the publications of an organization which at times openly called for and schemed their destruction. Privileging the left-wing press in this way is rather to overlook the repression to which the centre and right-wing press were subjected, especially after the *coup d'état* of May 1926.

The behaviour of the Polish authorities between 1918 and 1939, and increasingly from 1927 onwards, often showed a blatant disregard for law.[3] For instance, the 1938 Press Decree may justifiably be viewed as an fairly draconian piece of legislation. But even it does not tell the complete story: although it made no mention of preventive censorship, this was quite widely practised. The legislative or constitutional statement of press freedoms needs to be confronted with the real official procedure of any political system at every point.

The question of the reversion to previously existent legislation is especially intriguing and confusing in the context of independent Poland after 1918. Since inter-war Poland had to be carved out of the three empires of Prussia, Russia and Austria-Hungary, provisions for press freedoms over tracts of the country could prove significantly different. Reversion to Russian clauses in the area of the old Congress Kingdom inevitably meant a serious regression from liberal-democratic ideals. By contrast, the old German (Prussian) legislation was frequently much preferable to Polish bills and, indeed, served to bolster the independence of the oppositionist National Democratic (*Endecja*) press in the west of Poland against government incursions. Austrian legislation was poised midway between the two, more vague in its provisions than German, but certainly less restrictive than Russian legislation.[4]

The present paper is concerned, first, with the provisions made in legislation regarding freedoms of, primarily, the political press and, second, with the efficacy of these various laws in the light of official practice. Third, press controls as a system are also considered.

THE DEVELOPMENT OF LEGISLATION IN THE
SECOND REPUBLIC

The development of legislation concerning press freedoms became one of the most contentious political issues in the history of the Second Republic. As with all other areas of public life, the situation prevailing at the end of the First World War might be aptly described as chaotic. Just as the new government had to unify the three former zones of Austrian, German and Russian influence into a new state, it had likewise to streamline the heterogeneous legal codes (including vestiges of the Napoleonic Code promulgated in 1808) which remained in force across its territory. Even in times of relative quiet, this would have been a huge and complex undertaking. In conditions of unresolved border conflicts and the state of war which obtained with the Soviet Union in 1919–20, it proved to be an altogether greater problem. Yet it is fair to speak, on the one hand, of the clash between an imaginary ideal solution – the long-dreamed-of Polish state – which would avoid the repressive practices which the Poles had experienced under the partitioning powers during the previous century, and on the other the prosaic, laborious and sometimes bitter reality of building a new state essentially from scratch in such precarious conditions.

It is in these terms that the battle over a free press in liberated Poland may firstly be viewed: as a division between idealistic declarations of civil liberties, including, supremely, the Constitution of March 1921 at one polarity, and the subordination of such liberties – even if undoubtedly for a temporary period as its authors intended – to the greater good of the new state's survival at the other. The rapid institution of martial law at the end of 1919, and its reintroduction for short periods at later dates, led to the suspension of democratic freedoms. Although this was invariably of limited duration, from the authorities' perspective the convenience of a supine press seems to have been a much more attractive proposition than that of democracy in action. Emergency situations became in a sense the authorities' preferred *modus vivendi* with the press. This was especially the case in the eastern borderlands, for instance, where a state of emergency introduced over the whole of Polish territory in early 1919 lasted in that region until August 1921.

In terms of the general debate over freedom of the press, the question revolved as elsewhere around the practice of *preventive* as opposed to *repressive* censorship. 'Preventive' censorship, or 'prior restraint', involves the suppression of undesired writings before distribution, usually by administrative measures and secretly; 'repressive' censorship means their suppression subsequent to publication and distribution, generally through the courts and publicly. In a democratic society, based on the principle of freedom of speech, the latter option is normally the preferred one.

Preventive censorship had been the Poles' lot in the nineteenth century, particularly under the Tsarist autocracy. Encouraged by Piłsudski, the first Polish post-war government of Jędrzej Moraczewski moved quickly to abolish this mode of control. A state of almost unlimited freedom thereby prevailed for several weeks after the liberation. Under the force of criticism from journalists on the Right and Revolutionary Left, Stanisław Thugutt, the Interior Minister, felt moved to reprimand the press, unsurprisingly without effect, and instructed the Ministry of the Interior to prepare legislation in order to guarantee administrative supervision. During a cabinet session on 26 November 1918 a draft bill was presented detailing the conditions under which newspapers might be suspended and the penalties for attempts to circumvent control.[5]

The key distinction which the bill drew was between regulation of the press in stable political conditions and provisions to come into force during an emergency, which were intended to give swift, effective control over the press. Subsequently, two bills were produced for a further cabinet meeting on 2 January 1919, providing for, respectively, temporary press regulations and print works. The second government, that of Ignacy Paderewski, implemented these bills, introducing a 'notification' or 'registration' system for setting up newspapers, but these provisions covered only the territory of former Russian Poland.

The increasing political instability in Germany, combined with the mounting threat posed by Bolshevik Russia, inclined the Polish authorities to view the Polish revolutionary left as the most serious threat to Polish statehood and to act to suppress the activities of its press organs. Accordingly, the government prepared draft legislation intended to counter the presence of the 'enemy within'. An Interior Ministry circular of 14 February 1919 outlined the direction that the administrative authorities's thinking was taking:

> Freedom of speech is a precondition of developing statehood. However, in so far as the legislator's intention is to grant free play to those political forces which, regardless of their political tendency, base themselves upon Polish statehood and act within the limits of the law, those same constitutional freedoms should be applied with circumspection to the press which possesses an clearly anti-state hue. In relation to the press which has clear Communist tendencies, each *voievode* entrusted with the care of a particular territory should make use of the means at his disposal from the necessity of protecting the existing political system.[6]

During the proceedings of the 'legislative *Sejm*', preparing what would be the 1921 Constitution, the instructions provided by the Interior Ministry to *voievodes* (regional governors) closely echoed the demands of right-wing deputies who sponsored parliamentary motions to suppress the left-wing press. Such was the trend in the period up to the coup of May 1926.

After that date, however, it was the Right, which had been instrumental in the development of repressive legislation targeting the radical Left, that came to be viewed as the major enemy by the *Sanacja* regime and became the special focus of repression. The continuity in political life throughout the first decade of Polish independence, regardless of which grouping held power, stemmed from a fundamental clash between the legislative (*Sejm*) and executive (government) organs over which had primacy in the political system. Decisive government control over parliament and the press was only established with the elections of 1930.

The 1921 Constitution may rightly be regarded as the high-water mark of liberal tendencies in the battle over press freedoms. Since it was dependent upon the drafting and implementation of other pieces of legislation, however, which were never completed, it remained an idealistic *declaration*, not a substantial foundation on whose grounds press freedom might be defended. For example, Article 104 acknowledged the right of every citizen to the free expression of his thoughts and convictions in any manner he saw fit in so far as it did not infringe the rule of law. The principle of press freedom was established by Article 105, which rejected preventive censorship and a licensing system for the publication of printed works as being contrary to the principle of press freedom. Daily newspapers and printed works published in Poland could not be deprived of the right of circulation, nor were restrictions on their distribution to be tolerated on the territory of the Republic. Article 23 forbade the combination of the post of responsible editor with that of parliamentary deputy or senator, since parliamentary immunity would mean that a responsible editor could not be prosecuted for criminal acts without parliament's agreeing to remove the deputy's privilege of immunity.

The Constitution guaranteed the freedom to reprint and distribute reports from open sessions of the *Sejm* and *Sejm* commission. Article 31, which provided for the immunity of parliamentary reports, contained rather imprecise formulations: whilst forbidding the prosecution of persons publishing truthful reports from *Sejm* and Senate proceedings, it failed to ban the confiscation of those reports. This imprecision came to be exploited in the years 1925–8 as a means of circumventing the immunity of confiscated press articles, based on references to them in deputies' questions and interpellations in parliament and their subsequent distribution as parliamentary reports.[7]

Article 82 provided for the conduct of court proceedings in public, apart from exceptions foreseen in specific clauses. Reports of public court proceedings which represented truthful accounts could not result in the prosecution of persons publishing or distributing them, nor in their confiscation.

The implementation of the principles of press freedom depended to a large extent on the promulgation of new laws to replace the partition laws, which contravened the declarations of the Constitution. Such was the drift of Article 126, but in the absence of such legislation, which was supposed to be drafted and implemented within one year of the promulgation of the Constitution, legislation reverted to that existing under the partitions in the different regions. Whilst civil liberties and rights found a place in the Constitution, provision was also made for the possibility of their suspension (Article 124). This Article allowed the cabinet, with the President's agreement, to suspend the freedom of the press in the event of war breaking out, of internal disorder or of extensive plotting of a treasonous nature which presented a threat to the Constitution or the security of its citizens. Although the cabinet's decision had to be ratified by the *Sejm* and the principles for declaring a state of emergency were to be defined by a special clause, Article 124 was to be invoked solely in exceptional circumstances.

The fact that much of the additional legislation foreseen by the March Constitution was not drafted, let alone implemented, meant that its effectiveness was much reduced; its key provisions remained, in effect, at the level of desiderata rather than legal reality. Certainly by July 1921, the cabinet was instructing the Ministry of Justice to employ repressive measures against newspapers which 'undermined the authority of the administration'. The Interior Minister, in turn, called for greater scrutiny of the proliferation of Communist publications and, in August, the cabinet instructed justice ministers in the former Prussian sector to lecture their subordinates in the courts and prosecutor's office on the importance of combating Communist agitation. A Ministry of Justice circular on this matter (dating from September 1921) indicated the urgency and difficulty of the task:

> Crimes of a political nature against one's own state cannot be viewed in the same manner as the struggle by various elements and parties against the Partitioning states. This principle should be all the more forcibly emphasised given the ease with which certain less enlightened circles may succumb to a train of thought which they acquired during the period of the partitions. [...] I see it as my duty to bring this to the attention and to appeal to the sense of national and civic duty of prosecutors and judges. I call urgently upon the offices of the judiciary to carry out their duties in an uncompromising and fearless manner. Immediate, resolute repression is required [...] Each ill-considered step, particularly a restrained use of preventive or repressive measures, causes the state incalculable damage.[8]

This appeal acknowledged the difficulty of changing the habits of conspiracy ingrained in the Polish psyche over the course of a century of foreign rule. This awareness on the part of the new Polish administrative authorities demonstrated an anxiety that they might have replaced the detested imperial authorities of the three partitioning powers in the popular imagination. But the call for responsibility went largely unheeded, as the rapid drafting of fresh legislation by the Interior Ministry testified. On 4 November 1921, the Ministry brought new provisions designed to combat the Communist menace before parliament. Article 3 spoke openly of the true target of this legislation:

> Whosoever with the intention of preparing or facilitating in future the violent overthrow of the social order existing in the Polish Republic:
>
> (a) disseminates even privately, in print or any other form, views to that end, particularly concerning the introduction of the system of soviets;
> (b) incites others to avoid military service or encourage antipathy towards that service;
> (c) advocates hatred between specific classes or groups of the populace;
> (d) disseminates false news or uses other means with a view to foment sedition or provoke disquiet in the populace;
> (e) incites hatred or contempt for the authorities
>
> ... will be punished by a term of penal servitude of 2–10 years.[9]

As the left-wing deputies in the *Sejm* argued, these provisions could equally well be turned against other political groupings at a later date. The authorities strove to reassure deputies, however, that the sole target was Communist agitation. This legislation contained some alarming new developments indicative of an increasingly authoritarian trend in government thinking. These included the extension of penalties to all involved in the process of producing such literature and the equation of the intention to do any of the above with the actual deed. Typesetters, printers and distributors as well as those receiving such literature could receive up to five years' imprisonment. In short, it marked the introduction of preventive censorship, albeit for only one section of the political spectrum, and therefore stood in direct contravention of the terms of the Constitution.

The judiciary was charged with implementing these conditions and could be removed if they failed to do so, which compromised their independence. In cases where a solution satisfactory to the administrative authorities was not reached, the Court of Appeal could redirect a case to a different court outwith the original district, in order to ensure a more favourable outcome. The parliamentary Left fiercely contested these provisions in the *Sejm*; Herman Lieberman asserted that the Poles seemed now to be striving to outdo the partitioning powers in creating a police state. Although the bill was passed by the *Sejm*, it was not promulgated by the cabinet, now a government of specialists under Antoni Ponikowski, who wished to ensure the support of all the parliamentary parties for his economic programme. Ponikowski therefore encouraged the *Sejm*'s Juridical Commission responsible for work on the bill to slow the pace of its activity, so that it never became law during the lifetime of his government. Eventually, in January 1922, he prorogued the discussion until an executive decree on Article 124 of the Constitution could be presented by the government. It was May 1923 before a new draft of the bill came again before the *Sejm* and again became bogged down at the Commission stage.[10]

Press freedoms prior to the May coup continued to be guaranteed mainly by default, first and foremost by the fact that few governments lasted long enough to draft yet more stringent legislation or promulgate the previous government's. The *Sejm*'s active stance in overturning legislation or delaying work on bills also enabled more draconian impositions to be avoided. By the same token, however, the possibility of the *Sejm* producing a unified Press Law of a more liberal nature could be easily frustrated by the government and President (by proroguing parliament, for instance). This impasse reflected the general state of parliamentary life in the first half of the 1920s, fuelling Piłsudski's contempt for what he termed 'sejmocracy'. Certainly, the benefits of 'sejmocracy' were all too clear for the Polish press and saved it from greater administrative excesses.

The next government (Witos), angered by constant attacks in the press, pushed through the previous administration's draconian legislation. By the time the bill reached the *Sejm* (23 October 1923), however, another government (Grabski) was in place which quietly shelved the legislation. The drafting and presentation of legislation regulating press freedoms thus followed much the same course until May 1926: governments attacked by the press sought to implement legislation restricting press freedoms, whilst non-party cabinets, dominated by 'experts', sought to remain on friendlier terms with the *Sejm* and hence the press.

The coup of May 1926 produced key changes in this situation. In brief, the installation of a *Sanacja* government marked the triumph of the use of administrative controls, especially in view of Piłsudski's notorious antipathy towards both parliamentary democracy, as practised in Poland in 1918–26, and newspapers. The *Sanacja* rigorously eliminated certain political parties and their newspapers, especially those belonging to Ukrainian nationalists. In the aftermath of the coup, the National Democrats and their Peasant allies found themselves in the position of being the major opposition bloc. The *Endecja*, with its power centred chiefly in the west of Poland, now became the key target of press restrictions, particularly since it had the most extensive press network in the country. Its position was bolstered by the judiciary's general sympathies with the Democrats' programme, which led to the foiling of *Sanacja* attempts to initiate clampdowns on *Endecja* publications. Confiscations of its papers implemented by the administrative authorities were often overturned in the courts. The irremovability of judges meant that the government could not replace them quickly. This, in turn, necessitated the drafting of a new press law.

The first shot in this new campaign was fired with the Piłsudski government's decree of 4 October 1926, which introduced sanctions for slandering the state authorities and their representatives. In reflection of Piłsudski's distrust of the *Sejm*, the government came to rely increasingly upon presidential decrees, which had the force of binding legislation although they had to be ratified by the *Sejm*.[11] The *Sejm*, for its part, continued to overturn such decrees.

On 22 April 1927 two ordinances were passed by the cabinet, the second of which was a unified press law promulgated on 8 June 1927. This ordinance included a number of provisions which sharply increased the range of potential violations and penalties for infringing the law. Fines could now be imposed in cases where confiscated articles had been reprinted. Decisions regarding the repression of newspapers still lay with the courts, but the administrative authorities' scope for carrying out confiscations had been greatly increased. Judges who overturned administrative decisions were to be reported to the Interior Ministry (with a view to their removal at a later date).

Since it applied to the whole of Polish territory, the new law removed at a stroke the regional differences which had frequently worked in favour of the National Democrat press. One of the other major features of the ordinance was a gradual shift towards the use of economic sanctions to curtail press independence. Fines came to be preferred over closures by the administrative authorities, to be levied from a broad group associated with the paper's production whose collective responsibility ensured that fines could be collected.

When the bill came before the *Sejm*, it was thrown out by the legal commission. Owing to a technicality, however, it acquired legal status because the *Sejm* was prorogued before its decision could be published officially in the *Digest of Laws*. Its decision therefore remained only a *proposal*, not a *decree*.[12] The authorities used this distinction to pursue with alacrity recalcitrant editors and newspapers. Although the Supreme Court ruled in the *Sejm*'s favour concerning the interpretation of the status of its decision, this provided little real help, since that decision had yet to be recorded in the statutes. The authorities were able to pressurize editors into accepting a system of *voluntary* preventive censorship, who could thus avoid the catastrophic expense entailed by the confiscation of a whole edition. The threat of closure under the pressure of incessant confiscations brought many newspapers to heel. Due to the existent legal limbo, the authorities took the opportunity to remove several leading oppositional figures in the judiciary, thereby encouraging compliance on the part of their subordinates. The Press Decree remained in force until 1930, when Bartel's government, in a brief period of liberalization, allowed parliament to record its 1927 decision in the statutes.

In 1930, following the emasculation of parliamentary opposition, the government had a far more malleable *Sejm* at its disposal. In these conditions, the government managed to remove the immunity of deputies' statements in parliament. Accordingly, reports of their speeches could be censored from newspapers and the record of proceedings was vetted and cut by the Speaker. Furthermore, in 1932, the government managed to persuade parliament to abolish the principle of the irremovability of judges, thereby facilitating the replacement of *Endecja* sympathizers with its own appointees.

The government's subjection of the press reached its apogee in the new constitution of 23 April 1935, which reduced civil rights and liberties. The emphasis of the constitution fell on the citizen's duties towards the state. Article 5 provided for freedom of speech, within the limits of the 'common good', which was, of course, impossible to define satisfactorily in law. There was no mention of press freedoms, leading therefore to their loss of constitutional status. These were somewhat beside the point, given the widely established practice of 'prior restraint' in respect of taboo subjects, such as Polish–German relations, from 1934 onwards.

Although its impact was curtailed by the outbreak of war, the most serious legislative threat to press freedoms lay in the Press Law of 21 November 1938. Its 94 articles represented a reworking of the 1927 Press Decree. Some of its provisions were the reduction of the number of people who could become editors, the formalization of the obligation on the part of newspapers to publish official communiqués (or 'corrections'), increasing the fines to be paid for violations, and the limitation of the judiciary's role in decisions relating to press matters. Most of its responsibilities were to be transferred to the administrative authorities and the public prosecutor's office. In many respects, this made little difference to the existing situation.

The main trends in the development of legislation concerning press freedoms were, first, a drive towards uniformization across the whole country. Initially, it was hoped by those involved in newspaper production that this would follow the liberal provisions of the 1921 Constitution. If uniformization did take place, however, it represented a development detrimental to the usual role ascribed to the press in liberal democracies as a principal form of social control upon the activities of the administration. The state authorities accorded a subservient role to the press, which found expression in successive pieces of draconian legislation. Second, by contrast, the legislative reality was essentially a default position, either through reversion to laws created before the establishment of the new state – laws which, in many ways, contradicted the initial principles of that state's existence – or by the frustration of normal parliamentary procedure. Equally, in certain key respects, this heterogeneous legislation protected press freedoms, but only in so far as the authorities themselves respected the law. After 1926, this happened with ever-decreasing frequency.

REPRESSION AS A LEGISLATIVE ISSUE

One of the major principles in newspaper production was anonymity. At least part of the Interior Ministry's elaborate information-gathering exercises concerning the press can be seen to stem from the authorities' difficulty in establishing responsibility for either the editorship of newspapers or the authorship of articles. The principles of editorial secrecy and anonymity were established in the 1919 Decree on the Press: journalists could sign their articles, though they were not under any obligation to do so. This fact encouraged them to be critical of aspects of political and public life, since they could not easily be called to account. Similarly, to protect the identity of the real editor of a newspaper from answering before the law to any infringements, the post of 'responsible editor' was given to an individual who would frequently be in no way competent to perform the editor's function.[13] It was only with the Press Decree of 1938 that the authorities broke with the principle of an editor who was formally responsible for the production of a newspaper.

It was also in response to the principle of anonymity that the government tried to introduce legislation, based on Austrian laws from 1922, stipulating the collective responsibility of all those who worked on the editing of newspapers. In this way, the authorities could guarantee the payment of fines, regardless of who was actually responsible for the infringements. By the end of the 1920s, rather than attempt to close down an offending newspaper at one stroke the authorities began to move towards the practice of imposing economic sanctions upon publications. The central plank of this policy consisted in the wholesale confiscation of editions, thereby subjecting opposition newspapers particularly to substantial financial losses. The success of this policy did not depend on bringing the issue of confiscation to court in order to establish the responsibility for offences as the law provided. The rationale behind such practice was explained in an Interior Ministry circular of 1936:

> press infringements closely linked with confiscations belong to those categories of offences, whose legal qualification and judgement by the courts do not always proceed according to the intentions of the pertinent authority of the general administration and even of the public prosecutor, in view of which in practice only in exceptional cases do the administrative authorities take recourse to pursuing this kind of affair through the courts.[14]

Confiscation itself, although supposed to initiate a whole sequence of legal consequences, was deemed a self-contained punishment for press infringements. In the 1938 Press Decree it finally became firmly established as a deterrent.

Confiscation as a principle of official behaviour was subject to various refinements in practice, above all in conjunction with the legal requirements contingent upon a editor to supply the authorities (the local police) with obligatory copies of each edition once printing was under way. The question of at what stage the police received their copies in order to carry out repressive censorship was an issue debated furiously in inter-war Poland. The Interior Ministry was anxious to receive copies before the printing process was completed so as to prevent any leaving the print works and thus to be able to implement preventive censorship. Faced with the possibility of losing a whole edition, impecunious newspapers would submit voluntarily to preventive censorship in order to forestall massive losses and remove offending fragments before printing commenced. This undoubtedly facilitated the disguising of censorship interventions, the notorious blank spaces marking confiscated articles. With time, the administrative authorities grew concerned to conceal the evidence of their interventions and would insist that suitable articles be printed. Conversely, they could allow a whole edition to be printed before announcing their confiscation precisely in order to subject papers to severe economic penalties of this kind.[15]

THE SYSTEM OF ADMINISTRATIVE CONTROL

The rise of the Interior Ministry as the central body of press control came principally after the coup of 1926, when the *Sanacja* governments strove to fasten their hold on political life and, in particular, to curb the press. It had, however, been active in that capacity from the moment of liberation, being concerned first and foremost to gather information on press activity. This role was implicit in the setting up of its secret Press Department (*Wydział Prasowy*) on 3 March 1924, which had the responsibility of gathering political information about all people engaged in newspaper production – editors, publishers, printers – with a view ultimately to organizing the system in a manner favourable to the authorities. During the first few years of parliamentary democracy the targets of its activity depended precisely on which political grouping held power. None the less, the general principles of its activities remained the same: operating in conjunction with the *voievodes*, it sought to define newspapers in terms of their political orientation. In the early years, the process of information-gathering was greatly hindered, first, by uncertainty regarding the actual identity of individuals working in the press and, second, by the tardiness of the regional authorities in furnishing the requisite data. Nevertheless, all matters concerned with 'the press, authors, printing and performances' lay within its ambit from the very beginning of its existence and this remained the case throughout the Ministry's subsequent restructuring. In effect, its role was nothing less than the definition of the general guidelines of the state's internal policy.

While the Interior Ministry's various departments had a duty to inform the press about its own activities, its main business was rather to garner information about that press and organize various undertakings in the sphere of acquiring, supporting, neutralizing and combating individual publications. In addition, it sought to control newspaper content, first in a proactive sense, by encouraging the writing of articles on various subjects and, second, to steer newspapers away from other topics by the employment of censorship.[16] Essentially, the Ministry's powers enabled it potentially to control all stages of the process of newspaper production, from a paper's foundation to its distribution.

Although there was no licensing system which could allow the authorities to vet an application to set up a newspaper, there were always possible abuses inherent in the notification. Essentially, it required official acknowledgement or recognition from the judiciary. Here, such questions as economic criteria and the alleged intellectual suitability of the person proposed for the post of editor-in-chief could provide grounds for obstructing the foundation of a newspaper.

Following the coup, supervision of print works came to the fore as one of the key duties of the *voievodes*. In October 1926, on the basis of the 1919 decree on print works, the Interior Ministry sent instructions to each district ordering the monitoring of print works to be carried out at least once every quarter and, where the local authorities had a 'justifiable suspicion that the decree was being ignored, [they] should arrange to carry out monitoring more frequently, as they saw fit'.[17] Especially in the provinces, the failure to comply in even the most trivial respect or being suspected of printing anti-state publications could lead to constant intrusions into plants publishing opposition press. Sometimes this itself constituted a form of pressure upon the owners to abrogate contracts with clients 'disloyal' to the state, and could lead, in cases where the owners refused, to a print works being closed down.

Control could be imposed at an even earlier stage of the production process, namely by influencing the supply of paper. Although the state did not exercise a monopoly in this regard, information held by the Ministry enabled it to exert pressure on suppliers to cut off deliveries to a plant and thus induce a temporary halt in the production of unacceptable papers. Conversely, favoured print works and publications might be awarded additional supplies on favourable credit terms, thus enabling them to increase their output. These were tactics adopted particularly during elections, when the need to diminish the opposition's output and raise the government's own became paramount. Furthermore, during such critical moments as the 1930 election, legislation such as the 1927 Industrial Law laying down safety regulations and working conditions could be invoked as the basis for closing down a plant which printed opposition materials. The net result over the longer term was to turn the manager of the plant into an additional censor, who might refuse to publish materials which jeopardized the continued existence of his firm.

Although left-wing publications depended largely on readers' support, advertising constituted the majority of papers' chief source of revenue. During the 1928 election campaign the authorities were anxious to ensure that advertising revenue for insertions made by the government went to papers supporting the *Sanacja* line. Outwith elections, the idea of periodically sending lists of papers deserving of government support to the Polish Telecommunications Agency (PAT) was proposed by the Interior Ministry. Part of the authorities' concern was also to place adverts in papers with large readerships. With time, the question of profitability came to play an increasing part in the Ministry's deliberations about which papers to support via the placement of advertising.[18]

Public institutions associated with the *Sanacja* regime, such as the Army, wielded great influence in terms of providing mass subscriptions to journals and newspapers. Certain publications could be deprived of substantial revenue if Army chiefs decided that they had portrayed the armed forces in a poor light. Contrariwise, favourite papers such as *Strażnica* and *Nowiny* enjoyed substantial financial advantages. The administrative authorities were responsible for granting permission to distribute copies throughout the country by means of the 'debit'. The 1919 decree alone stipulated no limitation on this. There were definite trends towards monopolization of the distribution network by members of the political élite and their associates:[19] the Association of Railway Bookshops (*Ruch*) is the clearest example of this trend. Initially holding a major interest in kiosks at railway stations around the country, it came to monopolize the distribution business in Warsaw and eventually the distribution of journals from the capital into the provinces. An agreement signed on 6 March 1928 between *Ruch* and the Ministry of Communications foresaw thé exclusion of certain papers (usually of a left-wing nature) from sale in kiosks. In June 1929, on the instructions of the Interior Ministry, *voievodes* ordered police stations to 'gather precise information concerning the branches of the *Ruch* Association operating in railway stations with regard to the following points: [...] (3) what reasons might there be for the absence of certain papers with a pro-governmental slant, such as *Gospodarz Polski, Głos Prawdy, Epoka, Kurier Poranny, Przełom, Przedświt, Młoda Wieś*, etc. and finally (4) is there evidence of the favouring or boycotting of certain newspapers? It is pointed out that the *Ruch* Association should possess all newspapers.'[20] The Ministry was naturally not concerned with the widest possible provision of newspapers in the *Ruch* kiosks. As ever, it was pro-government publications that were to be promoted:

> The pro-government press should be supported by providing it with announcements and communiqués via the regional councils, communal coffers and we should prevail upon other authorities, such as the commercial departments of the courts, court chambers, etc., so that they too give the pro-government press appropriate announcements and communiqués. Above all it should be pointed out to the distribution offices of daily papers, such as 'Ruch', that it have all the pro-governmental press on sale, but it is not desirable that the above offices specially recommend oppositionist dailies.[21]

A further refinement of this position was recommended to *Ruch* in 1930, when it was encouraged to display prominently all its wares, that is, to demonstrate the full range of pro-government publications. Towards the end of the 1930s, closer relations formed between the Interior Ministry and *Ruch*. In December 1935 the Association with the Ministry's assistance, rapidly expanded its monopoly on distribution from the capital into the provinces. In effect, only in exceptional circumstances were permits to be granted to other distributors. In this way, *Ruch* also served the purposes of administrative control since its monopoly meant that it could select which publications were to be widely distributed. In addition, the practice of confiscations of politically unacceptable newspapers could be implemented more effectively. On 23 April 1936, a circular provided a list of banned newspapers, which if found in any *Ruch* kiosk would lead to the dissolution of the contract between the distribution network and the individual kiosk-owner.

The use of 'carrot and stick' tactics characterized most areas of the Ministry's activity. This was especially true of official news provision. By the early 1930s the Ministry had begun to take a very close interest in the existence of news agencies other than the Polish Telecommunications Agency on the territories of the *voievodeships*. As ever, the potential political affiliations and direction of these other agencies were recorded. Such an approach applied also to journalist associations. In short, the Ministry amassed data on every aspect of the press industry to facilitate the implementation of its actions.

From the end of 1924, the secret Press Department had been constantly monitoring all publications with the aid of the State Police. Within a fortnight of the May coup, the Interior Ministry was instructing *voievodes* to update lists on newspapers published in their regions, giving particular consideration to data about their political profile, financial situation and key figures associated with them. By the end of February 1927, the Ministry had extended the range of information it required to cover 'party membership, size of the print run and the paper's technical state and the sources of finance of the political press', together with such questions as ownership, the paper's self-sufficiency, and the source and amount of capital invested in it.[22] This information would then provide the basis for deciding which would be more effective in making opposition newspapers conform to the authorities' wishes: the use of economic pressure or, on the contrary, financial inducements. A key issue in this respect was determining whether the newspapers in question received information announcements – with a view to eliminating this source of revenue for papers hostile to the regime. This procedure represented an important development in the run-up to the elections of 1928 as a means of guaranteeing control over the portrayal of the government-sponsored, but technically independent Non-Party Bloc for cooperation with the Government (*BBWR*).

In terms of a positive programme, the *Sanacja* regime spent enormous sums either guaranteeing newspaper editors' quiescence during electoral campaigns or buying into the press industry itself. The Interior Ministry covered cash payments for these purposes from its discretionary fund.[23] It was during the election campaign of 1927–8 that the Interior Ministry mounted its first grand press venture. Even before the campaign had got under way the then director of the Press Department, Kazimierz Świtalski, had arranged meetings with hundreds of local officials, pro-government political activists and editors and journalists from various newspapers with a view to funding the running of the electoral campaign in accordance with the government's wishes. The kinds of actions implemented at a local level included the secret purchasing of opposition press or funding of papers to challenge it.[24] A key example here was the capture of the National Democratic paper *Słowo Polskie* in Lwów. A group of young National Democrat activists, the so-called '100 Team', which was ready to compromise with the *Sanacja* regime, took over the paper in December 1927 with 120,000 *złoty* they had received from the Interior Ministry. The number of new pro-government papers which sprang up at this time (from November 1927 to March 1928) in the provinces alone, almost certainly funded out of the Interior Ministry's coffers, has been calculated at 18 dailies and 20 weeklies.[25] The degree of financial backing that the Ministry supplied allowed it a proprietorial stance towards the boards of the papers. The Ministry made a direct decision concerning the post of editor, in effect ensuring that a political line favourable to the regime would be followed by the incumbent.

The regime's desire to guarantee its version of events had a number of dimensions. The first related to the inspiration of press content, particularly the idea that society needed to be educated in a state-minded spirit. The placing of official stories could not always be assured without using threats. In some cases, all versions other than the regime's would be censored, which left editors facing the dilemma of whether they should not mention the story at all, publish and expose the newspaper to severe financial losses or print the communiqué or commentary the official press office provided. An additional factor in this equation was that of basic competition with other newspapers for information, which sometimes swayed the editors to run the official version for want of an alternative. By the latter half of the 1930s one of the regime's key strategies in ensuring that the public received its own side of any story was the use of corrections. Newspapers were obliged to correct 'wrong' stories. In accordance with the terms of the 1938 Press Law, the government could require news-papers to print up to 250 lines of six words per line, which effectively made all newspapers into government mouthpieces, since commentaries distancing the newspaper from the official version were prohibited.

Less formal and even illegal solutions were often practised too. Prior to the 1928 election, Kazimierz Świtalski held instructional sessions nearly every day with journalists of pro-government papers, dictating what they could or could not write about. Input came from a variety of sources, although usually channelled though the cabinet's press office.[26] The chief practise, however, was that of preventive censorship, the proscription of certain topics in advance. A major concern of the authorities was to prevent the reportage of internal disorder. For example, during the May coup the Press Department of the Interior Ministry instructed the provincial authorities about the undesirability of any mention of the bloodshed that had occurred in Warsaw, since 'news and voices [...] from the recent period of fighting in Warsaw [...] might prove extremely harmful at the present moment and exacerbate the mood of society'. The administration also recommended as 'very desirable' the instilling of a 'sense of responsibility into the minds of newspaper editors' in addition to the intensification of press supervision.[27]

In the more socially polarized times of the 1930s, all mention of workers' and peasants' strikes and protests was to be banned. The régime practised *ad hominem* censorship by confiscating the press articles of certain former (opposition) politicians now in exile. The rationale behind such decisions was to block any positive publicity for such 'political criminals', since that would undermine respect for Polish courts.[28] Particular documents could also be subjected to a total ban. In the summer of 1939 the text of the Polish Socialist Party's memorandum to the President was unconditionally banned from the press, despite the fact that its original confiscation had been overturned by the Court of Appeal in Warsaw. Since it could not be legally banned again, however, the authorities used the pretext of banning another article in papers where the memorandum was due to appear in order to seize the whole print run. Such instructions were often of an *ad hoc* nature and issued by telephone, whereupon it became the news-papers' responsibility to communicate them to its journalists.[29]

Another key area in which the administrative authorities demons-trated continuity in their censorship policy concerned the portrayal of Germany's internal relations. According to the provisions of the Polish–German Press Agreement of February 1934,[30] the Polish side undertook to enforce a number of principles in respect of the Polish press in return for the suppression of revisionist and revanchist tendencies in the German press.[31] For its part, the German side promised to observe provisions in relation to daily newspapers, books, school textbooks, maps and public demonstrations (organizations, speeches, performances and monuments). In reality it did little, however. Although the Poles noted their fulfilment of the terms of the agreement to the letter,[32] this seems somewhat removed from the truth. In fact, despite the agreement, Polish newspapers published in Pomerania, for instance, portrayed German internal relations in a deeply unflattering light and did not desist from attacks on leading German political figures.[33] Even in the face of censorship the convention tended to be observed faithfully only by the *Sanacja* regime's own newspapers.[34]

The reality of the Polish authorities' practice in respect of the 1934 Agreement demonstrates a general point about the nature of the press control which they implemented, namely that it was never total, let alone totalitarian. Stringent provisions did not always entail stringent execution. Although in theory the administrative authorities had a large arsenal of repressive measures at their disposal, they did not consistently employ them in order to stifle public opinion and control dissent, except in regard to the Communist press and Ukrainian publications: in these cases it was largely to suppress perceived threats to the Polish state, either in the form of class struggle or of the expression of separatist tendencies. Opposition newspapers might be harassed for years on end, and every second issue subject to confiscation, but they often none the less continued to exist. In the years up to May 1926 nearly all sections of the press enjoyed substantial freedoms, and only with the establishment of *Sanacja* governments was a system of control instituted. With the hindsight of the next 50 years, its strictures might have appeared Arcadian.

NOTES

1. 'Zgromadzenie w obronie wolności słowa w Warszawie 26 XI 1929', *Rocznik Historii Czasopiśmiennictwa Polskiego* (henceforth: *RHCzP*) (1966), vol. 5, 2, p. 230.
2. There is a very extensive literature on the Polish press during the inter-war period. Substantial information on general background is given by Andrzej Paczkowski's *Prasa polska w latach 1918–1939* (Warsaw: PWN, 1980) and *Prasa codzienna Warszawy w latach 1918–1939* (Warsaw: PIW, 1983). The two major Polish monographs on press control, to which the present paper is indebted, are Michał Pietrzak's *Reglamentacja wolności prasy w Polsce (1918–1939)* (Warsaw: Książka i Wiedza, 1963), and Andrzej Notkowski's

Prasa w systemie propagandy rządowej w Polsce 1926–1939. Studium techniki władzy (Warsaw-Łódź: PWN, 1987). Pietrzak's account suffers more from official ideological requirements given the time when it was written, necessitating, for instance, the use of the appelative 'bourgeois' before 'democracy', and the generally hostile tone towards the *Sanacja* regime. For all that, it remains the standard work in the field. Given the Communists' relaxation of ideological requirements by the late 1980s, Notkowski can permit himself a more objective view of the period and conclude 'in interwar Poland, the political system never became completely totalitarian. As a result, neither opposition parties, nor their press, were made illegal' (p. 93). An invaluable source of archival documents and articles is *Rocznik Historii Czasopiśmiennictwa Polskiego*, later renamed *Kwartalnik Historii Prasy Polskiej* (Wrocław, Cracow, Warsaw: 1962–1994). Treatment of the issue of inter-war Polish press control in English has been at best sporadic. It arises occasionally in historians' accounts of the period as, for example, in Antony Polonsky's *Politics in Independent Poland 1921–1939* (Oxford: OUP, 1972), pp. 226, 257, 331–2, etc. Andrzej Paczkowski, in his article 'The Jewish Press in the Political Life of the Second Republic' raises the issue in relation to the Jewish press and makes comparisons with other sectors of the inter-war press. *Polin: Studies in Polish Jewry*, 8, 'Jews in Independent Poland 1918–1939' (London and Washington: The Littmann Library of Jewish Civilization, 1994), pp. 176–93.

3. The Polish authorities were not alone in censoring the Polish press. The German authorities of Gdańsk controlled Polish newspapers, published both in Polish and German, before it became a free city. See Andrzej Romanow, *Gdańska prasa polska 1891–1920* (Warsaw: Instytut Historii PAN, 1994), pp. 197–218.

4. A useful source of information concerning censorship under the Partitions are the two volumes of *Piśmiennictwo – systemy kontroli – obiegi alternatywne* (Warsaw: Biblioteka Narodowa, 1992). Essays in vol. 1 cover all three sectors.

5. Such as the practice of slightly changing the title of suspended papers, which had been a stratagem developed by newspaper editors and owners as a means of survival particularly under the Tsarist regime.

6. Pietrzak, *Reglamentacja walności prasy w Polsce*, p. 35.

7. Reports of proceedings from the *Sejm* were later also subject to confiscation, albeit only after 1930 and the infamous 'Brześć affair', when parliamentary candidates on the left were arrested *en masse* overnight prior to the elections, which severely compromised the representative nature of the subsequent parliament.

8. Pietrzak, *Reglamentacja wolności prasy w Polsce*, p. 44. The 'less-enlightened circles' to which this note refers are, of course, the National Democrats, whose power base was in the west of the country in the territories formerly occupied by Germany, which were coincidentally the areas where more liberal press controls applied. Western Poland was accordingly the area where most resistance to the administration was to be found: judges frequently overturned Interior Ministry confiscations.

9. Ibid., p. 47.

10. Ibid., p. 51. The new bill provided for preventive censorship, confiscations, the suspension of newspapers and closure of print works by the administrative authorities.

11. They also had the advantage of not being subjected to parliamentary scrutiny during their drafting and could be accepted or rejected by the *Sejm*, but not modified.

12. The decision was not published until 28 February, 1930, under the Bartel government, during a short period of liberalization when the government was looking to the *Sejm* for support. A major protest against this state of affairs took place in Warsaw on 26 November, 1929, in the form of the 'Assembly in Defence of the Freedom of Speech', which garnered support from all corners of the political scene (with the exception of the *Sanacja* regime's supporters). The protocol was published in *RHCzP* (1966), 5/2, pp. 229–251.

13. Pietrzak, *Reglamentacja wolności prasy w Polsce*, pp. 144, 152. Problems could arise for the editor if he were summoned to give evidence in trials. Article 308 of the Criminal Code obliged him to provide information about the authorship of an article.

14. Ibid., p. 168.

15. Ibid., pp. 200, 204. This could be done in the print works, at the newspaper offices, in kiosks and on the streets, and also when the newspaper was being distributed by post or transport.

16. Antoni Trepiński provides a first-hand account of the experience of *Sanacja* press controls in 'Cenzura w prasie warszawskiej przed drugą wojną światową'. *RHCzP* (1972), vol. 11, 1, pp. 115–28.

17. Instruction from the *Voievode* of Kielce to his *starostas*, 28 October 1926. Notkowski, *Prasa w systemie propagandy rządowej*, p. 272.

18. Eugeniusz Rudziński, 'Kształtowanie prasy kontrolowanej w Polsce w latach 1926–1939', *Dzieje Najnowsze* (1969), vol. 1, 1, pp. 104–6.

19. Decided on the basis of the extensive data with which the local authorities were required to furnish the Ministry.

20. *Voievode* of Kielce to his *starostas*, 12 June 1929. Notkowski, *Prasa w systemie propagandy rządowej*, p. 289.

21. Ibid., pp. 290, 291.

22. Document sent to the Department of Public Security of the Kielce *Voievodeship* Office on the 23 and 25 February 1927. Ibid., pp. 268–9.

23. In 1929 the Ministry was spending up to 250,000 *złoty* each month, whilst the cabinet made an official declaration of barely 17,000. Ibid., p. 277. Polonsky quotes Sławoj Składkowski's statement that, on Piłsudski's orders, Finance Minister Gabriel Czechowicz gave him 8 million *złoty* for the elections: *Politics in Independent Poland*, p. 246. These financial abuses provided the basis for the later 'Czechowicz Affair' (ibid., pp. 272–7).

24. The *Sanacja* set up the Silesian paper *Gazeta Zachodnia* at the end of 1926 to challenge *Polonia*, the newspaper belonging to the eminent *Chadecja* politician Wincenty Korfanty. See Edward Długajczyk, *Oblicze polityczne i własnościowe prasy polskiej w województwie śląskim 1922–1939* (Katowice: Muzeum Śląskie, 1990), pp. 119–22.

25. Notkowski provides figures showing the reduction in the scale of such activity by about a third in the 1930 election campaign (14 dailies and 9 weekly or fortnightly papers were set up then), but comments that this was due to the extensive network that had been established in the earlier election. *Prasa w systemie propagandy rządowej*, pp. 282, 288.

26. Within the government the Press Bureau of the Council of Ministers was the official press body of the government, to which all ministries had to submit their statements except for the Ministry of Foreign Affairs. One of the dimensions of its influence is considered later in connection with the Polish–German Press Agreement of February 1934.

27. Notkowski, *Prasa w systemie propagandy rządowej*, pp. 296–7.
28. Two Interior Ministry circulars (of 30 September 1933 and 14 November 1934) stated that 'articles and notes signed by Witos, Kiernik, Bagiński, Lieberman should not appear in the press regardless of their content [...]. The very fact of including these articles of the above Polish émigrés should be treated as a demonstrative gesture of solidarity on the part of the newspaper.' Ibid., pp. 298, 299.
29. Trepiński provides an annex containing the principal instructions received in this manner, the newspaper's 'black book', between 1935 and 1939, 'Cenzura w praise warszawskiej' pp. 129–47. By contrast, the Foreign Ministry provided briefings on the international situation. See 'Notatnik Mieczysława Krzepkowskiego z konferencji prasowych w Ministerstwie Spraw Zagranicznych (luty – czerwiec 1939)', *RHCzP* (1975), vol. 13, 2, pp. 335–74.
30. This agreement was concluded after a diplomatic conference held on 23–24 February 1934, and represented a cementing of the Non-Aggression Pact signed between the two countries in January that year. Like the Pact, the press agreement arose out of a German initiative. The specific provisions for the Polish authorities were: (i) to defend the person of the Chancellor and, as far as possible, of leading personalities in the Reich; (ii) to permit the free circulation of the previously confiscated *Mein Kampf*; (iii) to influence the press, as far as possible, to discuss the situation in Germany in an objective manner; (iv) to extend the previous bans in relation to émigré German press appearing in Poland; (v) to monitor closely the Jewish press with the aim of preventing infringements of the press agreement; (vi) to review the lists of books banned in Poland; and (vii) to confiscate the book *Ed. Hitler*. ('Dokumenty o porozumieniu prasowym polsko-niemieckim z 1934 r.', *RHCzP*, 1965, vol. 4, 2, pp. 174–5.)
31. The German response was to use the agreement for propaganda purposes, whereas the Polish delegates were strongly opposed to any exploitation of the agreement in this way, aware that it would be difficult to square the agreement with Polish public opinion. In the event, the Polish side successfully prevailed upon the Germans to avoid any mention of the content of the agreement when announcing its conclusion. Pietrzak, *Reglamentacja wolności prasy w Polsce*, p. 449.
32. *RHCzP* (1965), vol. 4, 2, p. 177.
33. The Interior Ministry declared itself unable to act as effectively as the Foreign Ministry desired owing to the lack of appropriate legislation under which confiscations could be made. Pietrzak, *Reglamentacja wolności prasy w polsce*, p. 450. Notkowski, however, points out that a fundamental conflict of interests arose between the ministries over the Polish–German Press Agreement due to the Interior Ministry's need to counteract the German minority's anti-Polish propaganda: *Prasa w systemie propagandy rządowej*, pp. 304–5.
34. Ryszard Michalski, *Obraz rzeszy niemieckiej na łamach polskiej prasy pomorskiej w drugiej rzeczypospolitej 1920–1939* (Toruń: Uniwersytet Mikołaja Kopernika, 1995), pp. 37–95.

6 Poland's Defence Preparations in 1939

Andrzej Suchcitz

There have been countless histories written about the Second World War; there have been numerous television serials made about it. Strangely, the opening campaign of this most written-about conflagration remains little known and little understood in the English-speaking world. It is shrouded in ignorance, legends and a seeming obliviousness to its impact on the further development of the war. The campaign in question is the Polish Campaign which began on 1 September 1939 and came to an end five weeks later, on 5 October, when the Independent Operational Group 'Polesie' under Major General Franciszek Kleeberg laid down its arms after the battle of Kock.

The last two decades have seen a slight improvement in the English-language literature concerning the Polish Campaign, though this welcome if belated recognition of its importance still leaves much to be done.[1] However, one aspect still remains sadly neglected, although in many ways it is the core to understanding the operations which ensued when Germany attacked Poland. This aspect is the planning and preparations made by the Polish Government and military authorities to counter the expected German invasion.

Contrary to general belief, the Polish Army was not the backward, cavalry-dominated organization that has often been portrayed, even by such noted military historians as Basil Liddell-Hart.[2] It is true that Poland was primarily an agricultural country, where motorization and the infrastructure needed for it was in the early stages of expansion, though there was a steady annual increase in the number of motor vehicles on the expanding road system. In 1937 there were some 6,000 lorries in Poland, of which the Army could expect to receive 1,500 on mobilization. Polish planners foresaw the necessity of the army having some 12,000 lorries. Some could be purchased, but about 10,000 would have to come from mobilization. To achieve this number there would have to be at least 40,000 lorries in the private sector.[3] The main arm of the army was the infantry, the cavalry forming some 10 per cent of the men under arms. In any case, the cavalry was primarily used as a mobile force whose main advantage was its manoeuvreability. Armed with anti-tank guns and heavy machine guns, it fought dismounted, the horses being used for quick changes of position following an action.

In 1939 Poland was halfway through a six-year military expansion plan aimed at modernizing and strengthening the armed forces. Part of this plan involved the partial motorization of the cavalry brigades. The strain on the state budget was enormous, especially when one takes into consideration that, in percentage terms, Polish military spending was second only to that of the USSR. However, it is important to underline that the whole of the state budget was smaller than that of the city of Berlin. Another illustration would be that the Polish defence budget in the years 1935–9 was not more than 10 per cent of the *Luftwaffe*'s budget just for 1939.[4] Thus, the main impediment to modernizing the armed forces was the financial poverty of the country. This only serves to further underline the positive achievement made in this direction in a relatively short space of time.

Throughout the inter-war period, the Polish military believed that the greatest danger to Poland lay from the east. The Treaty of Versailles effectively reduced the threat from Germany for the forseeable future. This attitude was to change only after the rise of Hitler and the initiation of a rapid expansion of Germany's military strength. Whilst the defence plan in the event of a Soviet invasion was given priority, a new study of Germany's capabilities was ordered in 1936. The introduction in 1935 of two-year compulsory military service, and a new organizational and training structure in Germany, were the main motives for this new study. A new operational study was initiated at the General Staff which became the basis for a provisional plan of operations drawn up by the Inspectorate General of the Armed Forces. The study made foreboding reading. To Poland's 39 infantry divisions and 11 cavalry brigades the Germans were expected to muster 110 divisions, of which 70 would be directed against Poland.

The first alarm bells about Germany's long-term plans rang less than a month after the signing of the Munich agreement (September 1938) in which Czechoslovakia and the western democracies capitulated to Germany's demands.[5] The German Foreign Minister, Joachim von Ribbentrop, in conversation with the Polish Ambassador in Berlin, Józef Lipski, mentioned that in a general settlement between Germany and Poland, the Free City of Danzig would have to be incorporated into Germany, an extra territorial highway and railway built across Polish Pomerania (the so called 'Polish Corridor') and Poland join the anti-Comintern pact.[6] The matter was not raised again until the end of January 1939, when it was done so by Hitler himself during a brief visit of the Polish Foreign Minister, Józef Beck. The Polish Foreign Minister turned the proposals down, and on his return to Warsaw considered it his 'duty to warn the President of the Republic and Marshal Edward Śmigły-Rydz, the Inspector General of the Armed Forces, of these alarming symptoms which could result in war'. There was general agreement at the highest level that 'if the Germans continue to put pressure on matters which to them are of secondary importance, such as Danzig and the motorway, then there can be no illusions that we are threatened with conflict on a grand scale and that these objectives are only a pretext.' The lack of a decisive response would only serve to put Poland on the slippery slope, resulting in Poland losing sovereignty and becoming a vassal state of Germany.[7]

Political considerations were to seriously influence and hamper the military preparations. The backbone of the defence plan took as read that the war had to be a coalition war. Under no circumstance could Poland find herself politically isolated and forced to fight alone. The cornerstone of this policy was the Franco-Polish Alliance of February 1921, which envisaged mutual military aid in the event of an attack on one of the parties by Germany. By the 1930s the French were half-hearted about the alliance, and Georges Bonnet, the French Foreign Minister in 1938–9, was eager to dilute it further. In this, however, he did not succeed. When the situation markedly deteriorated in March 1939, Poland still only had the alliance with an unenthusiastic France, though growing Italian ambitions in North Africa did revive French interest in the alliance as a check on Germany. Following the German takeover of Bohemia and Moravia, the formation of an independent Slovakia friendly to Germany, and possible signs of further German interest in Poland and Rumania, the British Government announced its famous guarantee to both countries in the event of a German invasion (30 March 1939). Foreign Minister Beck quickly seized the opportunity given, and during his visit to London turned it into a reciprocal Anglo-Polish Agreement on 6 April. A formal Treaty of Alliance was signed on 25 August 1939. Britain promised to 'aid Poland if her independence should be threatened'. The decision as to what constituted a threat to her independence was left entirely in the hands of the Polish Government.

The British guarantee and subsequent agreement is seen by some historians as a break with the erstwhile policy of appeasement, by others as its continuation, aimed at turning any German attack in an eastward direction.[8] The guarantee was to bolster Polish resolve to fight. If this indeed was the case, then it showed that the British Foreign Office was totally out of touch with Polish political thinking. From Warsaw's point of view, the turning of the unexpected guarantee into a bilateral agreement was a notable diplomatic success. Not only did it provide Poland with a second official ally bound in duty to aid Poland, but, it was thought, it would strengthen wavering French resolve. More importantly, it made sure that a German–Polish conflict was a European, not a local conflict. In the Polish Government's eyes, Poland's best hopes for the future lay in ensuring that the conflict was a general one, against Germany. This would better guarantee that the Polish question could not be ignored or sidestepped, as a local conflict threatened to do. It did lead to a confirmation of the Franco-Polish Alliance in all its aspects by Daladier, the French premier, in the Chamber of Deputies on 13 April.[9] It was now necessary to pin down both France and Britain as to what aid they could and would give if Poland were attacked. In the middle of May, the Polish Minister of War, Lt. Gen. Tadeusz Kasprzycki, travelled to Paris, where on 19 May he signed with France's General Maurice Gamelin a military protocol in which it was agreed that if Germany attacked Poland, or if Poland's interests in Danzig were endangered in such a way as would lead to military action by Poland, the French army would immediately begin operations by their different services. This would entail that the French Air Force would begin operations immediately in accordance with a pre-arranged plan.[10] On the third day of general mobilization, France would begin land operations with limited aims. The French Army would undertake a major offensive from the fifteenth day of French general mobilization. When Gamelin was asked by Col. Józef Jaklicz, Deputy Chief of Polish General Staff, how many divisions would be used in this offensive, he replied, 'Half of those on the north-east front.' This meant about 38 divisions.[11] This was what Marshal Śmigły-Rydz wanted. He now had, or rather thought he had, a clear picture of what the French would do. The war would be a coalition war, as he had planned.[12] However, there was one hitch. The military convention was not to come into force until the political convention had been signed, and this was continuously delayed by Bonnet under various pretexts. The fear that the French would try to evade their political obligations at the slightest excuse led Marshal Śmigły-Rydz to take very seriously both French and British warnings not to do anything which might provoke the Germans. In the event, the political convention was not signed until 4 September 1939, the military convention becoming immediately operative.

A British Military Mission arrived in Poland in the last week of May to discuss what aid Britain could give Poland in the event of a conflict. It was by British standards a low-level mission, headed only by a temporary brigadier, a former military attaché in Warsaw, J. B. Clayton. It was soon made apparent that there was little practical help which Britain could or would give. Certainly there would be no military or naval support. On the latter point, agreement was reached to send three Polish destroyers to

British ports before hostilities began to operate alongside the Royal Navy: this was advantageous to the British side, which was desparately short of destroyers for convoy escorts. The advantage for the Poles was that it was a way of preventing the destroyers being sunk or interned, which would have been their fate if they had remained in the Baltic.[13] There was no question of the Royal Navy entering the Baltic: at most, individual submarine raids were not excluded. On the other hand, it was agreed that the RAF would initiate attacks on Germany even if the territory of the British Empire was not violated. Initially, only strictly military targets were to be bombed, and these were severely limited to prevent the deaths of civilians. Brigadier Clayton made clear that the moment the *Luftwaffe* bombed Polish civilian installations, the hands of the RAF would be freed. Essentially, the British Military Mission, apart from a promise to use the RAF to assist Poland, gave no other binding assurances. In fact, the British military attaché, Lt.-Col. Edward Sword, was quite frankly appalled. In his diary for 26 May he wrote: 'They [the three senior officers of the British Mission] tell me that they have accepted invitation to visit COP [Central Industrial Region]. Was horrified to hear this as proces verbal not complete, and what with the Horse Show on Saturday seems little time either for discussion of remaining points, or discussion with me.'[14] However, Brigadier Clayton did support Polish aims at continuing the Staff talks, and proposed that the Chiefs of Staff invite a Polish delegation to London and that the talks be carried out at a senior level on the British side. Nothing came of this.

Throughout the summer Polish missions in France and Britain tried to obtain cash credits to enable them to purchase badly needed equipment, especially tanks and aircraft. The talks progressed slowly and achieved little of substance. From Britain, a material credit of £8 million was obtained, but so late that no material reached Poland before the outbreak of war.[15] A 430-million-franc credit loan was obtained from France, from which one battalion of R.35 tanks was delivered to Poland in August.

In July 1939 British worries as to Poland's intentions in the event of any German actions sent General Sir Edmund Ironside, Inspector General of Overseas Forces, to Poland to pin down the Poles on the above question. He was also to reassure the Polish High Command about British support. The visit took place between 17 and 21 July 1939. From the report which he wrote on his return, it transpires that he was ill-prepared by the Foreign Office about Polish politics, the report being full of naive comments about the way Poland was governed. He did secure assurances that Warsaw would not do anything rash. However, it was impressed upon him by Col. Beck and Marshal Śmigły-Rydz that any action in Danzig would not be initiated by the government of the Free City. It would definitely be led from Berlin.[16]

Ironside's visit was regarded as a success, especially bearing in mind the disappointment of the Polish Government at

> the difficulties met with in the course of the discussions in London with Colonel Koc regarding a cash loan for Poland, and the fear had been expressed to me that His Majesty's Government had not sufficiently realized the urgent necessity of translating into military and financial terms the political collaboration established as long ago as April between Poland and Great Britain. The assurances which the General [Ironside] was able to give on behalf of His Majesty's Government did much to remove this impression, at least so far as the military sphere is concerned.[17]

Yet when all is said and done, the Polish Government and military authorities had been double-crossed and betrayed by their Western allies. There was no intention of giving Poland any effective military support at the beginning of the war. There was no question of a rapid response to German aggression and of fighting a coalition war, which would have given the allies their best opportunity of quickly defeating Germany at minimum cost. For one, the British and French military had a totally different view on how the war should be prosecuted successfully. Secondly, the political willpower, especially in France, simply was not there. The conscious abandonment of Poland to her fate had been more or less decided barely three days after Chamberlain's House of Common's guarantee to Poland. On 2 April, the British Chiefs of Staff prepared a paper in which they concluded that neither France nor Britain could guarantee Poland direct military aid or even a supply of armaments. On 3 June the Chiefs of Staff made a more detailed report entitled 'Anglo-French action in support of Poland'. In it, the military chiefs reiterated that neither France nor Britain could give direct support. Moreover, they agreed that no rapid and spectacular success against the Siegfried Line would be undertaken. Any rapid attack in the West against this line was totally unacceptable and was not envisaged. At most, limited air action against specific targets would be considered. Poland's fate had been effectively sealed on 4 May 1939, a fortnight before Generals Kasprzycki and Gamelin had signed the Franco-Polish military convention. At a meeting between representatives of the French and British General Staffs, agreement was reached on the policy of how the coming war should be prosecuted. It was taken as read that the war would be a long one, and that in its first years France and Britain would concentrate on building up their forces to guarantee an overwhelming superiority against the Germans. Only when this had been achieved would the Western allies go over to the offensive. Poland's defeat was regarded as a question of time only, and her fate would depend on the outcome of the war, which in turn would depend on Britain's and France's ability to defeat Germany and not on their ability to reduce the pressure on Poland at the beginning of the conflict.[18] At no time was a two-front war envisaged at its outset.

During the summer of 1939, half-hearted and totally unrealistic attempts were made to secure the support of the USSR against Germany. This policy of clutching at straws was being executed out of context of the existing framework of international agreements. Britain and France were trying to obtain Soviet aid, without reference to the main party concerned – Poland. The Polish Foreign Ministry had made it plain that it would not allow the Red Army onto its territory without guarantees which, of course, were not forthcoming. In any case, the Soviet request was directed towards the Franco-British Mission in Moscow. As the Polish Foreign Minister Józef Beck noted, why did the Soviets not direct their demand directly to the Polish Government through normal diplomatic channels? The question of entry into Polish soil was but an excuse to bring these unsatisfactory talks to a quick end. How prophetically true, in view of 1945, rang the words of the British ambassador in Warsaw, Sir Howard Kennard, who, in the autumn of 1938, wrote that if once the Red Army was to find itself on Polish soil it would be necessary to prosecute a new war to expel them, even if both the USSR and Poland were to be in a common anti-German coalition.[19] The victorious Red Army would not depart from ethnic Poland, let alone the pre-war frontier, of its own volition. As far as the Polish planners were concerned, the Soviet Union hardly came into the equation, either politically or militarily. The Poles had a valid non-aggression pact with the USSR. Polish–Soviet relations were cool but correct. During a brief visit by Potemkin, Deputy Commissar for Foreign Affairs, to Warsaw on 10th May, he told Col. Beck that in the event of a Polish–German conflict the former could count on a benevolent Soviet attitude. This was repeated many times by the new Soviet ambassador in Warsaw, Sharanov. Polish optimism that the Soviets would be willing to supply arms and raw materials was based on Warsaw's belief that the USSR was interested in the continued independence of the border states, and that the last thing they wanted would be to have a victorious German army on their frontier. It was an optimism which had little foundation.

When the German–Soviet pact was signed on 23 August 1939 it shocked everyone, though such a possibility had been foreseen by the

British Foreign Office. When the pact was announced, Beck did not believe that the situation had changed in any fundamental way. To him, it proved what he had maintained all along: that the Russians had been playing a double game. He did not believe, nor did any other Polish politician or general as far as it is known, that the non-aggression pact was anything more than it appeared. They believed it was inconceivable that two such contradictory ideologies could strike a bargain. It would be impossible to explain such a bargain to the German population, which for years had been indoctrinated with hatred for all things Communist. Whatever the explanations for this attitude, one is left with the impression that in this particular case the Poles were burying their heads in the sand. Russia and Germany were Poland's traditional enemies. Their co-operation had always been at Poland's expense. Beck should have known that national interests transcend all ideologies. Having said this, however, even had it been suspected or believed that there was a secret anti-Polish clause, there was little that could have been done. The main difference would have been that the High Command would have known that there was no chance of winning the war on Polish soil. The decision to fight would have been unaltered. At most, the eastern frontier would have been strengthened, obviously at the cost of the armies facing the Germans. In the event of a war on two fronts, the attitude taken by Marshal Śmigły-Rydz was the same as that of his predecessor, Marshal Piłsudski: 'Our fight would be an armed demonstration against a new partition of Poland.' The Soviet aspect in the historiography of the coming of the Second World War is a prime example of how each country perceived the matter from their own point of view. Thus, in French and British historiography, this is an important element; but from the Polish point of view in 1939, the Soviet aspect was at best marginal.

Let us turn to the actual military preparations which were given top priority from the spring of 1939. Until the autumn of 1938 the main assumption on which planning had been based was that, in the event of a conflict, the main German attack would come from the north-west in the direction of Bydgoszcz, Kutno and Dęblin, south of Warsaw. A subsidiary attack would be launched from Silesia towards Częstochowa and Dęblin. A third, minor thrust would be launched from East Prussia in the direction of Warsaw. The takeover of the Sudetenland increased the danger from the Lower Silesia front and was regarded as on par with that from western Pomerania. Accordingly, the planned concentration area of the Reserve Army was moved from the Kutno area west of Warsaw in a south-easterly direction into the triangle Kutno–Tomaszów Mazowiecki–Warsaw. This would allow for its use in either direction as necessity arose.

In the autumn of 1938, the Polish Inspector General of the Armed Forces (C-in-C Armed Forces in the event of war), Śmigły-Rydz, agreed to the carrying out of a special course for army chiefs of staff and army quarter-masters, using the actual material which would be available in war conditions. For those present, it was an unpleasant eye-opener. Col. Stanisław Lityński, the exercises' organizer and later Chief of Staff of Army 'Poznań', said that 'it was a breeze of the true Polish military doctrine – a doctrine of poverty.'[20]

From March 1939, attention was focused on the details of Plan 'Z' (Plan 'West', as it was called). It was defensive by nature, and was based on the understanding that the war would be a coalition war. The Polish Commander-in-Chief's main aim was to preserve his armies intact as far as possible and await the offensive in the west, which would relieve pressure in the east and hopefully allow for a stabilization of the Polish front. With the disappearance of Czechoslovakia in March 1939, the whole weight of Poland's defence shifted from the north-west to the south-west. Already in an unenviable strategic position, overnight the situation worsened drastically, exposing the whole of Poland's southern flank. Even before the war had started, Poland was enveloped by the German pincers. The main task of the Polish Army, which was to be concentrated along Poland's borders, was to prevent being smashed and defeated in separate pockets of resistence before the offensive began in the west. At the same time, maximum losses were to be inflicted on the enemy. All concentration was given over to the preparations of the first stage of the battle. This itself was divided into three phases. The first phase involved fighting a delaying action along the border. The aim was to give more time for the preparation of the main defence lines, and to gain more time for the carrying out of general mobilization. The second phase was to be the battle on the actual lines of defence; the third was to be the counter-offensive by the reserve army in the most endangered direction, against German forces coming from Lower Silesia and aiming for Warsaw.

Marshal Śmigły-Rydz hoped that he would hold this line until the offensive in the West took place. However, he realized that it was likely that he would have to withdraw to the Vistula. This would be the second part of the battle. It would entail a general disengagement and backward jump, taking up new defensive positions on the Vistula. The withdrawal was to be begun by Army 'Pomorze', which was the most exposed in the north-west. This army would be joined by Army 'Poznań'. These two armies would cross the Vistula between Modlin and its confluence with the Pilica. Army 'Łódź' and the reserve army were to withdraw so as to cross the river between the confluence of the Pilica and Vistula and the town of

Sandomierz. The pivot of this south-easterly movement was to be Army 'Kraków', whose main line of defence ran very close to the border along the frontier's fortifications. This army was to hold out the longest, and finally withdraw along both banks of the Vistula, its southern wing on to the river Dunajec, and its northern wing on to the river Nida, and then on to the Vistula between its confluence with the Dunajec and the town of Sandomierz. The success of the withdrawal of the Polish Army depended on the ability of Army 'Kraków' to hold its position for as long as possible. The two northern armies, 'Modlin' and Independent Operational Group 'Narew', were also to hold their main defence positions during the second stage. If necessary, it was foreseen that they would withdraw on to the Bugonarew river–river Bug–Białystok Forest, possibly even to the Białowieża Forest. 'The execution of the withdrawal would enable the carrying out of the basic conditions of the plan: *not allowing oneself to be crushed* [Piątkowski's emphasis] before the Western Allies acted.'[21]

The second stage of the battle was not worked out in detail, either by the General Staff or in the field. The explanation for this is given by General Stachiewicz. The Marshal believed that the better the first stage was prepared, the greater were the chances of its success. If all three stages were to be worked upon simultaneously, then the efforts would be dispersed and the preparations for the first stage would not be so advanced, or properly worked out. Śmigły-Rydz believed he could hold out on the Vistula if forced to withdraw to it, until the Western offensive would reduce the pressure on his armies. This would allow him to reorganize and regroup the Polish Army, and if conditions permitted, he would then go over to the counter-offensive on the Polish front.

If a further retreat was inevitable, the general direction of this retreat would continue to be south-eastwards, so as to consolidate the Army on the Rumanian frontier. Since the latter was an allied country, it was the safest route for French and British war supplies to reach Poland. No preparations were made for the second or third stages of the battle.[22]

The Inspector General believed that Germany might do one of two things: either attack Poland with the aim of destroying and occupying her, or attack at one point in a local action, for the annexation of Danzig, Polish Pomerania (the so-called Polish Corridor) and Poznania. If this happened, Hitler could then announce that this was his last conquest. In any future war, Poland's position would be even worse, due to the direct connection which would exist between the Reich and East Prussia.

This was the problem which faced the High Command. If territories, which from the purely military point of view, were not defended (Pomerania, Poznania), then the Germans could occupy them, and announce to the world that they had no more ambitions. The West, whose resolve to stand up militarily to Hitler was weak, might easily accept this and renege on their obligations to their ally, with the excuse that the Polish government and Army did not defend these areas. On her own, Poland could not defeat Germany, and Śmigły-Rydz knew this. That is why he was adamant that no actions should be taken which could be used as an excuse by France or Britain to avoid carrying out their obligations.

The above was the overall aim of Marshal Śmigły-Rydz in the defensive war against Germany. His plan has come in for much criticism, especially the decision to defend the whole frontier zone. Yet he had little choice. As already stated, it was politically essential to defend the whole of Polish territory from the outset, even though it might have been militarily wiser to abandon Polish Pomerania and Poznania. A possible alternative, once it was known that the whole of Poland was to be attacked, was to withdraw armies 'Pomorze' and 'Poznań' from their exposed positions and form two smaller independent corps, one of which would be placed in Polish Pomerania, the other in Poznania. There could be little doubt that these two corps would be on a suicide mission. However, they would be strong enough to put up a tough, if short, resistance against any invader. It would be a symbolic action, but strong enough to prevent the Germans from claiming that there had been no defence of the areas claimed by Germany. At the same time, it would have given Śmigły-Rydz up to eight divisions for use elsewhere. However, such an alternative was never taken into consideration.

There were two other major reasons why it was decided to defend the whole of western Poland. It was economically the richest part of the country. Most of the major industries were situated in the west. Silesia, the most important industrial complex, was on the actual border. It was only in 1936 that a four-year plan had been introduced to build an industrial complex away from the borders, and so the Central Industrial Region (C.O.P. – *Centralny Okręg Przemysłowy*) was developed. It lay on both banks of the Vistula, in the area of Radom–Lublin–Jarosław–Rzeszów–Tarnów–Kielce. However, it was still not powerful or large enough to take over the role of Silesia. Poland's industrial dispersion was admirably suited for war with the USSR, but far less so for a war with Germany. It was essential to defend the economic base of the country so as to carry on the war. Thus Silesia, defended by Army 'Kraków', was to hold out the longest, and no withdrawal was foreseen for this army in the first stage of the battle. If the Polish Army was forced to withdraw to the Vistula, then the main economic base of the country would be lost. Moreover, the western areas of the Central Industrial Region would also be lost. It would leave the

Polish Army reliant on allied supplies coming through Rumania. If the army was forced to withdraw to the south-east of Poland, then it would be totally dependent on allied supplies. This was the second reason why the western territories, and especially Silesia, had to be defended.

A third reason for defending these territories, at least justifiable in the initial stages of the war, was that they were important mobilizational centres of the Army. Until general mobilization was completed, reservists would be gathering at various points in western Poland. This was fully realized by the General Staff, and just before the outbreak of war thousands of reservists who could not be equipped were evacuated from Polish Pomerania and Poznania. These were the three reasons, especially the first and second, which made the defence of the western territories essential, even if from the purely unadulterated strategic point of view it made little sense. But, then, war is never confined to pure military strategy. Thus, while in theory it might have been far better to abandon the western provinces, and concentrate the Army along the Vistula, this made little practical sense.[23]

It should be underlined that the central tenet of the defence plan was to hold out until the offensive in the West. Śmigły-Rydz did not envisage a large-scale counter-offensive west of the Vistula, as this would have eaten up badly needed divisions.

Entangled in the overall defence plan lay the problem of Danzig, and what is regarded by many Western historians as the foolhardy decision to defend the so-called 'Corridor' often portrayed as a result of Polish pride and wild over-confidence.[24] It is time for this whole episode to be explained.

The justification for intervention in Danzig in the event of a surprise coup by Germany or the Danzigers was purely political. There was no military justification for it, and this was recognized by Poland's politicians and by Śmigły-Rydz. Poland's reaction to any surprise action by the enemy in Danzig was seen by the Poles as the test case for Western Europe and Europe as a whole regarding the adherence to the decision to stand up against German aggression. For this reason, it was decided that there had to be an immediate reaction to any kind of attempted coup in Danzig. At the same time, it was felt that due to its geographical position, any reaction could be only symbolic. If the Germans attempted to annex it, then military action would be undertaken by the Poles. This amounted to the sending of the Pomeranian Cavalry Brigade into the territory of the Free City from the south, the Navy co-operating from the sea, and a battalion entering from the north-west. There was no plan to attempt to occupy the actual city. This plan was valid up to the end of May 1939. By early June, there were clear indications that Danzig was arming itself. During the summer, a corps was supplied with arms from East Prussia. Fortifications were built along the southern and western borders of the Free City. Intensive military training in Danzig was noticed, as well as the smuggling of *Wehrmacht* detachments into the city as tourists.[25] This led Warsaw to strengthen its reactions. The one cavalry brigade would no longer be enough to break the strong and well-prepared defences in a short time, and the idea of sending one or two divisions was explored. In August, when the situation in Danzig was such that an incident might occur at any moment, the decision to mobilize the Interventionary Corps was taken. On 13th August this corps, consisting of the 13th and 27th Infantry Divisions, was mobilized and transported to the area of Bydgoszcz-Fordon (at the base of the 'Corridor'). The new plan of reaction was not fundamentally different. The occupation of the city was still not envisaged. The two divisions were to enter from the south, from the Starogard-Tczew region. The Fleet and Land Coastal Defence were to cooperate form the north and north-west. The aim of the action would be to take the hills in the Emaus-Langfuhr region, south-west and west of the city. The plan of intervention in Danzig was only valid if the Germans resorted to a local action and not a full-scale invasion of Poland. If the latter occured, or it was made clear beforehand that this was Germany's aim, then the whole Danzig intervention plan was automatically cancelled. In that case, the Interventionary Corps was to be evacuated from the 'Corridor' immediately.

Initially, it was not intended to place the Interventionary Corps north of the Bydgoszcz-Fordon region. However, when it became apparent that due to difficult communications in Polish Pomerania it would take three or four days before the Corps could intervene after a German action in Danzig, Śmigły-Rydz reluctantly decided to move the 27th Infantry Division north, just south of Starogard. At the same time, the units which were to cover the possible intervention from the west, the 9th Infantry Division and the Pomeranian Cavalry Brigade of Army 'Pomorze', were sent north into the 'Corridor'. When Śmigły-Rydz took the decision to move the 27th Infantry Division north, deep into the 'Corridor', he said to his Chief of the General Staff, Gen. Stachiewicz, 'This is an operational absurdity, to which I have been forced by political motives.'[26]

The Danzig intervention was never part of the operational plan of the Inspector General. It was a totally separate action necessitated by political motives. The Marshal was never happy about sending badly needed divisions into the 'Corridor'. On 31 August, when it was apparent that Poland was going to be faced with a full-scale invasion, the Interventionary Corps was ordered to be evacuated. The 13th Infantry Division was evacuated on 1st September to the Supreme C-in-C's reserves. However, the 27th Infantry Division, which had been given to General Bortnowski as his reserve, could not be evacuated immediately, and it was trapped together with the 9th Infantry Division and the Pomeranian Cavalry Brigade in the 'Corridor', a development which, but for the political importance of Danzig, would never have happened. Yet, when all is said and done, the position on 1 September was that the Danzig plan had led to a further extension of the already overstretched front, and to a further dispersal of Polish forces needed elsewhere. It is also clear that the reasons for the existence of such large forces in the 'Corridor' are very different from those put forward by Western military historians such as Liddell-Hart, and that they were not there as a result of an inexplicable Polish whim.

At the end of February, Śmigły-Rydz gave directives to the Chief of the General Staff, General Stachiewicz, on the preparations of Plan 'Z', and ordered that it should be worked out in detail. On 20 March, Plan 'W' (*Wschód*, east) was finally completed and locked away. All attention was given to Plan 'Z', on which work had begun on 4 March. The underlying assumption on which the plan was based was that the danger from German Pomerania and from Lower Silesia was equal. This was to be drastically altered by the takeover of Czechoslovakia. Poland's already disadvantageous strategic position worsened overnight. On 21 March, Ribbentrop presented German proposals in the form of a demand to Ambassador Lipski. On 26 March came the official rejection from Warsaw, though the latter wanted to discuss a settlement both of the Danzig question and greater transport facilities for the Germans which would satisfy both sides. On 6 April Lipski was told by Baron von Weizsäcker, the Secretary of State at the German Foreign Office, that the German proposals were no longer on offer. Lipski told Weizsäcker that the Anglo-Polish Agreement, signed that day, did not aim at surrounding Germany and that Poland desired to continue the non-aggression pact. Lipski was not to set foot in the German Foreign Office until 31 August, the day before war broke out.

The annexation of Memel on 23 March, barely a week after the takeover of Czechoslovakia, led Polish officials to fear that action might be taken against Danzig. That same day, 23 March 1939, Śmigły-Rydz gave the western army commanders their instructions for the first stage of the battle. The main line of defence from north-east to south-west was: Augustów Forest–river Biebrza–river Narew–river Bugonarew–river Vistula with the Modlin and Toruń bridgeheads–Bydgoszcz–Żnin Lakes–Inowrocław Lakes (Lake Gopło)–the Gopło-Warta Canal–river Warta with the Koło bridgehead–river Widawka–Częstochowa–Silesian

Fortifications–Oświęcim–Bielsko-Biała–Żywiec, Jordanów and Chabówka– Nowy Sącz.

In greater detail, the division of the front was as follows. The northern armies were Independent Operational Group 'Narew' (Major-General Czesław Młot-Fijałkowski) and Army 'Modlin' (Major-General Emil Krukowicz-Przedrzymirski) were to defend the northern theatre of operations, closing the way into the deep rears of the Polish Army from East Prussia and closing the shortest route to Warsaw. It was not expected that the Germans would maximize their flanking attack into the deep rears in the first stages of the campaign. Each army had two infantry divisions and two cavalry brigades. To the west of Army 'Modlin' was Army 'Pomorze' (Lieutenant-General Władysław Bortnowski). This army, and its southern neighbour, Army 'Poznań' (Lieutenant-General Tadeusz Kutrzeba), were to defend the north-western and western territories and prevent them being occupied unopposed. Army 'Pomorze' was to prevent for as long as possible the linking-up of enemy forces operating on both sides of the Vistula. (a major line of attack would be from German Pomerania in the direction of Bydgoszcz. A secondary line of attack was expected from East Prussia in the direction of Grudziądz.) Its main line of defence was the Bydgoszcz bridgehead–Toruń–river Vistula. The army consisted of five infantry divisions and one cavalry brigade. Army 'Poznań' was initially unlikely to have to deal with any large-scale attacks. It was to cover the Poznanian mobilizational centers, and protect the flanks of the neighbouring armies, from which it was not to allow itself to be pushed away. To its south was Army 'Łódź', (Lieutenant-General Juliusz Rómmel), which was to bear the main brunt of the enemy attack. Army 'Łódź' was to unconditionally hold the Łódź and Piotrków regions. It was concentrated in such a way that it would be able to carry out a counter-attack from the Sieradz area (right flank of the army) in a westerly direction. On its left flank, it was to keep contact with Army 'Kraków' and patrol the Radomsko-Skarżysko route. The main lines of defence of Army 'Łódź' were along the Warta and Widawka rivers. It had five infantry divisions and two cavalry brigades. The army had to hold its positions as long as possible, to create the conditions for the most advantageous use of the reserve army.

To the south lay Army 'Kraków' (Major-General Antoni Szylling). This was the pivot army of the whole defence plan if the necessity arose to withdraw to the Vistula. No withdrawal was foreseen for this army in the first stage of the battle. Its main lines of defence ran very close to the frontier. It was to maximize the advantage of the Silesian fortifications, resting its left flank on the Carpathian Mountains. As with Army 'Łódź', so with Army 'Kraków': its success would create the best conditions for the use of the reserve army. Initially, Army 'Kraków' was given seven infantry divisions, one cavalry brigade, and fortification crews. It was later given the 1st Mountain Brigade 'Żywiec' and the 10th Motorized Cavalry Brigade. The size of this army denotes its importance; yet two of its divisions were not due to be ready until the second phase of general mobilization. This meant that General Szylling, the army commander, was to be deprived of badly needed reserves in the initial stages of the war. As events were to show, the lack of those divisions would already be sorely felt on the second day of the war. It might have been better to have exchanged these two divisions (the 11th Infantry Division and the 45th Reserve Infantry Division) with two divisions from Army 'Poznań' which were mobilized under alarm mobilization. Army 'Kraków', as the army which was to remain in its positions the longest, and would be defending its main line of defence from the outset, should have been given all the conditions for it to be completely ready before the outbreak of hostilities. However, Śmigły-Rydz believed that the forces available to this army before the reserves would be ready were adequate. This was characteristic. He overestimated the ability of his forces, heavily reliant on foot- and horse-drawn supplies, to operate against a mobile enemy equipped with panzer and light divisions. He believed he would have time to disengage and withdraw. Yet once the main line was broken a dangerous situation would develop unless reserves were available immediately.

Another problem facing Szylling was his right flank, which consisted of the 7th Infantry Division defending the Częstochowa area, hanging in limbo. Between it and its right-wing neighbour, the Volhynian Cavalry Brigade of Army 'Łódź', there was a gap of about 25 kilometres. This joint was the most vulnerable area of the front. Intelligence reports indicated a massive build-up of enemy forces opposite Army 'Kraków's right wing, at the joint of armies 'Kraków' and 'Łódź'. The isolated 7th Infantry Division had little chance of covering Częstochowa effectively. Once the enemy smashed his way through this joint, there would be nothing between it and the reserve army, which would still be mobilizing and concentrating (full readiness was envisaged for the 14th day of general mobilization). It was highly unlikely that the right wing of Army 'Kraków' and the left wing of Army 'Łódź' would be able to halt the identified ten German divisions in this area for any considerable amount of time. Despite this, no changes were made in the Częstochowa area by G.H.Q. in Warsaw. Army 'Prusy' (the reserve army), under Lieutenant-General Stefan Dąb-Biernacki, was to operate in the direction of the joint of armies 'Łódź' and 'Kraków', and shake and halt the enemy thrust, allowing the Polish north-western armies to begin the process of withdrawal. Initially it had seven infantry divisions, one cavalry brigade, one armoured motorized brigade, and two tank battalions.

Except for General Dąb-Biernacki, commander of Army 'Prusy', each of the prospective army commanders received their directives from the Inspector General on 23 March, and was informed of the task for his army, given executive indications, as well as limited information about neighbouring armies. None of the army commanders was informed of the operational plan as a whole. The reason for this was that the Inspector General had an exaggerated fear of possible leakages of military secrets, and he wanted the army commanders to give their full concentration to the first stage of the battle plans. Whilst the importance of military secrets was and is of great value, the danger is that it will be exaggerated. This is what happened here. None of the army commanders knew the overall plan; thus vital time would have been lost if the necessity arose to withdraw to the Vistula in the communication of information about such matters as the directions of withdrawals. Moreover, each army commander was given only the minimum information about his neighbours. To make matters worse, army commanders were forbidden to discuss their plans, or even inform neighbouring army commanders of them. On 27 March Śmigły-Rydz issued a long order on the subject of the importance of secrecy.[27] This, in practice, meant that each army commander knew next to nothing, except what concerned his own army during the first phase of the battle. The importance attached to secrecy is revealed by this telling episode. In May 1939, Lieutenant-Colonel S. Mossor, Chief of Staff of Army 'Poznań', was given a dressing-down by General Stachiewicz and dismissed from his post because he had informed the neighbouring army commanders of the main plans of his own commander. Instead, Mossor was given the command of a cavalry regiment. The paranoia over secrecy had other consequences. The tasks of the south-western armies, 'Łódź', 'Kraków' and the Reserve Army 'Prusy', which was to counterattack at the joint of those two armies to halt General von Reichenau's Tenth Army, were most crucial for the success of this battle; yet neither General Rómmel of Army 'Łódź' nor General Szylling of Army 'Kraków' was informed about how Reserve Army 'Prusy' was to be used, and no plan of cooperation between these three armies was made.[28] The result of this secrecy was that it overburdened the already overworked Inspector General. As the army commanders did not know his overall intentions, most of the initiative was taken out of their hands. All relied on good communications with G.H.Q. to keep them informed during the operations.

Marshal Śmigły-Rydz further overburdened himself through the command structure. No fronts were created.[29] Thus he would have directly to control seven armies and one independent operational group, as well as several other smaller operational groups. This necessitated an excellent system of signals and communications. Whilst in the last years this was being modernized and expanded, it was far from being adequate. Communications between G.H.Q. and army H.Q.s were especially vulnerable to bombing. No general, however capable – and Marshal Śmigły-Rydz was arguably the best general in the Polish army – could possibly carry the burden of directly controlling eight armies whilst also preparing and planning the future prosecution of the campaign. It was simply too much for one person to make it an efficient command structure, and this was to be shown clearly during the September days.

Preparations for war can also be seen in other fields of the government's and High Command's moves and decisions. Among them was the decision to share with the French and British even before the outbreak of war the secret of the breaking of the German cypher machine 'Enigma' – arguably the most important contribution to ultimate Allied victory. At a top secret meeting in late July 1939 of Polish, French and British intelligence code-breakers, the Poles supplied each with a copy of the enigma machine, with usage instructions and up-to-date information on the subsequent work being carried out to crack the new changes introduced by the Germans.[30]

Another valuable contribution which was available to the Allies thanks to the foresight of the Polish government was the Polish merchant fleet. In the summer of 1939, it consisted of 42 vessels of some 120,000 BRT. The Ministry of Industry and Trade had prepared a special instruction to all vessels to head for western ports in the event of war. Of 42 vessels, 38 served the Allied cause at the side of the Polish Government-in-Exile.[31]

One of the main difficulties for the Polish authorities was the timing of mobilization. The German Army could be mobilized as a whole without declaring general mobilization. The Polish mobilization Plan 'W' of 1938, modified in May 1939, allowed for the secret alarm mobilization of 75 per cent of the infantry divisions, all 11 cavalry brigades and 75 per cent of the rest of the armed forces, the remainder being called up under general mobilization.

The same day that the army commanders received their directives (23 March), Marshal Śmigły-Rydz ordered mobilization for colours red, yellow, a part of green in Military District IX (Brest-Litovsk) and parts from Military District IV (Łódź).[32] This effectively mobilized four divisions (the 9th, 20th, 26th and 30th Infantry Divisions), the Nowogródek Cavalry Brigade and some extra-divisional units. This was in answer to Hitler's demands of 21 March and the annexation by Germany of the Lithuanian port of Memel on 23 March.

Three days after the first measures of partial mobilization were carried out, a further four battalions of Frontier Defence Corps troops (*Korpus Ochrony Pogranicza*) were strengthened and sent to the Slovak border. Also, eight cavalry squadrons of this Corps were sent to Army 'Łódź' where they formed a cavalry regiment. More importantly, the divisions and brigades stationed near the border with Germany were strengthened, so that in an emergency they could provide some cover. The staffs of five armies and the independent operational group were partially mobilized, and all of them with their army commanders (except for the staffs of Army 'Modlin' and 'Poznań') left for their operational territories. In May 1939, Mobilizational Plan 'W' was modified to encompass a further two divisions (the 2nd and 22nd Infantry Divisions) into alarm mobilization. The formation of new reserve divisions proved difficult: there were plenty of reservists, but a shortage of equipment, armaments and ammunition. Despite these difficulties, two reserve divisions, the 35th and 38th Reserve Infantry Divisions, were formed in the summer of 1939 as well as three mountain brigades.

The military authorities were aware of the need for maximum preparedness, as was made quite clear by the reports of the II Bureau (Intelligence) of the General Staff. However, there were two braking factors: first, the political one, by which the government was continuously warned by France and Britain not to make any provocative moves. The reasons why these warnings were taken so seriously have already been discussed. Second, there were the economic factors. Mobilization would inevitably put a great burden on the Treasury. The international crisis could last for months, and further mobilizational measures would increase the burden and, if completed, would in a short time lead to a breakdown of the Polish economy. Thus the question of further military preparations on a wide scale were not solely military decisions.

In May 1939, the Polish High Command secured a verbal Lithuanian promise of neutrality from General S. Raštikis, the Lithuanian Commander-in-Chief. This meant that Operational Group 'Grodno', formed in April to keep guard on the routes from Lithuania, could be used to safeguard the right wing of Independent Operations Group 'Narew', which itself was strengthened by two extra regiments (cavalry and infantry). Despite these changes, the commander of Ind. Oper. Gr. 'Narew', General Młot-Fijałkowski, was still not informed about the formation and task of Oper. Gr. 'Grodno' under General J. Olszyna-Wilczyński.

From March onwards, close attention was paid to the southern, Slovakian front. Initially, it was not thought that the Germans would launch large-scale attacks from Slovakia. However, intelligence reports clearly indicated the growing danger from the south. Thus, the already over-extended front was extended by a further 300 kilometres. On 11 July, Army 'Karpaty' (Lieutenant-General Kazimierz Fabrycy) was formed. Its task was to cover the Central Industrial Region, the flank and rears of Army 'Kraków', as well as to guard routes leading from Hungary to Eastern Małopolska, especially to the Borysław oil fields. The new army for the moment had only the 2nd and 3rd Mountain Brigades, plus some extra divisional units. It was expected that large-scale operations from Slovakia would be carried out in the latter stages of the campaign. If the Germans came in strength here, Fabrycy reckoned he would need four divisions and a cavalry brigade. Yet the southern reserve group which he was to have at his disposal consisted of only two divisions (the 22nd Infantry Division and the 38th Reserve Infantry Division). Moreover, the 38th Reserve Infantry Division was due only under general mobilization.

In early July, the concentration area of Reserve Army 'Prusy' was moved southward to the area Tomaszów Mazowiecki–Radom–Kielce. In August, the Marshal planned to move it furhter south, on a level with Kielce, so as to be in a better position to help Army 'Kraków' if the necessity arose. The build-up of German forces in Lower Silesia made necessary the change in the concentration area of the reserve army. However, the outbreak of hostilities prevented this move.

Since spring, fortification works had been going on along the western front. The Silesian fortifications were expanded, whilst old forts along the rivers Narew and Biebrza, at Ossowiec, Nowogródek and Wizna among others, were strengthened. However, this was a case of too little too late. The reason for this was that until the spring, fortifications were being completed on the eastern front. To have abandoned them before they were completed would have been militarily nonsensical, and it was too expensive to fortify both fronts simultaneously.[33] Flooding was to have played a major role in the creation of defence barriers. Extensive preparations were made, but the exceptionally dry summer invalidated them. On 24 June, Śmigły-Rydz, through the General Staff, issued an order concerning the preparation of field positions. Even at this late date, work on agricultural land was forbidden. This limited field works to state forests and wastelands. Fortunately, on 12 July, in a new order, this restriction was rescinded.

On 13 August the Interventionary Corps was mobilized and transported to Pomerania. On the night of 22/23 August, after a conference between Śmigły-Rydz, General Stachiewicz, Colonel Jaklicz and Colonel Wiatr (Chief of the I Bureau (Organization and Moblization) of the General Staff), the Marshal ordered full alert in military and civil offices,

return of all troops on exercise to their barracks, mobilization of II echelons of staffs and signal units, and mobilization of certain special units
from the green colour. After conferring with President Mościcki, the
Marshal ordered the mobilization of all colours in the six Military Districts
which had a common border with Germany on the night of 23/24 August.
Those not encompassed, Military Districts VI (Lwów) and X (Przemyśl),
were mobilized on 27 August. This meant that in the six border Military
Districts in the north, west and south, all 18 regular divisions and 7 cavalry
brigades were mobilized, as well as two and a half reserve divisions. In the
north-west, mobilization was complete (except for a number of army services, such as supply column) as all formations were mobilized by alarm.

On 24 August Śmigły-Rydz ordered the 27th Infantry Division north
into the 'Corridor'. The following day army commanders flooded the
General Staff with requests to be allowed to concentrate their divisions in
their respective starting positions. In response to this Stachiewicz explained
the Marshal's position, which was that the mobilization was to be regarded
as a preventive act and was to prepare the Army against any surprises.
It was not the same as taking up war operations. During the night of
25/26 August, Slovak and German units attacked the Jablonowski tunnel
in the Carpathians. The invaders were repelled. The above incident, the
largest of a whole series of border incursions by the Germans, probably
took place as a result of the cancellation of the invasion orders by Hitler
for 26 August not reaching all their destinations in time.

From dawn on 27 August the transportation of the mobilized formations
to their areas of concentration began. That day, all remaining units under
alarm mobilization were called up.

Meanwhile, German penetration of Slovakia was complete. As a result
of this, on 28 August, a reserve group was formed in the area of Pilzno–
Szymwald–Tuchów to support Army 'Karpaty'. For this group the 22nd
Infantry Division was taken from Army 'Łódź'. This was hardly wise,
considering this was the army which was supposed to hold out against the
main enemy attack. In exchange it was given the 44th Reserve Infantry
Division, mobilized only during the second phase of general mobilization.
With mounting German war provocations reaching their peak in the
last week of August, and with the concentration of Polish divisions and
brigades called up under alarm mobilization well under way, the General
Staff and the Marshal believed that the time for general mobilization had
come. The leading military chiefs had little doubt that war was inevitable,
and would probably follow within 24 hours of Poland declaring general
mobilization. Politically, it was a difficult decision, as it would give
Germany a propaganda ace. Germany had mobilized and concentrated

without declaring general mobilization. In the afternoon of 29 August, allied diplomats and military representatives intervened to halt Polish general mobilization, which had been declared earlier that day. Śmigły-Rydz agreed to a maximum 24-hour delay, and the morning decrees were cancelled. That same day, army commanders received orders to take up their combat starting-positions, troop movements for which were to begin immediately. Generals Kutrzeba, Przedzymirski, Dąb-Biernacki and Fabrycy were ordered to their wartime H.Q.s. Meanwhile, some transportation difficulties of units stationed in the east became apparent.[34] The delays of 29–30 August could not be made good.

On the morning of 30 August general mobilization was declared, again with 31 August the first day of mobilization. In connection with the belief that the Germans would attack within 24 hours of general mobilization being declared in Poland, all army commanders received the following order in the evening of 30 August: 'The Inspector General of the Armed Forces has instructed the drawing of your attention, General, that the night of 30/31 August is especially risky and demands a strengthened vigilance.'[35] In addition, Generals Szylling and Fabrycy of armies 'Kraków' and 'Karpaty', respectively were permitted to carry out demolitions directly on the Carpathian frontier, though leaving intact the larger bridges for the moment. During this night, Gen. Rómmel moved Army 'Łódź' in front of his prepared positions so as to give himself greater operational depth. The Volhynian Cavalry Brigade was moved south outside the operational area of the army to gain direct contact with the vulnerable right wing of Army 'Kraków' (the 7th Infantry Division). Plan 'Pekin', the sailing of three destroyers to British ports, was activated that day. They arrived at Leith in Scotland on 1 September.

On the last day of peace, 31 August, the Interventionary Corps was disbanded and ordered out of the 'Corridor'. Anti-aircraft defences were placed on alert, whilst the squadrons of the Polish Air Force moved to their wartime airfields, leaving behind on their peacetime aerodomes only training planes and those under repair. The Air Force High Command had undergone a complete reshuffle in March 1939, which, with the growing danger of war, was a risky move. The C-in-C Air Force and Anti-Aircraft Defences, Gen. Zając, an army general, halted production of the modern and excellent PZL 37 Łoś medium bomber. In his eagerness to build up a fighter force quickly, he agreed to the purchase of 160 Morane 406 fighters and 100 Fairey Battle light bombers (Poland had no prototype of a fighter ready for immediate serial production). Both planes were far from being the best choice, especially the latter. However, despite their many disadvantages, they would have been of great use; but none arrived in Poland before the war. Thus, Poland entered the war with 447 combat aircraft (36 PZL Łoś bombers, 162 PZL 7 and PZL 11 fighters and 120 PZL 23 Karaś recce/light bombers: the remainder were observation planes). Meanwhile, military transports were running normally again. The transportation of the divisions and brigades mobilized on 24 August was nearly completed, whilst those of 27 August were in full swing. All armies were in their combat starting-positions, but still waiting for some of their divisions and brigades which were in transports or due under general mobilization.

At 4.45 a.m. on 1 September 1939, the Germans invaded Poland on land, air and sea without declaring war. The conflict for which the Polish High Command had been preparing since March 1939 had come. The following days and weeks were to show both the advantages and the inadequacies of Polish military planning and preparations. Firstly, the campaign was to show that Poland and her allies were preparing for two totally different types of war, and that the latter had no intention of carrying out their obligations to Poland. This effectively destroyed Poland's overall strategic plan. On her own, there was no doubt as to the outcome of the Campaign. It was only to be a question of time. Moreover, the form of warfare used by the Germans, the *Blitzkrieg*, was totally new. The Polish cordon defence was to prove inadequate very early on. The lack of a defence in depth meant that once the enemy broke through it would be difficult to plug the gaps and contain enemy incursions. The operational plan depended largely upon Army 'Kraków' staying on its main line of defence. Yet already in the late hours of 2 September it had to withdraw, thus seriously undermining the whole plan. Along the whole front, the pace of the campaign was proceeding much faster than anticipated by Marshal Śmigły-Rydz. Time was of the essence. A matter of hours could change the situation. The lack of a defence in depth meant that new forces had to be hastily formed to defend the Vistula until the front-line armies fell back. However, being reliant on foot and mainly horse-drawn vehicles, they often found themselves behind the motorized and panzer enemy formations which had thrust deep into to the country. Reserve Army 'Prusy' was committed to battle on 5 September whilst still not completely ready. The cordon defence along the frontiers led to a faster collapse of organized resistance along the whole front. Instead, individual battles became the norm, whilst the G.H.Q. attempted to prepare new lines of defence further back. The Polish armies became cut off from one another by powerful panzer thrusts, and were encircled or had their routes of withdrawal cut off. Despite all these points, the preparations made before the war, though inadequate (like those of all other countries attacked by Germany), allowed the Polish Army to give stiff resistance to the enemy from the first moment of the invasion, and to continue it for 35 days, just a week less than France, which was so much economically richer, militarily more powerful and geographically better placed than Poland. When the ultimate collapse of any chances of defending Poland on Polish soil came with the Soviet invasion, on 17 September, the Polish strategic plan, which based its ultimate support on Rumania, allowed some 100,000 Poles to cross the Rumanian and Hungarian frontiers and make their way to France and Syria to carry on the war alongside their allies.

There is little doubt that Poland's government and military authorities had taken the threat from Germany seriously and undertaken as much as they believed could be done in the circumstances to prepare Poland for war from the moment Germany turned her demands against her in spring 1939. With the advantage of hindsight, it is easy to say that more could have been done and that some things could have been done differently. However, history should be understood and judged not from the vantage of hindsight, but as far as possible from the position as known at the time. In that case, it can be argued that few of the allied nations had undertaken so many steps to prepare for their defence. These in turn show that rarely in history have allies differed so fundamentally as to a war's prosecution and understanding of the moves and decisions prior to its outbreak. It is hoped that this paper has, at least in part, put forward the Polish point of view of the run-up to the war. Without this point of view, all histories of the origins of the Second World War are inevitably incomplete and unbalanced in their understanding of the topic.

NOTES

1. The only full account of the Polish Campaign remains Steven Zaloga's and Victor Madej's book, *The Polish Campaign 1939*, published in New York by Hippocrene in 1984. The first English-language book is the much-dated account written by Lt. Gen. Mieczysław Norwid-Neugebauer, *In defence of Poland (September 1939)*, published by M. I. Kolin in 1942. Zygmunt Bielecki's and Ryszard Dąbrowski's *In Defence of Independence: September 1939*, published by Interpress in Warsaw in 1972 is a typical product of Communist historiography and has to be treated carefully. There is also Major Robert Kennedy's (US Army), *The German Campaign in Poland (1939)* (Washington, 1956), which, though useful, does not use any Polish sources and is based on German documents only. The air force aspect is covered in several books, notably Jerzy Cynk, *History of the Polish Air Force 1918–1968* (London, Osprey, 1972). An introduction to the naval side of the story can be found in Michael A. Peszke,

A history of the Polish Navy in the Second World War. A historical sketch (London, The Polish Naval Association, 1989). Michael Peszke has recently published a book about the Polish Forces during the war. The second chapter covers the September 1939 Campaign: Michael A. Peszke, *Battle for Warsaw 1939–1944* (East European Monographs, Boulder, New York, 1995). The diplomatic and political side is somewhat better represented in English-language historiography. The following should be noted: Wacław Jędrzejewicz (ed.), *Diplomat in Berlin 1933–1939* (Papers and Memoirs of Józef Lipski, Ambassador of Poland, New York, London, Columbia University Press, 1968); Edward Raczyński, *In Allied London* (London 1962); Philip Cannistraro, Edward Wynot, Theodore Kovaleff (eds), *Poland and the Coming of the Second World War. The Diplomatic Papers of A. J. Drexel Biddle Jr., US Ambassador to Poland 1937–1939* (Ohio State University, 1976); Edward Raczyński, *The British–Polish Alliance. Its Origin and Meaning* (London, 1948); Piotr Wandycz, *Polish Diplomacy. Aims and Achievements, 1919–1945* (London, 1988); Antoni J. Bohdanowicz, *1939–Poland, the Abandoned Ally* (London, 1989); Anita Prażmowska, *Britain, Poland and the Eastern Front 1939* (Cambridge University Press, 1987); Antony Polonsky, *Politics in Independent Poland 1921–1939* (London, 1972); Anna Cienciała, *Poland and the Western Powers, 1938–1939. A Study on Interdependence* (London, 1968).

This paper is based on the author's MA dissertation, University of London (1981), and the documents held by the Archives of The Polish Institute and Sikorski Museum in London. Of the latter, the most important are the papers of the General Staff for 1938–1939, and the written depositions of senior army officers, written mainly in the months following the 1939 defeat.

2. Basil Liddell-Hart, *History of the Second World War* (London, 1973), p. 29
3. Wacław Stachiewicz, 'Pisma tom I. Przygotowania wojenne w Polsce 1935–1939', *Zeszyty Historyczne* 40 (Paris, 1977), pp. 90–1.
4. Steven Zaloga and Victor Madej, *The Polish Campaign 1939* (New York, 1985), p. 11.
5. Andrzej Suchcitz, 'A brief survey of the military planning and preparations for the defence of Poland October 1938–August 1939' (MA dissertation, University of London 1981).
6. Some historians, notably Anna Cienciała, in her excellent book, *Poland and the Western Powers 1938–1939* (London, 1968), p. 162, believes this was no more than German diplomatic pressure to refrain from any actions leading to a common Polish–Hungarian frontier. Others such as Henryk Batowski, *Kryzys dyplomatyczny w Europie* (Warsaw, 1962), pp. 145–6, and Richard Watt, *Bitter Glory. Poland and Its Fate 1918–1939* (New York, 1979), p. 390, take Ribbentrop's words at face value.
7. Józef Beck, *Ostatni raport* (Warsaw, 1987), pp. 162–3.
8. Note should be made of the following books which show the differing interpretation of the guarantee to Poland, how it came about and how Poland's role is perceived by western historians in the run up to the outbreak of war: A. J. P. Taylor, *The Origins of the Second World War* (London, 1961); Simon Newman, *March 1939: The British Guarantee to Poland* (Oxford, 1976); Donald Cameron Watt, *How War Came. The Immediate Origins of the Second World War, 1938–1939* (London, 1978); Sidney Aster, *1939: The Making of the Second World War* (London, 1973).
9. *Le Livre Jaune Français. Documents Diplomatique 1938–1939*, p. 132.

10. On 27 May 1939, an Air Agreement was signed after talks between the representatives of the two Air Force Staffs. During the talks, Gen. Josephe Vuilleman, the French Chief of Air Staff, said that the French Air Force could *agir vigoureusement* ('act vigorously') from the begining of hostilities. See *Polskie Siły Zbrojne w drugiej wojnie światowej, tom I. Kampania wrześniowa 1939*, cz. 1 (London, 1951), p. 97. If Germany attacked Poland, the majority of the French Air Force was to be used at the critical moment of the battle in Poland. Vuilleman also agreed to send 60 bombers to Poland to operate from there. Needless to say, they never arrived.

11. Wacław Stachiewicz, *Pisma*, tom I, p. 217.

12. J. Lukacs is mistaken when he wrote in his book *The Last European War, September 1939-December 1941* (London, Henley, 1977), on p. 55, that despite assurances given to Kasprzycki by Gamelin in May 1939 about attacking in the west 16 days after the Poles were attacked, 'these were little more than words: There was no exact agreement to that effect'.

13. Teresa Skinder-Suchcitz, *Rok 1939. Polsko-brytyjska polityka morska* (Warsaw, 1997), pp. 81–2.

14. Diary kept by Lt. Col. E. R. Sword. Extract quoted by kind permission of his daughter, Mrs. Elizabeth Turnbull.

15. Teresa Skinder-Suchcitz, *Rok 1939*, pp. 99–123; The Polish Institute and Sikorski Museum (PISM), A.I.4/1 file containing documents relating to the Mission's activities in London. Similar files can be found in the Navy and Air Force archival groups.

16. Andrzej Suchcitz, 'Wrażenia generała Ironside'a z wizyt w Polsce w 1925 i 1939', *Mars*, t.I (London-Warszawa, 1993), pp. 62–3.

17. Public Record Office (PRO), FO. 417/40. Clifford Norton, British *chargé d'affaires* in Warsaw, to Viscount Halifax, endorsing Lt. Col. E. Sword's view on Gen. Ironside's visit to Poland, dated Warsaw 25th July 1939.

18. Jan Ciałowicz, *Polsko-francuski sojusz wojskowy 1921–1939* (Warsaw, 1970), pp. 301–2; J. R. M. Butler, *History of the Second World War, Grand Strategy*, vol. II (London, 1957), pp. 11–12.

19. Tadeusz Piszczkowski, *Anglia a Polska 1914–1939* (London, 1975), p. 428; Andrzej Suchcitz, 'Pakt Ribbentrop–Mołotow', in Józef Jasnowski and Edward Szczepanik (eds), *Napaść Sowiecka 1939* (London, 1985), p. 43.

20. Wacław Chocianowicz (ed.), *W 50-lecie Powstania Wyższej Szkoły Wojennej w Warszawie* (London, 1969), p. 82.

21. Henryk Piątkowski, *Kampania wrześniowa w Polsce 1939* (London, 1946) p. 31 (author's translation).

22. In his book, *Kampania Wrześniowa 1939* (Grenoble, 1942) Col. Jaklicz, who in 1939 was Deputy Chief of General Staff, claimed that he had worked out the routes of the withdrawal to the Vistula and the division of the new front into defence sections for the armies. Jaklicz wrote that he had done this alone on the express orders of Gen. Stachiewicz. The likely explanation is that the problem of the second phase of the battle was discussed between Stachiewicz and Jaklicz as a basis for future decisions to be made by the Inspector General if the necessity arose. (See P. S. Z. Tom I, część I, pp. 278–81.) Col. Jaklicz went even further, when he claimed that the third phase of the battle, after the withdrawal into southeastern Poland, was worked out in detail. (See J. Jaklicz, *Kampania Wrześniowa 1939*, p. 47). There is no corroborative evidence to support this last view.

23. Andrzej Suchcitz, 'A brief survey', pp. 6–7.
24. Basil Liddell-Hart, *History*, p. 30; Henri Michel, *The Second World War* (London, 1975), p. 33.
25. Wacław Stachiewicz, *Pisma*, tom I, p. 207.
26. *Polskie Siły Zbrojne w drugiej wojnie światowej. Tom I. Kampania wrześniowa 1939*, cz. 1 (London, 1951), p. 380. According to Col. J. Jaklicz, Marshal Śmigły-Rydz wrote in the spring of 1939, when no large-scale action over Danzig was envisaged, 'On this strategically eccentric direction I will not use any larger forces, as it would be the equivalent to their destruction.' See J. Jaklicz, *Kampania Wrześniowa 1939* (Grenoble, 1942), p. 69 (author's translation).
    Not all western officers negated the strategic importance of Danzig to Poland. Lt. Col. E. Sword, Britain's military attaché in Warsaw, wrote a whole report on its importance to Poland's strategic position (9th May 1939, PRO FO 371/23019). He ended his report with the words, 'It has often been said in the past that Gdynia and Polish Pomerania are indefensible. This may ultimately be true, but the considerations to which I have referred clearly show that the occupation of Danzig by Germany would have a very adverse effect on Poland's strategical position in this area and render still more difficult the question of defence. Poland could not reasonably be expected to make such a sacrifice as it would involve a surrender of her rights in Danzig without adequate compensation.'
27. PISM, A. II 3/1/13 Order of Marshal E. Śmigły-Rydz on the importance of military secrets, 27th March 1939.
28. For example, Gen. Rómmel knew the probable *ordres de battaile* and area of concentration of Res. Army 'Prusy'. He did not know the timing and exact forces with which the counter-offensive would be taken. All this secrecy led Rómmel to draw up his own suppositions – wrong ones. He believed his task was to tie down the enemy frontally and gain time to allow the Supreme C-in C to mount a major counterattack on the enemy flank using Army 'Poznań' in the north and Res. Army 'Prusy' in the south. See J. Wróblewski, *Armia 'Łódź' 1939* (Warsaw, 1975), p. 35. This supposition of Rómmel's did not coincide with the plans of the Marshal who did not aim for a decisive battle on the western bank of the Vistula.
29. Col. Kirchmayer, in his *Kampania wrześniowa* (Warsaw, 1946) correctly criticized the lack of fronts, but the solution he gave on p. 57 is devoid of reality as it negates the planned use and roles of armies 'Kraków', 'Łódź' and 'Prusy'. Kirchmayer's solution placed armies 'Karpaty' and 'Kraków' in one front, armies 'Łódź', 'Poznań' and 'Pomorze' in another, whilst the reserve army was placed under a separate commander for all the reserves. Thus the three most important armies would be totally separated as far as the issuing of orders was concerned. This was not a recipe for good cooperation, co-ordination and efficiency.
30. Józef Garliński, *Intercept. The Enigma War* (London, 1979), pp. 38–47.
31. Jerzy Pertek, *Druga mała flota* (Poznań, 1959), pp. 17–19.
32. The Polish mobilization plan was such that it divided the process of mobilization into three periods: danger, alarm (secret) and general mobilization. The alarm mobilization worked on the basis of individual call-ups. It was divided into six groups, each denoted by a colour (green, brown, red, blue, yellow and

black). In this way, it was possible to mobilize individual colours in individual districts, of which there were ten. The plan was constructed in such a way that all the colours could be mobilized independently of each other or all at once; alarm mobilization could be undertaken before, partially or wholly, together with general mobilization. Overall alarm mobilization (time limit for mobilizational readiness in all colours was up to 72 hours, except for the colour green, where readiness was from 12 to 48 hours) put about 75% of the Polish Armed Forces (that is, 27 infantry divisions, parts of 4 other infantry divisions, 11 cavalry brigades, 1 motorized-armoured brigade, the Air Force, the Anti-Aircraft Defences and 60% of extra divisional formations) on a war footing. General mobilization accounted for the remaining 25% of the Armed Forces. It was carried out by putting up placards decreeing general mobilization across the country. Completion of mobilization and concentration for forces from general mobilization was 14 days (16 days for units earmarked for the southwest). Piotr Zarzycki (ed.), *Plan Mobilizacyjny 'W'* (Pruszków, 1995), pp. 11–19; Eugeniusz Piwowarski, *Plan Mobilizacyjny 'W'*, in Myśl Wojskowa, nr 4 Warsaw, July–August 1996, pp. 151–2.

33. Gen. Kutrzeba's fortification plan for the west would have cost 12 milliard złoty. The Polish military budget was about 1 milliard złoty annually, whilst the state budget was not much more than 2.5 milliard złoty annually.

34. For example, Gen. Fabrycy waited in vain for the 22nd Inf. Div. which was to unload in the afternoon of 29th August. Gen. Szychowski, the General Officer Commanding Communications, could not find the explanation for the delays until it became apparent that the Ministry of Communications was at fault. It had not reduced enough goods transports, and had failed to transfer enough rolling stock from the west to the east. When that was sorted out, new delays occured when not enough hands were found for the unloading of troop transports. This was due to the fact that some local civilian authorities failed to realize that it was their duty to supply these hands. (See P. S. Z. Tom I, część I, pp. 414–15.)

35. See P. S. Z. Tom I, część I, p. 415.

Appendix I
Principal Officers of the Second Polish Republic, 1918–39

A. PRESIDENTS

Józef Piłsudski (1867–1935), Head of State	1918–22
Gabriel Narutowicz (1865–1922)	1922
Stanisław Wojciechowski (1869–1953)	1922–6
Ignacy Mościcki (1867–1946)	1926–39

B. PRIME MINISTERS

Ignacy Daszyński	1918 (of a Provisional Government in Lublin, 7–14 November)
Jędrzej Moraczewski	1918–19
Ignacy Paderewski	1919
Leopold Skulski	1919–20
Władysław Grabski	1920
Wincenty Witos	1920–21
Antoni Ponikowski	1921–2
Artur Śliwiński	1922
Julian Nowak	1922
Władysław Sikorski	1922–3
Wincenty Witos	1923
Władysław Grabski	1923–5
Aleksander Skrzyński	1925–6
Wincenty Witos	1926
Kazimierz Bartel	1926
Józef Piłsudski	1926–8
Kazimierz Bartel	1928–9
Kazimierz Świtalski	1929
Kazimierz Bartel	1929–30
Walery Sławek	1930
Józef Piłsudski	1930
Walery Sławek	1930–31
Aleksander Prystor	1931–3
Janusz Jędrzejewicz	1933–4
Leon Kozłowski	1934–5

Walery Sławek	1935
Marian Zyndram-Kościałkowski	1935–6
Felicjan Sławój-Składkowski	1936–9

C. FOREIGN MINISTERS

Stanisław Głąbiński	1918
Władysław Wróblewski	1918
Leon Wasilewski	1918–19
Ignacy Paderewski	1919
Władysław Wróblewski	1919
Stanisław Patek	1919–20
Eutachy Sapieha	1920–21
Jan Dąbski	1921
Konstanty Skirmunt	1921–2
Gabriel Narutowicz	1922
Aleksander Skrzyński	1922–3
Marian Seyda	1923
Roman Dmowski	1923
Karol Bertoni	1923–4
Maurycy Zamoyski	1924
Aleksander Skrzyński	1924–6
Kajetan Dzierżykraj-Morawski	1926
August Zalewski	1926–32
Józef Beck	1932–9

Appendix II
Chronology:
Poland, 1914–39

1914

8 August	Declaration of loyalty to the Tsar by the Polish Circle in the Russian Duma
14 August	Proclamation by the Russian Commander-in-Chief, the Grand Duke Nicholas, with vague promises of limited autonomy for the Poles under Tsarist tutelage
16 August	Formation of the Polish Legions by Józef Piłsudski (1867–1935)
25 November	The Polish National Committee established in Warsaw by Roman Dmowski (1864–1939) to promote the Polish Cause with Russia

1915

5 August	German forces expel the Russians from Warsaw

1916

5 November	The Central Powers restore the Kingdom of Poland in close union with them

1917

6 January	The Central Powers set up in Warsaw a Council of State with limited authority
22 January	President Wilson publicly intimates his support for an independent Poland
30 March	Manifesto of the Provisional Government in Russia promising an independent Poland, linked militarily to Russia
4 June	France allows the creation of a Polish army on its soil
22 July	Piłsudski imprisoned by the Germans in Magdeburg for refusing to help set up a Polish army (*Polnische Wehrmacht*) to aid the Central Powers
15 August	The Polish National Committee re-established in Lausanne, then Paris
15 October	Regency Council created in Warsaw by the Central Powers, comprising Prince Zdzisław Lubomirski, Archbishop Aleksander Krakowski and Count Józef Ostrowski, Mayor of Warsaw

1918

8 January	President Wilson's 14 Points include a commitment to an independent Poland with access to the sea (Point 13)
3 June	The Allies recognize Poland as 'an Allied belligerent nation' and affirm their support for an independent Poland

139

1 November	Beginning of Polish–Ukrainian struggle for Lwów and Eastern Galicia
7 November	'Provisional People's Republic of Poland' set up in Lublin under the Galician socialist, Ignacy Daszyński (1866–1936)
8 November	Piłsudski released from German captivity
9 November	Revolution in Germany
10 November	Piłsudski arrives in Warsaw
11 November	Piłsudski appointed C-in-C of Polish forces by the Regency Council; official Polish Day of Independence
14 November	Piłsudski appointed Provisional Head of State; Regency Council dissolved
18 November	Government formed under the socialist, Jędrzej Moraczewski (1870–1944)
22 November	Poland declared a Republic
23 November	Social reforms introduced, including the 8-hour day
16 December	Establishment of the Communist Workers' Party of Poland
26 December	Arrival of Ignacy Paderewski (1860–1941) in Poznań leads to Polish rising on 27th December to expel German forces from western Poland

1919

5 January	Abortive right-wing coup against the Moraczewski government; Polish and Soviet Bolshevik military units clash in Wilno, marking the start of the Polish–Soviet War (1919–20)
16 January	Paderewski appointed Prime Minister (and Foreign Minister)
18 January	Opening of Paris Peace Conference
23 January	Czechoslovakia reneges on agreement with Poland and seizes Cieszyn
26 January	Elections for a Constituent *Sejm*
30 January	Poland formally recognised by the USA
10 February	First session of Constituent *Sejm*; decree on compulsory primary education
20 February	Provisional (Small) Constitution passed; Piłsudski confirmed as Head of State
26 February	Polish Army officially established
7 March	Conscription introduced
15 April	Dissolution of Polish National Committee in Paris
19 April	Polish forces liberate Wilno from Soviet Bolsheviks
28 June	Treaty of Versailles, signed for Poland by Paderewski and Dmowski
20 July	Polish forces finally crush the Ukrainian nationalists to secure Eastern Galicia
1 August	*Sejm* re-establishes the Virtuti Militari as Poland's foremost military decoration
16 August	First Polish Rising in Upper Silesia
13 December	Leopold Skulski (1878–1940) new Premier, Paderewski having resigned 27 November
18 December	Sunday Rest Law introduced as an important social reform

1920

15 January	The Polish Mark standardized as the national currency
19 March	Piłsudski awarded title of 'First Marshal of Poland' (conferred in November)
21 April	Polish alliance with the Ukrainians under Semen Petliura against Soviet Russia
7 May	Polish forces occupy Kiev
9 June	Skulski cabinet resigns; replaced (23 June) by Władysław Grabski (1874–1938)
10 July	Spa Conference; Allies refuse support to Poland against the Soviet Bolsheviks
11 July	Plebiscites in Allenstein and Marienwerder (East Prussia) favour Germany
11 July	'Curzon Note' on Poland's eastern border (the 'Curzon Line')
15 July	Agrarian Reform Act
24 July	Grabski resigns; cabinet of national unity under Wincenty Witos (1874–1945)
13–19 August	Battle of Warsaw ('Miracle on the Vistula'); momentous Polish victory over the Red Army; hereafter 'Polish Soldiers' Day', celebrated annually on 15 August
19 August	Second Polish Rising in Upper Silesia
22 September	Polish victory at the Niemen completes defeat of the Red Army
9 October	Polish forces under General Lucjan Żeligorski (1865–1947) retake Wilno

1921

21 February	Franco-Polish alliance
3 March	Polish-Romanian alliance
17 March	New Constitution passed by *Sejm*
18 March	Treaty of Riga ends Polish-Soviet War and fixes the eastern border as it was more or less after the Second Partition of 1793
20 March	Plebiscite in Upper Silesia
2 May	Third Polish Rising in Upper Silesia, led by Wojciech Korfanty (1873–1939)
13 September	Antoni Ponikowski, Rector of Warsaw Polytechnic, replaces Witos as Premier
25 September	Assassination attempt on Piłsudski in Lwów by Stefan Fedak, a Ukrainian terrorist
30 September	First National Census records Polish population of 27.2 million

1922

6 June	Poniakowski cabinet resigns over Treaty of Rapallo; Artur Śliwiński takes over
31 July	Śliwiński replaced as Premier by Julian Nowak, Rector of Jagiellonian University
13 September	*Sejm* approves building of new port of Gdynia (opened 1927)
5–12 November	First parliamentary elections under the new electoral law

9 December	Gabriel Narutowicz (1865–1922) elected first President of Poland (5 candidates)
16 December	President Narutowicz assassinated by ultra-Nationalist Eligiusz Niewiadomski
16 December	General Władysław Sikorski (1881–1943) replaces Nowak as Premier
20 December	Stanisław Wojciechowski (1869–1953) elected President of Poland

1923

15 March	Ambassadors' Conference recognises Poland's eastern border (incl Wilno, Lwów)
28 May	Witos heads new cabinet
30 May	Piłsudski resigns as Chief of General Staff
2 July	Piłsudski resigns as Head of the Inner War Cabinet and goes into retirement
3 November	General strike in response to hyperinflation crisis
6 November	Serious rioting in Kraków leaves 32 dead
19 December	New government under Władysław Grabski

1924

14 April	Bank of Poland created; the złoty to be the new currency
18 April	Unemployment Insurance Act
31 July	Statute on Schools

1925

10 February	Polish–Vatican Concordat
15 June	Polish–German Tariff War begins (until 7 March 1934)
7 July	Agreement (Ugoda) between Polish Government and Jewish Club in *Sejm*
16 October	Locarno Pact, but no guarantee of Polish–German border
13 November	Grabski gives way as Premier to Aleksander Skrzyński
28 December	Second Agrarian Reform Act

1926

24 April	Treaty of Berlin between Germany and Soviet Union alarms Poland
5 May	Skrzyński resigns as Premier; replaced by Witos (10 May)
12–14 May	Piłsudski coup
14 May	President Wojciechowski resigns
15 May	Kazimierz Bartel (1882–1941) heads new cabinet; Piłsudski Minister of War
1 June	Ignacy Mościcki (1867–1946) elected President of Poland
2 August	Consitutional amendments strengthen the Executive at expense of *Sejm*
27 August	Piłsudski appointed Inspector General of the Polish Armed Forces
30 September	Bartel resigns as Premier; replaced by Piłsudski (until 25 June 1928)
25 October	Piłsudski courts the aristocracy at meeting at Nieśwież, the Radziwiłł estate

4 December	Formation of the right-wing Camp of Great Poland under Dmowski

1927

8 June	Russian ambassador, Piotr Woykov, assassinated in Warsaw by Russian emigré
14 October	'Stabilization Loan' of 62 million US dollars to Poland

1928

20 January	Creation of Non-Party Bloc for Cooperation with the Government (BBWR)
4–11 March	Parliamentary elections; BBWR 130 (444) seats in *Sejm* and 46 (111) in Senate
25 June	Piłsudski resigns as Premier; Bartel takes over

1929

20 March	Treasury Minister Gabriel Czechowicz resigns over financial scandal
14 April	Bartel resigns as Premier; Kazimierz Świtalski takes over
16 May	Exhibition (to 30 September) in Poznań of Polish achievements since 1918
6 December	New cabinet under Bartel

1930

January	The Depression era begins in Poland
17 March	Bartel resigns as Premier; Walery Sławek (1879–1939) takes over
29 June	Congress of opposition parties ('Centrolew') in Kraków denounces Piłsudski
23 August	Sławek resigns and is replaced as Premier by Piłsudski
10 September	Arrest and internment in Brześć of opposition leaders, including Witos and Korfanty
16 September	'Pacification' of Eastern Galicia by Polish forces in response to Ukrainian terrorism
16–23 November	Parliamentary elections produce 247 *Sejm* and 76 Senate seats for BBWR
4 December	Piłsudski resigns as Premier; replaced by Sławek

1931

13 March	Abolition of anti-Jewish legislation dating from the Tsarist era
15 March	A united Peasant Party (SL) formed
27 May	Sławek resigns; Aleksander Prystor is new Premier
29 August	Tadeusz Hołówko, BBWR vice-president, assassinated by Ukrainian terrorists
9 December	Second National Census; Polish population now 31.9 million

1932

Spring	Government dismisses over 50 university professors who are political opponents
25 July	Polish–Soviet Non-Aggression Pact

2 November   Józef Beck (1894–1944) replaces August Zalewski (1883–1972) as Foreign Minister

1933
March   Piłsudski advocates a 'preventive war' against Germany because of the Hitler regime
22 March   The right-wing political organization, Camp of Great Poland, banned
8 May   Mościcki re-elected President of Poland; Janusz Jędrzejewicz is new Premier
6 October   Military parade in Kraków to commemorate 250th anniversary of King Jan Sobieski III's victory over the Turks at Vienna (12 September 1683)

1934
26 January   Polish–German Non-Aggression Pact
14 April   The far-right National Radical Camp (ONR) set up, but soon banned
14 May   Leon Kozłowski new Premier
15 June   Bronisław Pieracki, Minister of the Interior, assassinated by Ukrainian terrorist
2 July   Internment camp for subversives opened at Bereza Kartuska
13 September   Poland repudiates the Minorities Treaty

1935
28 March   Sławek Premier once again
23 April   Introduction of new Constitution
12 May   Death of Marshal Piłsudski
8 September   Parliamentary elections boycotted by most opposition parties (turnout 46.5 per cent)
12 October   Premier Sławek replaced by Marian Zyndram-Kościałkowski
30 October   Dissolution of BBWR

1936
21 February   'Front Morges' founded as oppositional group by Paderewski, Witos, Sikorski and General Józef Haller (1873–1961)
29 February   Pastoral Letter on the 'Jewish Question' from Cardinal August Hlond (1881–1948), Primate of Poland
15 May   New cabinet under Felicjan Sławój-Składkowski (1885–1962)
1 July   Launch of government industrial strategy around the new Central Industrial Region

1937
21 February   Camp of National Unity (OZON) set up by government to rally all patriotic forces
16 August   42 killed during strike organised by the Peasant Party (SL)
19 October   Introduction of 'Aryan Paragraph' and 'ghetto benches' in Polish universities

1938
10 January   General Stanisław Skwarczyński replaces Adam Koc as leader of OZON

August	Communist Party of Poland dissolved on Stalin's orders
2 October	Poland recovers Cieszyn
6–13 November	Parliamentary elections bring major success for the government

1939

2 January	Death of Roman Dmowski
31 March	British guarantee to Poland
23 August	Nazi–Soviet Pact
25 August	Anglo-Polish Treaty
1 September	Germany invades Poland
3 September	France and Britain declare war on Germany, but do not aid Poland
17 September	Soviet Union invades Poland
28 September	Fall of Warsaw to German forces
5 October	Surrender of the last regular Polish army units following the Battle of Kock, bringing the Polish–German campaign to an end

Select Bibliography

This list is restricted to books published in English, and is designed to provide an introduction to the most important aspects of the history of the Second Republic.

Abramsky, C. *et al.* (eds), *The Jews in Poland* (Oxford, 1986)

Bromke, A., *The Meaning and Uses of Polish History* (Boulder, Col., 1987)

Cienciała, A. M. and Komarnicki, T., *From Versailles to Locarno. Keys to Polish Foreign Policy, 1919–1925* (Lawrence, Kan., 1984)

Davies, N., *White Eagle, Red Star. The Polish-Soviet War, 1919–20* (London, 1972)

Davies, N., *God's Playground. A History of Poland. Volume II. 1795 to the Present* (Oxford, 1981)

Davies, N., *Heart of Europe. A Short History of Poland* (Oxford, 1984)

Dziewanowski, M. K., *Josef Pilsudski. A European Federalist, 1918–1922* (Stanford, 1969)

Dziewanowski, M. K., *The Communist Party of Poland. An Outline of History* (Cambridge, Mass., 1976)

Gromada, T. V. (ed.), *Essays on Poland's Foreign Policy, 1918–1939* (New York, 1970)

Gutman, Y. *et al.* (eds), *The Jews of Poland Between Two World Wars* (Hanover, New England, 1989)

Jędrzejewicz, W., *Pilsudski. A Life for Poland* (New York, 1982)

Karski, J., *The Great Powers and Poland, 1919–1945. From Versailles to Yalta* (New York, 1985)

Komarnicki, T., *The Rebirth of the Polish Republic. A Study in the Diplomatic History of Europe, 1914–1920* (London, 1957)

Korbel, J., *Poland Between East and West. Soviet and German Diplomacy Towards Poland, 1919–1933* (Princeton, 1963)

Landau, Z., and Tomaszewski, J., *The Polish Economy in the Twentieth Century* (London, 1985)

Latawski, P. (ed.), *The Reconstruction of Poland, 1914–1923* (London, 1992)

Leslie, R. F. (ed.), *The History of Poland since 1863* (Cambridge, 1983)

Lundgreen-Nielsen, K., *The Polish Problem at the Paris Peace Conference. A Study of the Policies of the Great Powers and the Poles, 1918–1919* (Odense, 1979)

Marcus, J., *Social and Political History of the Jews in Poland, 1919–1939* (New York, 1983)

Miłosz, C., *A History of Polish Literature* (London, 1969)

Modras, R., *The Catholic Church and Anti-Semitism: Poland, 1933–1939* (New York, 1994)

Narkiewicz, O. A., *The Green Flag. Polish Populist Politics, 1867–1970* (London, 1976)

Pease, N., *Poland, the United States, and the Stabilization of Europe, 1919–1933* (New York, 1986)

Polonsky, A., *Politics in Independent Poland. The Crisis of Constitutional Government* (Oxford, 1972)

Prażmowska, A., *Britain, Poland and the Eastern Front, 1939* (Cambridge, 1987)
Riekhoff, H. von, *German-Polish Relations, 1918–1933* (Baltimore, 1971)
Roos, H., *A History of Modern Poland* (London, 1966)
Roszkowski, W., *Landowners in Poland, 1918–1939* (Cambridge, 1991)
Rothschild, J., *Piłsudski's Coup d'Etat* (New York, 1966)
Stachura, P. D. (ed.), *Themes of Modern Polish History* (Glasgow, 1992)
Taylor, J. J., *The Economic Development of Poland, 1919–1950* (New York, 1952)
Wandycz, P. S., *Soviet–Polish Relations, 1917–1921* (Cambridge, Mass., 1969)
Wandycz, P. S., *The United States and Poland* (Cambridge, Mass., 1980)
Wandycz, P. S., *Polish Diplomacy 1914–1945. Aims and Achievements* (London, 1988)
Watt, R. M., *Bitter Glory. Poland and Its Fate, 1918 to 1939* (New York, 1979)
Wiles, T. (ed.), *Poland Between the Wars, 1918–1939* (Bloomington, 1989)
Wynot, E. D., *Polish Politics in Transition. The Camp of National Unity and the Struggle for Power, 1935–1939* (Athens, Georgia, 1974)
Wynot, E. D., *Warsaw Between the World Wars. Profile of the Capital City in a Developing Land, 1918–1939* (Boulder, Col., 1983)
Zamoyski, A., *The Battle for the Marshlands* (Boulder, Col., 1981)

Index